Performing Grand-Guignol: Playing the Theatre of Horror

The third volume in this ground-breaking series on Grand-Guignol and the 'theatre of horror', *Performing Grand-Guignol* provides unprecedented practical grounding for any theatre ensemble wishing to perform Grand-Guignol. The book provides eleven classic Grand-Guignol plays representing the genre's classic mixture of horror and comedy. The plays are mainly first translations and adaptations of masterpieces from across all eras of the French repertoire but also included are two from the London experiment in Grand Guignol in the 1920s (one of these being the first publication of a horror play that was banned by the British theatre censor). In addition, the authors provide a detailed description of exercises and rehearsal processes which lead the reader through the Grand-Guignol performance journey in an accessible and encouraging way.

Richard J. Hand is Professor of Theatre and Media Drama at the Cardiff School of Creative and Cultural Industries, University of Glamorgan. His interests include adaptation and translation in performance media, particularly in historical forms of popular culture.

Michael Wilson is Professor of Drama at Loughborough University; he was previously Professor of Drama at University College Falmouth. His main areas of research lie within the fields of popular vernacular theatre and storytelling.

Also by Richard J. Hand and Michael Wilson, and published by University of Exeter Press:

Grand-Guignol: The French Theatre of Horror (2002)
and
London's Grand Guignol and the Theatre of Horror (2007)

Exeter Performance Studies

Series editors: Peter Thomson, Professor of Drama at the University of Exeter; Graham Ley, Professor of Drama and Theory at the University of Exeter; Steve Nicholson, Professor in Twentieth-Century and Contemporary Theatre at the University of Sheffield.

A complete list of books published in the series is available from the publishers, University of Exeter Press, www.exeterpress.co.uk.

The Censorship of British Drama 1900–1968: Volume One 1900–1932
Steve Nicholson (2003)

The Censorship of British Drama 1900–1968: Volume Two 1933–1952
Steve Nicholson (2005)

Freedom's Pioneer: John McGrath's Work in Theatre, Film and Television
edited by David Bradby and Susanna Capon (2005)

John McGrath: Plays for England
selected and introduced by Nadine Holdsworth (2005)

Theatre Workshop: Joan Littlewood and the Making of Modern British Theatre
Robert Leach (2006)

Making Theatre in Northern Ireland: Through and Beyond the Troubles
Tom Maguire (2006)

"In Comes I": Performance, Memory and Landscape
Mike Pearson (2006)

Theatres of the Troubles: Theatre, Resistance and Liberation in Ireland
Bill McDonnell (2008)

The Censorship of British Drama 1900–1968: Volume Three, The Fifties
Steve Nicholson (2011)

British South Asian Theatres: A Documented History
edited by Graham Ley and Sara Dadswell (2011)

Critical Essays on British South Asian Theatre
edited by Graham Ley and Sara Dadswell (2012)

Victory Over the Sun: The World's First Futurist Opera
edited by Sara Dadswell and Rosamund Bartlett (2012)

Marking Time: Performance, Archaeology and the City
Mike Pearson (2013)

Singing Simpkin and Other Bawdy Jigs: Musical Comedy on the Shakespearean Stage
Roger Clegg and Lucie Skeaping (2014)

Ancient Greek and Contemporary Performance: Collected Essays
Graham Ley (2014)

The Censorship of British Drama 1900–1968: Volume Four, The Sixties
Steve Nicholson (2015)

Eighteenth-Century Brechtians: Theatrical Satire in the Age of Walpole
Joel Schechter (2016)

Forms of Conflict: Contemporary Wars on the British Stage
Sara Soncini (2016)

Performing Grand-Guignol: Playing the Theatre of Horror

Richard J. Hand
and
Michael Wilson

UNIVERSITY
of
EXETER
PRESS

First published in 2016 by
University of Exeter Press
Reed Hall, Streatham Drive
Exeter EX4 4QR
UK
www.exeterpress.co.uk

British Library Cataloguing in Publication Data
A catalogue record for this book is available
from the British Library.

Hardback ISBN 978 0 85989 995 6
Paperback ISBN 978 0 85989 996 3

Typeset in Sabon, 10 on 12
by Carnegie Book Production, Lancaster
Printed in Great Britain
by Short Run Press, Exeter

To Sadiyah, Shara, Danya and Jim (RJH)

To Matthew, Rosie, Jake and Sophie
– the Next Generation (MW)

Contents

List of Illustrations ix

Preface xi

SECTION I: A Brief History of the Théatre du Grand-Guignol 1

SECTION II: The Grand-Guignol Laboratory 9

A Gallery of Production Photographs from the Grand-Guignol Laboratory

SECTION III: Prefaces and Plays 49

First Programme 51

The Haunted House (*La Maison hantée*) by Marc Bonis-Charancle 60

The Kama Sutra or Never Play with Fire … (*Kama Soutra, ou Il ne faut pas jouer avec le feu*) by Régis Gignoux 70

Blind Man's Buff by Charles Hellem and Pol d'Estoc 83

The Light in the Tomb/Gott mit uns! (*La Lumière dans le tombeau/Gott mit uns!*) by René Berton 98

Second Programme 123

Progress by St. John Ervine 130

A Silk Dress (*Une Robe de Soie*) by Henriette Charasson 146

The Great Terror (*La Grande épouvante*) by André de Lorde and Henri Bauche 156

Third Programme 189

The Wax Museum (*Figures de Cire*) by André de Lorde and Georges Montignac 202

The Lovers (*Les Amants*) by Octave Mirbeau 221

The Man Who Met the Devil (*L'Homme qui a vu le diable*) by Gaston Leroux 232

The Man Who Killed Death (L'Homme qui a tué la mort) by René Berton 256

Bibliography 277

Index 281

Illustrations

A Gallery of Production Photographs from the Grand-Guignol Laboratory
between pages 48 and 49

1 Suspense
2 Despair
3 Ecstasy
4 The Two Masks of the Grand-Guignol
5 Dark Laughter
6 Fury
7 Madness
8 Eye-Catching Publicity

9 Poster for the premiere of René Berton's *Gott mit uns!* (*The Light in the Tomb*) at the Théâtre du Grand Guignol in 1928 59
10 Film poster for *The Brain That Wouldn't Die* (Joseph Green, 1962) 200
11 Poster for the premiere of René Berton's *L'Homme qui a tué la mort* at the Théâtre du Grand Guignol in 1928 201

Preface

It is now more than fifteen years since we first began this project to explore the extraordinary, but largely forgotten, theatre in Montmartre that was the Théâtre du Grand-Guignol. In that time we have run numerous exploratory workshops with students, some of whom are now older than we were when we started all of this. Some of those workshops led to productions; some didn't. But all the work we have done with our student collaborators over the years has led to more knowledge and fresh insights into the Grand-Guignol.

We have also, over the years, witnessed something of a revival of interest in horror theatre more generally and Grand-Guignol specifically amongst amateur enthusiasts and passionate professionals alike. We have been fortunate enough to meet with, discuss with and watch the productions of many of these individuals and companies. We have also published two previous books on the Grand-Guignol. The first of those, *Grand-Guignol: French Theatre of Horror* (2002), dealt exclusively with the history and practice of the Théâtre du Grand-Guignol in the Pigalle district of Paris from 1897 until 1962. The second volume, *London's Grand Guignol and the Theatre of Horror* (2007), concerned itself with the attempt by José Levy to establish a British version of the form at the Little Theatre in John Adam Street from 1920 to 1922, in which the Thorndike-Cassons and a young Noël Coward were amongst the collaborators. Both of these volumes were primarily histories and, although this volume also starts with a brief history of the Parisian theatre (for the benefit of those readers who have not read, or do not wish to read, the earlier volumes), this latest volume has a different focus.

In all our work on the Grand-Guignol we have always tried to be responsive to those who have read the books and corresponded or worked with us, and we have been consistently asked to address two issues.

Firstly, we have been asked to provide some insights into the way that we ourselves have worked with students within the context of the Grand-Guignol Laboratory, which we set up at the University of Glamorgan (now the University of South Wales) when we started this project. The Lab has always been an ad hoc entity that has allowed us to contextualize our explorations of the Grand-Guignol within a research and teaching framework. The introductory section to this book describes some of the ways we have worked with students over the years. This practice can be broken down into three main elements: the repurposing of standard drama and actor training exercises with a particular focus on horror performance; an engagement with other forms of horror performance (especially film) as a point of reference; and close textual work (including in the areas of translation and adaptation) in recognition of the Grand-Guignol as writers' theatre.

The second request we have had is for more (and more) plays. This delighted us, as it gave us the perfect excuse to hunt down more obscure and out-of-print texts and translate them, and we are pleased to include a further eleven plays, significantly adding to the repertoire of Grand-Guignol plays available in the English language. We very much look forward to hearing about the performance of these newly available scripts in professional, amateur or pedagogical production contexts and may even get to one or two productions ourselves. We would merely repeat the request we have made before: we would be glad to hear from any companies working with the Grand-Guignol and would happily receive copies of production materials for our own (ever-growing) archives.

The selection here is a deliberately eclectic mix. It includes some pieces that we wanted to tackle in *Grand-Guignol: French Theatre of Horror* and *London's Grand Guignol and the Theatre of Horror*, but were unable to do so because of space. We are also including some plays we have discovered for ourselves over the intervening years. Alongside classics from the golden era of the rue Chaptal, there are also plays from the very early years, as well as three comedies – an important, but often neglected, part of the Grand-Guignol recipe.

We were also keen to include some new writers in our corpus of translations alongside old favourites such as André de Lorde, without whom no collection of Grand-Guignol plays would be complete. We have deliberately sought out plays by writers who had established reputations elsewhere, so you will find plays here by Gaston Leroux, Octave Mirbeau and René Berton, as well as a short comedy by Henriette Charasson, one of the few women to write for the rue Chaptal.

The majority of the plays included here are from the repertoire of the Théâtre du Grand-Guignol, but we have also included two plays from the London repertoire of 1920–22 – or, rather, one play that was actually staged by Levy's company and one that was refused a licence by the Lord Chamberlain, so was never presented publicly.

The greatest source of Grand-Guignol plays is undoubtedly Agnès Pierron's formidable collection of scripts published in 1995. Whilst this volume is now unfortunately out of print and is accessible only to the reader of French, a number of enthusiasts and companies, hungry for scripts, have tracked down copies and begun to commission new translations and adaptations for performance. With a few notable exceptions, therefore, we have, in this volume, given preference to plays that do not appear in the Pierron collection in order to enrich the number of plays available to the English reader. Many of these were published around the time of their stage premiere in cheap editions by *La Librairie Théâtrale* or within the pages of *La Petite Illustration*, a literary journal that was published weekly from 1913.

One brief word about the translations. In our translations of the original French texts, although we aim to adhere closely to the original French we have always prioritized *dramatic* or *theatrical* purpose over literary accuracy. Our aim here has been to provide workable scripts that are of value to the modern student, teacher or company of theatremakers wishing to make practical explorations of the Grand-Guignol genre. We must remember that these were originally plays for different places and different times, so there have been some rare occasions where we have made minor changes in order to clarify the dramatic intention of the author, such as the anglicization of a French cultural or historical reference that might otherwise have required a lengthy footnote. We have also dispensed with the French practice of marking every entrance and exit as a scene change, but have retained the integrity of separate acts, marking either a change of setting or a significant passage of time. In this sense we have deliberately blurred the lines between translation and adaptation and we would encourage readers to treat these scripts as working texts and to make adjustments as necessary.

Furthermore, in *The Light in the Tomb* we have made some judicious cuts to the dialogue. This is a long play and unlikely to be tolerated in its original form by a modern audience; we would not wish to create a translation of a play that then lies dormant within the pages of this book because it is too unwieldy to perform. It was a strategy we adopted earlier for Maurice Level's *The Final Kiss*, but we mention it here so that readers wishing to read the full script can return to the original.

In previous volumes we arranged the plays in chronological order, according to their date of first performance. This seemed like a reasonable strategy when dealing with the history of either the Théâtre du Grand-Guignol or London's Grand Guignol. For this volume we have adopted a rather different approach. We have divided the plays up into three 'programmes', presenting a kind of 'douche écossaise' of horror and comedy plays and a slow ratcheting up of horror from one play to the next. This is really a bit of playfulness on our part – we are not suggesting that this is how the plays here *should* be grouped or performed, but simply how they *could* be organized to create three separate nights at the Grand-Guignol. We wanted to find a way of allowing the reader to experience the plays as if they were sitting on the front row (or, if you are an adventurous type, in a *loge grillée*) in the rue Chaptal, the smallest theatre of its day in Paris. Each of the programmes is preceded by a short preface which we hope will situate the group of plays within the wider context of both Grand-Guignol and horror performance more generally.

In case there is any confusion, we have adopted the following 'rule' when referring to the titles of plays. For all plays we have used the published French title, followed by the English title in brackets, on the first occasion of its use. Thereafter we have used the English title only for plays that we have published in translation, either in this volume or elsewhere, and the French title only for all other plays.

For readers coming to the Grand-Guignol for the first time, we should also explain our approach to the issue of the troublesome hyphen. The term Grand-Guignol in French usually (but not always) appears in its hyphenated form. However, references to London's Grand Guignol are always without the hyphen. Therefore, we have used the non-hyphenated form only when we are referring specifically to the London seasons of 1920–22. In all other cases, whether referring to the Théâtre du Grand-Guignol or to the Grand-Guignol genre more widely, we have implemented the hyphen.

As ever with a project of this kind there are many people who have contributed in one way or another and without whose help and support our work would not have been possible. We have acknowledged a number of these in our previous books and our indebtedness continues. In addition, on our ongoing journey into the exquisite terrors of the Grand-Guignol we continue to meet wonderful people from the worlds of theatre, education and fandom who share with us their insights and activities in exploring the Grand-Guignol. We would like to thank them for their never-ending enthusiasm and generosity in sharing their questions, ideas and successes with us.

Finally, we owe a particular debt of gratitude to a certain group of experts. This book emerges out of work undertaken with students in the Grand-Guignol Laboratory in South Wales. Over many years, these students have immersed themselves into the Grand-Guignol with boundless passion and energy. They have helped us refine our translations and adaptations of the classic French repertoire by riding roughshod over them in the studio. They have spilt, thrown and swallowed copious amounts of stage blood. They have made us laugh, jump and shudder with hundreds of productions of classic and all-new horror plays. In Pontypridd, Cardiff and on numerous tours they have brought that long dead theatre in the rue Chaptal back to full-blooded life. They have deserved every ovation. Therefore, our greatest thanks and most sincere appreciation go to all you students, too numerous to mention individually by name (but you know who you are), who have contributed to the Grand-Guignol Lab over the years. It has been hellishly good fun.

RJH & MW
December 2015

SECTION I
A Brief History of the Théâtre du Grand-Guignol

Montmartre at the end of the nineteenth century was a lively, if morally complex, place where artists and intellectuals rubbed shoulders with dancers, cabaret artistes, prostitutes and addicts. It was the Montmartre of Aristide Bruant and Henri Toulouse-Lautrec, of Le Rat Mort (The Dead Rat), the famous cabaret venue on the notorious Place Pigalle, and of Le Moulin Rouge, where the highest-paid performer was Joseph Pujol, Le Pétomane, whose claim to fame was his extraordinary ability to play tunes and perform impersonations by farting (Nohain and Caradec, 1992). It was also the birthplace of stage naturalism, where André Antoine founded the Théâtre Libre in 1887 and scandalized audiences with his radical approach to staging.

Amongst Antoine's compatriots was the somewhat imposing and characterful Oscar Méténier, a playwright and novelist who specialized in stories of Parisian low-life. His 1896 play *Mademoiselle Fifi*, adapted from a short story by Guy de Maupassant, was the first play in France to feature a prostitute. Méténier was also a Secretary to the Police Commissioner of Tour Saint-Jacques in the fourth arrondissement, a job which involved being an official witness at the public execution of murderers. After the Théâtre Libre finally closed its doors, following some years of financial difficulty, small studio theatres in the same spirit were evidently viable and Méténier was able to acquire a small theatre and former Jansenist chapel at the end of a small alleyway of the rue Chaptal, a short walk away from the bright lights of the Place Pigalle. He named it Le Théâtre du Grand-Guignol and it was to be the new home for naturalism in the Zola mould. Méténier was already a controversial figure and his new theatre soon built upon 'his reputation for scandal, contradiction, and a taste for the forbidden' (Deák, 1974, 36).

Méténier's stewardship of the theatre lasted barely two years, and it was his successor, Max Maurey, who transformed the theatre into a theatre of horror – not by abandoning the Grand-Guignol's naturalist origins, but by blending them with the melodramatic conventions of the sensationalist press of the day, such as *Le Petit Journal* or *Le Petit Parisien*, and their gory depictions and descriptions of true-life crime stories. Maurey, ever the enterprising impresario, recognized that behind Méténier's initial success with the Grand-Guignol lay a public taste for scandal, thrills and chills, and built upon the foundations laid by his predecessor not only to establish a commercially successful theatre but also to develop a whole performance genre that became synonymous with the name of the theatre itself. Today the term Grand-Guignol is used to describe any heightened act of performed horror, and French children who are accused of overreacting or having a tantrum might be told, "Ne joue pas au Grand-Guignol!"

Maurey took two innovations in particular from Méténier, both of which became defining features of the Grand-Guignol and critical components of its success. The first was the adoption of the *douche écossaise*, or hot and cold shower, as a structuring device for the evening's entertainment. This involved the alternation of shocking dramas and comedies throughout an evening's carefully structured programme of up to five short plays. This alternation of styles became one of the theatre's trademarks.

Secondly, Maurey was quick to realize that a theatre of horror needed to be, above all else, a playful theatre, where actors and audience willingly engaged in the game that was being played. Maurey would have witnessed Méténier's nightly antics during which, dressed in a flamboyant black cape and flanked by two burly bodyguards, he would appear outside the theatre and regale the waiting audience with horrific tales of the latest crimes that had been committed in Paris.

Part of the game was, of course, the journey to the theatre itself: from the bright lights of the Place Pigalle and along the seedy and salacious rue Pigalle right into the sudden quiet of rue Chaptal until, suddenly, the cobblestoned alleyway of the cité Chaptal appears with the theatre at the end, emerging from the shadows. Although the area around the rue Chaptal has spruced itself up somewhat in recent years, the walk can still, to this day, recapture a hint of a clandestine atmosphere, a slight frisson, especially if done under cover of night.

Maurey was also, in the spirit of playfulness, the person who created the myth and the public image of the Grand-Guignol as the theatre of horror through the use of horrific imagery on the posters and programmes promoting the theatre (sometimes bearing no more than a passing resemblance to the productions that were being advertised) and, perhaps most famously, the introduction of a house doctor, the *médecin de service*, to take care of those patrons who were taken ill on account of the on-stage horrors they were witnessing.

There is no doubt that Maurey was an exceptional theatre manager and publicist who succeeded in turning what was the smallest theatre in Paris at the time into its most notorious. But he was not alone in creating the foundations of the theatre's success. He recruited Paul Ratineau, an actor and director with an extraordinary talent for designing and creating stage lighting and sound effects – essential weapons in the Grand-Guignol's armoury and reputation – and André de Lorde, the librarian at the Bibliothèque de l'Arsenal, a playwright who had submitted plays to André Antoine and a friend of Méténier's. De Lorde became the Grand-Guignol's most prolific writer of horror plays and, although he also wrote for other theatres, it is the Grand-Guignol with which he is eternally associated as the 'Prince of Terror'. He was an exceptionally skilled writer of the carefully wrought horror play, sometimes working on his own and sometimes working collaboratively, often with men of science and medicine to add authenticity to his plays.

Although de Lorde made it clear that the Grand-Guignol was a theatre for writers, the Théâtre du Grand-Guignol did not treat its writers with any particular deference. By all accounts the rehearsal rooms at the

Grand-Guignol under Maurey's stewardship were riotous, with scripts rewritten and arguments erupting on all sides at regular intervals around production and scripting decisions. According to René Berton, Maurey would reduce writers to tears with his demands for amendments: 'With tears in their eyes, they watched their torturer cover the pages of their manuscripts with blue crossings-out' (quoted in Antona-Traversi, 1933, 33). Reading some of the accounts, it seems a wonder that productions were put together at all, especially given the need to maintain a high turnover of new plays to keep audiences coming back. A rehearsal period of two weeks for each play, comedy or drama was normal, during which time 'the author, the actors, the director, all worked relentlessly' (Antona-Traversi, 1933, 34). It was clearly a place of great creative energy, excitement and, above all, common purpose.[1]

Maurey was, above all else, a businessman. In 1914, with the First World War barely into its terrible course, Maurey was convinced that the real-life horrors that were unfolding on the fields of Northern France would put an end to the public taste for on-stage horrors. He sold his stake in the Grand-Guignol and took over as director of the Théâtre des Variétés, where he remained until his death in 1947 (except for the years of Nazi occupation, 1940–44). He left an enduring legacy at the Grand-Guignol, however, having set down the foundations of a new theatrical genre by counter-intuitively blending the traditions of melodrama and naturalism, establishing the mythology of the rue Chaptal and the formulaic structure of the evening's programme there, and confirming the centrality of the writer to the enterprise. This last point is critical. Although Maurey was quite wrong about the impending demise of the Grand-Guignol in 1914 – indeed, its best days were still to come – many of the plays that were written under his stewardship became the cornerstones of the Grand-Guignol canon and were returned to and reprised throughout the theatre's history.

A partnership now took over the running of the Grand-Guignol. Camille Choisy fulfilled the role that Maurey and Méténier had previously undertaken, whilst Charles Zibell financed the enterprise, but took no direct interest in the theatre. Choisy presided over what is generally thought of as the Golden Age of the Grand-Guignol, a period when its reputation was cemented internationally and significant new plays were added to the repertoire, with de Lorde at his most prolific. Two things in particular came together to play in Choisy's favour.

First, contrary to Maurey's expectations, rather than quenching the public's demand for horror theatre the end of the War in 1918 seemed to increase its appetite for it. The public's demand for thrills and chills seemed insatiable in the post-war years, evidenced by the hedonism of the 1920s

---

[1] For a fuller account of the febrile atmosphere of the Grand-Guignol rehearsal rooms, see Berton's account in Antona-Traversi, 1933, 30–36.

and the arrival of the Jazz Age.[2] Across the channel in London the theatres struggled to meet the demand for new thrillers. This was the age of Bulldog Drummond and the emergence of the detective novel as a significant genre in popular literature (see Barker and Gale, 2001). It is no coincidence that London's Grand Guignol ran successfully from 1920 to 1922, until the stringencies of the official theatre censor, the Lord Chamberlain's Office, effectively put an end to what it had always regarded as a most 'troublesome' theatre.

The second element that contributed to the Grand-Guignol's success at this time was undoubtedly the recruitment of Paula Maxa as the theatre's leading lady, and, specifically, her on-stage partnership with Georges Paulais. Whilst Maurey had established the primacy of the writer, the Grand-Guignol was also a form that made great and very specific demands on its actors. Maxa soon attracted the moniker of 'the most assassinated woman in the world' (a reputation she revelled in) and was celebrated for her trademark bloodcurdling scream.[3]

Maxa was born Marie-Thérèse Beau in 1898 and, after marrying the aristocratic but impecunious writer le comte Charles-Gustave-Joseph Le Clerc de Bussy de Vauchelles in 1912, a few weeks before her fourteenth birthday, she joined the Théâtre du Grand-Guignol in 1916 (Pierron, 2011, 50–51), making her debut in Marcel Gerbidon's comedy *Le Grain de poivre* (*The Peppercorn*) (Pierron, 2011, 52).[4]

Throughout the 1920s Maxa dominated the stage at the rue Chaptal, but she is indelibly associated with the Choisy years. When, in 1926, Charles Zibell was forced to sell his share in the theatre to Jack Jouvin, a tricky two years followed as Jouvin attempted to assert his authority at the rue Chaptal, resulting in an acrimonious relationship between him and Choisy. Choisy finally left the Grand-Guignol in 1928 and established the short-lived Théâtre du Rire et de l'Épouvante (Theatre of Laughter and Fear) at the Théâtre Saint-Georges, a mere five-minute stroll from the rue Chaptal. Meanwhile, Maxa was contractually obliged to remain with Jouvin and endured five more difficult years. According to Maxa, Jouvin wanted to create a more anonymous company and resented Maxa's 'star' status. He also wanted to stamp his own identity on the theatre and was notorious for getting involved in all stages of production, including writing numerous plays under a variety of pseudonyms. One gets the feeling, however, that

2 The 1920s Paris jazz scene benefited from substantial numbers of black American artists, some of whom chose to remain in non-segregated France after the end of the War, and others, such as the dancer and singer Josephine Baker (1906–1975), who arrived in the years following.

3 It is perhaps ironic that Maxa finally succumbed to throat cancer in 1970.

4 According to Pierron (2011, 52), Choisy had a policy of trying out unproven actors in comedies before letting them perform in horror plays, which was considered a greater risk to the theatre's precious reputation.

what was happening was a monumental clash of egos. Maxa finally broke free of her contract in 1933 and set up her own Théâtre de la Vice et de la Vertu. This too was unsuccessful, however, and she soon made peace with Jouvin and returned to her spiritual home.

Jouvin's tenure at the Grand-Guignol is often blamed for the slow and lamentable decline of the Grand-Guignol from the 1930s onwards. It is a judgement, however, that is perhaps a little unfair. Times were changing and gone were the optimistic, carefree days of the Roaring Twenties, to be replaced by the Wall Street Crash of 1929,[5] the subsequent Depression and the encroaching cloud of fascism in Europe. At the same time, the talkies had arrived and, in a foretaste of what was to come, the Grand-Guignol found that, following the phenomenal success of Universal Picture's horror films in the 1930s, including James Whale's *Frankenstein* (1931), it had a rival in the emerging horror film genre.

In response Jouvin experimented with the programme, staging an evening of *Quinze Couples* in 1933, in which Henriette Charasson's *Une Robe de soie* (*A Silk Dress*) was one of the plays performed, and introducing a new emphasis on psychological horror and a 'certain seductive eroticism' (Rivière and Wittkop, 1979, 91) into the general programme. At the same time he remained faithful to many of the classics of the genre and de Lorde continued to write plays for him. Exhausted from his efforts, Jouvin gave up the Grand-Guignol in 1938 and, after a brief stint at the helm by Clara Bizou, the following year it was taken over by an Englishwoman, Eva Berkson.

Before long, however, war broke out in Europe again and, following the fall of Paris in 1940, Berkson returned to England for the duration of the conflict. During those difficult years of occupation Choisy and Maxa returned to the Grand-Guignol and staged seasons made up largely of the classics from the Grand-Guignol repertoire, but in March 1945 Choisy died and in 1946 Berkson returned to reclaim ownership.

The Théâtre du Grand-Guignol had, by all accounts, been a big hit with both the occupying German forces and the Allied liberators, but, after the War, the decline that had begun in the 1930s became more evident. Paul Ratineau may have returned to direct three seasons of plays in 1946 and 1947, but André de Lorde had died in 1942 and with him a whole tradition of Grand-Guignol writing. Maxa, too, was no longer able to perform and it was rumoured that her voice had been permanently damaged by the many continuous nights of on-stage screaming. The old team was no more and Berkson abandoned the theatre again in 1951, fleeing this time not from the invading Germans but from mounting debts (Pierron, 1995, 1395).

The final eleven years of the Théâtre du Grand-Guignol were characterized

---

[5] One consequence of the 1929 crash was the exodus from Paris of many of the Americans who had made it their homes in the post-war period and who now faced financial ruin.

by a series of different owners and managers. Max Maurey's sons, Denis and Marcel, took over for a while, as did Raymonde Marchard and Christiane Wiegant, but not even the efforts of the populist Eddy Ghilain, who wrote, directed and acted in entire programmes at the rue Chaptal in its final years, could prevent its terminal decline. Increasingly desperate attempts to revive its popularity merely succeeded in, at best, rendering it a mere shadow of its former self, and, at worst, presenting an outrageous self-parody.

Writers and critics have speculated on the reasons for this decline. It might be reasonably assumed that the theatre's staying open during the Occupation and its popularity with the occupying German forces cannot have endeared it to a post-war Parisian audience. Some have speculated that, following the War, there was little appetite for the contrived horrors of the Grand-Guignol, which Anaïs Nin described as seeming 'laughable and infantile' (Pierron, 1995, XXXIII) after the realities of the concentration camps. As the curtain came down on the rue Chaptal for the final time, Charles Nonon, who had been brought in as an administrator by Berkson, gave an interview to *Time* magazine. Quite simply, he said, 'we could not compete with Buchenwald. Before the War everyone believed that what happened on stage was purely imaginary, whereas now we know that it – and much more – is possible' (30 November 1962).

It is tempting to accept Nonon's simple explanation for the demise of the Grand-Guignol, but there were other factors at play. Henri-Georges Clouzot's *Les Diaboliques* (1954), Georges Franju's *Les Yeux sans visage* (1959) and Alfred Hitchcock's *Psycho* (1960) all helped to redefine horror performance in ways with which the Grand-Guignol could not compete. The spirit of the Grand-Guignol's closing years may even be best captured in the popular horror output of the Hammer Studios from the late 1950s to the early 1970s, with its strong reliance on both the Gothic and Melodramatic traditions of theatre.

Perhaps ultimately, however, by the 1960s the Grand-Guignol was simply no longer relevant. It emerged in a specific place and at a specific time in history – *fin-de-siècle* Montmartre – and it perished for equally specific reasons of time and place.

But, whilst the Théâtre du Grand-Guignol has permanently closed its doors, its legacy has proved robust and can be discerned in many subsequent film and TV horror performances. There have even been occasional attempts to stage programmes of Grand-Guignol plays, both in France and elsewhere, and particularly in the last two decades there has been something of a revival of interest in Grand-Guignol theatre, with the establishment of several professional, semi-professional and amateur companies, including Thrillpeddlers in San Francisco, Molotov in Washington DC, Vigor Mortis in Brazil, Tin Shed Theatre Company in Newport and compagnie acte6 in Paris, to name but a few. Fifty years after the final show at the rue Chaptal, a new age of Grand-Guignol is being born.

SECTION II
The Grand-Guignol Laboratory

Hilarious Horrors: Rehearsal Strategies and the Grand-Guignol

The Grand-Guignol investigates many themes on the bleaker side of existence and it does not flinch from making its audience witness cruelty, terror and nihilism. Grand-Guignol writers drew inspiration from *faits divers* news items in the popular press of the time, from historical incidents and from the extrapolation of scientific discovery. It also reflects the influence of literary phenomena such as *contes cruels*, most famously in Auguste Villiers de l'Isle-Adam's 1883 collection, but also as a more widely detectable genre influenced, not least, by the cultural revolution of Zola-inspired naturalism. In this regard, the horrors of the Grand-Guignol are emphatically non-supernatural and 'non-Transylvanian', exploring instead the disturbing paradox of 'human inhumanity' and the human capacity for monstrosity: extrapolating, as it were, *la bête humaine* into *le monstre humain*. However, an essential element in an evening of Grand-Guignol is comedy, whether as a release valve of tension, a welcome break from horrors or, on the contrary, a devious strategy to increase the impact of the next horror play. The importance of humour is most blatantly evident in the farces and comedies that interleave the horror plays in the genre's trademark structure of *la douche écossaise*, the 'hot and cold shower'. In addition, most of the horror plays themselves contain some element of sardonic humour and irony which may often evoke a wry smile or knowing titter from the spectator.

This horror/comedy dynamic finds a distinct resonance in popular genres of cinema. In his discussion of the horror film genre Paul Wells talks of comedy as being horror's 'allied genre' (Wells, 2000, 1). Similarly, although he is describing a specific contemporary horror film context (the late 1970s and early 1980s), Philip Brophy's term 'Horrality' (Brophy, 1986) – the hybridization of horror, hilarity, morality and textuality – is a term that it is tempting to requisition for the Grand-Guignol. To shift to another closely allied genre, in writing about thrillers Martin Rubin stresses that 'the thriller thrives on emotionally conflicting responses, and laughter and suspense can easily coexist and even intensify each other' (Rubin, 1999, 34–5). Rubin argues that:

> The thriller involves not just the presence of certain feelings in excess but also a *combination* of those feelings. Just as a roller coaster makes us laugh *and* scream, the thriller often works to double emotions, feelings, sensations: humor *and* suspense, fear *and* excitement, pleasure *and* pain. (Rubin, 1999, 6)

A Grand-Guignol horror performance is likewise a vehicle of 'feelings in excess', but it is also a thrilling combination of diverse emotions, and humour can be an important part of that. Indeed, this exploitation of double genre and double emotions in the Grand-Guignol exists both in the macrocosm of *la douche écossaise* and the microcosm of a single play. Arguably the greatest success of the Grand-Guignol was to bring together and reconcile a range of seemingly contradictory genres (Naturalism, Melodrama, Realism and the Gothic) and emotions (fear and laughter).

To return to cinema, we might consider that most Grand-Guignolesque of movies, a film which abides as a genuine milestone in both the thriller *and* horror genres: Alfred Hitchcock's *Psycho* (1960). While the movie industry and film reviews were initially lukewarm if not hostile towards Hitchcock's film, audiences flocked to see it in droves and made it a box office phenomenon. Moreover, contemporary audience accounts reveal that while spectators gasped and screamed they also laughed. In fact, they laughed so loudly that in some scenes important dialogue was drowned out. According to Anthony Perkins (who played Norman Bates in the film), the scale of hilarity caught the usually shrewd and farsighted 'Master of Suspense' by surprise, making him feel 'confused, at first, incredulous second, and despondent third' (quoted in Rebello, 2013, 163). This is rather ironic given Hitchcock's legendarily mordant sense of humour. In fact, he himself insisted that he 'could never have made a film like *Psycho* without a sense of humor' (quoted in Rebello, 2013, 174): it was, he claimed, intended to be a 'fun picture' in which the iconic director would lead the audience on a journey through 'the haunted house at the fairground or the roller-coaster' (quoted in Rebello, 2013, 168). *Psycho*'s delectable horrors embodied in its carefully scripted narrative, consummate performances and manipulated responses of terror and laughter clearly make it a close relation to the thrill ride of a night at the Grand-Guignol. Moreover, one of the key influences on the style and hybridized genre of *Psycho* was the French film *Les Diaboliques* (Henri-Georges Clouzot, 1954), a preeminent example of Grand-Guignol-influenced cinema and a film the typically critical Alfred Hitchcock much admired.[1] The appearance of *Psycho* and *Les Diaboliques* in the twilight phase of the Théâtre du Grand-Guignol gives a sense of the 'torch being passed on' when it comes to the thrills and chills of popular horror culture: the audiences that shuddered and tittered at the French theatre of horror would find what they desired on the rapidly evolving cinema screen.

When it comes to putting Grand-Guignol into practice, the space of comedy can be an important oasis in the realm of horror for the ensemble itself. When a team of actors has to present brutal scenes of assault, mutilation and murder, it is advisable to inculcate an atmosphere

---

[1] Hitchcock's interest in French thrillers is also reflected in the fact that *Vertigo* (1958) was based on Boileau-Narcejac's crime novel *D'entre les morts* (1954). Hitchcock certainly had his own admirers in France: his films were not only hugely popular, the critical advocacy of Hitchcock as one of cinema's greatest *auteurs* began in France.

of trust and conviviality: the grim intensity and pitiless cruelty enacted in many Grand-Guignol plays needs, in a rehearsal and performance context, to be nurtured in a framework of support and good humour. To this end, rehearsing Grand-Guignol can be – and probably should be – approached in such a way as to make it enormous *fun*. After all, the Grand-Guignol can be understood as belonging to a *popular theatre* tradition wherein the audience is all-important as co-creators, whether that was, in the original venue, the regular clientele of *Grand-Guignoleurs* or Grand-Guignol 'virgins'. The original Grand-Guignol venue may be long gone, but equivalent audience relationships can still be detected: watching Grand-Guignol today, on a 'good night out' spectators can (in)voluntarily make their presence felt by gasping in shock, wincing in excruciation or laughing (nervously or uproariously). This popular theatre potential of a dynamic and participatory audience should be borne in mind by the ensemble itself during rehearsal.

By the time a production reaches its audience, the atmospheric blend of familiarity and strangeness, of knowingness and surprise, is all part of the playfulness of the Grand-Guignol (see Hand and Wilson, 2002, 69–72) and critical to the ability of the actor to draw the audience into the action as witnesses and, therefore, collaborators (Hand and Wilson, 2002, 44–46). We would therefore suggest that the notion of playfulness, so evident in performance, should find its genesis early in the rehearsal process. By all accounts, rehearsals at the rue Chaptal were at times wild and torrid affairs, full of laughter and arguments.

There are countless ways to develop actors when mounting a production. Grand-Guignol performances have emerged across a range of amateur, academic and professional contexts and different rehearsal and production methods are necessary and chosen. Our discussion here is not intended to propose a particular 'system', but rather to share some of the things that we have done in the rehearsal studio over the years and felt worked well. The practical experiments conducted by the authors of this book are based primarily on experiences with undergraduate and postgraduate students of theatre studies and make use of an eclectic mix of standard rehearsal exercises, adapted to suit the genre and enhance the playful and intimate atmosphere we wanted to encourage. All this has been complemented with occasional workshops with youth theatres, further education colleges, high school groups (usually at A-level, rather than younger levels, given the 'adult' subject matter) and trainee actors. Each ensemble – or, more conventionally, director-led theatre company – will, no doubt, have its own repertoire of training methodologies and rehearsal processes. Moreover, the nature of the chosen or available space will also dictate the nature and purpose of rehearsal, whether this is a studio in an educational environment, a community rehearsal room, an improvised or requisitioned location, a fringe venue or a professional theatre context. In addition, the approach taken to the Grand-Guignol repertoire – whether it is a historical reconstruction set when the plays were first performed or a strategic updating – will also have an impact on how the plays are developed and staged. It must not be forgotten that the Grand-Guignol is a mode of theatre that should be carefully scripted. Devising and improvisation may be an excellent way into developing all-new Grand-Guignol plays for the twenty-first century, allowing an ensemble to pool news stories (in the spirit of the *faits divers*), personal anecdotes, anxieties or phobias as a source for creating a contemporary horror play. However, it is strongly advised that any devising process culminates in a carefully scripted play. Much of the dramatic suspense and tension heading towards an inexorable dénouement in the Grand-Guignol is achieved by the *playwright*. Most emphatically, when a play incorporates acts of physical violence, strict choreography is paramount. Indeed, the strict discipline of stage combat combined with the legerdemain of stage magic is an ideal recipe for Grand-Guignol set pieces.

Voluptuous Panic: Grand-Guignol Gaming

In the context of a discussion of theatre games that exploit the themes of 'Vertigo' or the 'Victim', Clive Barker[2] argues that:

> The horror movie exploits our appetite for 'voluptuous panic', the intention being to take the audience to the point of almost screaming out in imagined terror. (Barker, 1977, 86)

'Voluptuous panic' is a perfect term for the mood of the Grand-Guignol, particularly as regards its playfulness and the importance of using games when developing it – at least in the experiences of the Grand-Guignol Laboratory.[3] One possible way to ensure that the process of rehearsing a performance of Grand-Guignol plays is enjoyable is the use of a range of theatre games. In the following sections we will highlight a number of processes and exercises that we have found to be useful in the Grand-Guignol Laboratory and in developing horror productions with university ensembles of various sizes. They are merely options, which readers may find more or less useful, but

---

2 The authors would like to point out to readers that Clive Barker (1931–2005), author of *Theatre Games* and co-editor with Maggie B. Gale of *British Theatre between the Wars, 1918–1939*, was a highly regarded British theatre academic, teacher and editor of *New Theatre Quarterly* and is not to be confused with the Clive Barker, familiar to horror fans as a writer, film director and producer, perhaps best known for *Hellraiser* (1987), *Candyman* (1992) and the stage play *Frankenstein in Love; or, The Love of Death (A Grand Guignol Romance)* (1982).

3 Interestingly, Mel Gordon – author of *The Grand Guignol: Theatre of Fear and Terror* (1988; rev. ed. 1997) – titled his study of 1920s Germany *Voluptuous Panic: The Erotic World of Weimar Berlin* (2008)

they have certainly provided us with beneficial ways into exploring spatial environments, rehearsal strategies and fully developed performances.[4]

Interestingly, there is a close link between theatre exercises and many traditional playground or party games. Many such games exploit aspects of suspense, shock and hilarity. In this regard, they can be easily adapted to Grand-Guignol work, just as many familiar and frequently used theatre games can easily be given a neo-Gothic, Halloween or Grand-Guignol twist. Traditional party games such as 'Sardines', 'Hide and Seek', 'Murder in the Dark' and 'Wink Murder' exist in countless variations and can be easily and constructively appropriated for a Grand-Guignol rehearsal process. For example, versions of 'Wink Murder' are described by Augusto Boal (1992, 156) and Jessica Swale (2012, 74–5), and the game is sometimes known as – in a title worthy of the Grand-Guignol – 'Kiss of Death', wherein the killer blows a kiss rather than winks (Goulding, 2003, 33–4). In regard to playground games, Clive Barker cites 'What's the Time, Mr Wolf?' as a children's game that can be highly effective in drama rehearsal. In this game, a character designated as the 'wolf' walks around a space in which he is taunted by a group who ask him what the time is. The wolf lists off the time ('one o'clock', etc.), eventually announcing that it is 'Dinner time!', at which point the other players are chased and caught unless they reach a designated safe zone. In analysing the game, Barker writes:

> On one level this is a speed-of-reaction game involving quick, direct, strong movements but it also offers a framework in which the child can explore the emotional sensations of rising tension and fear in a safe release situation, which is enjoyable. (Barker, 1977, 86)

Related to this are numerous 'Tag', 'Stuck in the Mud' or other 'Cat and Mouse' chase games, including some identified by Boal as group 'integration' games (1992, 118–19). Jessica Swale describes a version of this type of game called 'Flying Sheep' (2012, 10–11) in which one player is selected as a 'wolf', one is a 'sheep' and the rest are 'rocks'. The wolf chases the sheep. When the sheep jumps over a rock, the latter becomes a wolf, the original sheep becomes a rock and the original wolf becomes a sheep. It is a frenetic and noisy game and the performers should be encouraged to make the transformations as large as possible. It is easy to give Grand-Guignol twists to this game, exploring different types of monstrosity and archetypal victims in transformation.

Somewhat less frantic – but an excellent way into aspects of concentration and suspense – is a game such as 'Grandmother's Footsteps'. This

---

[4] There are many resources for theatre games: here we cite Clive Barker (1977), Augusto Boal (1992), Jessica Swale (2012) and others, but there are also excellent on-line resources such as http://dramaresource.com/games.

classic playground game, in which players attempt to creep up unseen on 'grandmother', is used by Boal (1992, 81) and becomes, for Jessica Swale, 'Grandma's Hat', in which players need to collect a hat *en route* to grandmother and change their physicality to create the character who might sport the chosen headgear (2009, 104). Other variants include 'The Graveyard Game', in which 'corpses' attempt to silently revive – in suitably grotesque 'undead' form – and stalk a lone 'cemetery attendant' without being detected. Such exercises can build characterization and physicality as well as suspense. In whatever variation, 'Grandmother's Footsteps' has the potential to be excruciatingly suspenseful.[5]

Games such as 'Grandmother's Footsteps' – as well as party games such as 'Sardines' – exploit the discipline of *silence*. The exploitation of silence and stillness is as important in the Grand-Guignol as working on sudden noises and bloodcurdling screams. The well-known children's game 'Sleeping Lions' – also known as 'Dead Soldiers' (Goodland, 1969, 57–8) – is one in which participants need to lie motionless and are 'out' once any movement is detected. For Boal, this becomes 'The Bear of Poitiers' (Boal, 1992, 79), in which all but one performer mime being lumberjacks until the extra performer roars like a bear and everyone lies down, motionless. The bear can approach any lumberjack and can nudge, tickle and sniff, and once movement is elicited that lumberjack becomes another bear, until there is a large sleuth of bears stirring the final passive lumberjack. As Boal observes:

> (The) exercise is very curious in that it produces an effect exactly opposite to its guiding principle. The principle is: if the woodcutter can send his senses to sleep, if you can feel nothing, see nothing, hear nothing, if he can 'play dead', the bear will not attack because bears don't eat dead people. The instruction 'Feel nothing' provokes exactly the opposite reaction, and all the senses become extraordinarily highly developed – you sense much more, hear much better, etc. Fear hypersensitises us! (Boal, 1992, 79)

As with the other games mentioned, it is easy to give the game a Grand-Guignol twist if desired, changing the bear into horror archetypes or characters from the Grand-Guignol plays the ensemble are producing.

Closely affiliated to these games of silence and stillness are other games that develop concentration and focus. In the 'Guarding Captives' game, two

[5] Although a game with ancient roots, 'Grandmother's Footsteps' continues to exist through different media: for example, the indie-produced digital game *Five Nights at Freddy's* (2014) is a simple but extremely suspenseful digital version of 'Grandmother's Footsteps'. The player serves as a nightwatchman monitoring a themed restaurant through numerous CCTVs where the malevolent animatronic animals seem to have a life of their own, only moving when not being watched.

lines of chairs are set up facing each other, each with a 'guard' standing behind each of them. A number of participants are chosen to sit in chairs and await a signal to be released: a wink from the guard of a vacant chair. The released person needs to move to the guard's chair as swiftly as possible, as the guard behind them can trap them with a tap on the shoulder. The game develops excellent focus and tension.[6] A similarly useful game is Jessica Swale's 'Eyes Up!' (2012, 61). In this game, players stand in a circle staring at the ground. A game coordinator counts to three and then all the performers immediately look up at another player in the circle. If the player they have chosen is staring back at them they are both out of the game. In a macabre variant sometimes called 'The Ghost Game' players sit in a circle with their eyes closed, except for one player who is the 'ghost' and moves around the outside of the circle. The players in the circle count aloud to ten: when ten is reached a player who senses the ghost is behind them exclaims 'There is a ghost behind me!': if they are correct, the ghost is defeated and out of the game and a new round begins with the perceptive player as the new ghost. If a player is mistaken they are 'out', as is a player who fails to notice the ghost behind them. The game continues with a reducing number of players until there is a final winner.

The games described in this section are useful to energize a team or to develop a sense of ensemble identity. They also succeed in building skills of focus and dramatic tension. They can be used as team-building exercises, divorced from the theme and content of the Grand-Guignol plays being worked on, but they can also be reworked in order to map them onto the production being developed in terms of character, mood and even narrative. However, as important as the interpersonal and ensemble dynamics in a Grand-Guignol production are, there are other considerations in regard to the spatial dynamics and the 'packaging' of a Grand-Guignol event.

Packaging the Grand-Guignol: Preshow and Hosts

In his book on popular theatre, *A Good Night Out* (1981), John McGrath talks of the attention that must be given to all of the elements that surround the actual performance itself: venue, posters, ticket price, foyer decoration and so on. All of these communicate important messages to the audience and the Grand-Guignol was one theatre that paid particular attention to its para-performative language.

One of the most distinctive achievements of the original Théâtre of the Grand-Guignol in Paris was its creation of a preshow. This was, in fact, the result of the fortunate happenstance of Oscar Méténier's conversion

---

6 We would like to thank Kevin Johnson, theatre practitioner and drama academic at the University of St Mark and St John, Plymouth, and veteran of the Grand-Guignol Laboratory for recommending this game for Grand-Guignol work.

of a small, deconsecrated chapel in the salacious Pigalle district of Paris into a theatre in 1897. Although the interior of the original theatre was stripped out after it closed in 1962, the cobbled dead-end lane that leads up to the façade of the original Grand-Guignol remains, and still has an eerie aura all of its own. This location, setting and atmosphere served to start the performance before the audience had even taken their seats inside the auditorium. Indeed, original spectators of the Grand-Guignol are on record describing the *frisson* of the Parisian journey to the theatre itself. Once inside, the intimate interior of the auditorium retained the carved angels in the rafters and, so it is said, the smell of ecclesiastical incense and candlewax remained imbued into the walls. Although the theatre started as a venue presenting naturalism, it was soon discovered that its 'slice of life' plays were less popular than its 'slice of death' drama, for which 'sacrilegious' displays the setting was ideal. Similarly, an important ingredient in a successful Grand-Guignol show can be finding a way to explore this notion of preshow.

The Thrillpeddlers theatre company in San Francisco has, as its residence, its own customized venue: the Hypnodrome, a truly remarkable horror theatre embellished with neo-Gothic and sideshow artefacts and a range of themed viewing 'booths' for patrons (like the grilled back-row boxes in the original venue, but fully decked out as a padded cell, visions of heaven or hell and so on), as well as general audience seating. Although not all productions can be blessed with such a venue, appropriate locations and suitable venues can sometimes be found. When we performed *A Night at the Grand-Guignol* at the Edinburgh Fringe in 1999, the fact that the performances began at the stroke of midnight in the crypt of an old church served to enhance the performance immeasurably. More simply, in 2014, the Liverpool-based Licence to Thrill horror company used the Lantern Theatre, an ideally suitable venue seating only sixty people, evocatively located in a side street in the docklands area of Liverpool. Although the prominently located Theatre Royal Plymouth (albeit the suitably intimate Drum auditorium) may not have been, on the face of it, an ideal Grand-Guignol venue for the production of Carl Grose's *Grand Guignol* (2009), the 2014 revival did an inventive job of creating an effective nod to preshow: as the audience entered The Drum auditorium they had to walk around the back of the raked seating, navigating a little alleyway lit with imitation gas lamps before stepping out into the ominous splendour of the auditorium and taking a seat. When the production transferred to London it played at the Southwark Playhouse, located away from the bright lights of the West End and involving a suitably dark walk from Borough Tube Station towards Elephant and Castle.

Most importantly, whatever the venue, strategic decisions can be taken to enhance a production in terms of the choice of venue or its preparation. Signposting can be achieved outside the venue, in the foyer or before the actual show begins. In a Grand-Guignol production, the particular use of lighting and sound to create inventive effects and atmosphere in the foyer, refreshment and other vestibule areas can be highly effective. At the London premiere of *Ghost Stories* at the Lyric Hammersmith in 2010 eerie sound effects were used in the bar to create, almost subliminally, an unnerving atmosphere. With our own productions we have used the evocative sounds of cobbled streets or distinctively Parisian music, such as recordings of classic *chansons* or live accordion, to conjure up the environment of the legendary theatre. It is all part of the game.

It goes without saying how effective publicity can be, particularly in terms of striking imagery and 'health warnings' on the posters and fliers and the tactical use of 'rumours' and teasers on social media. Online trailers for Jeremy Dyson and Andy Nyman's stage play *Ghost Stories* focused on post-show audience responses and film of audience reactions during the performance, a decision which focuses everything on the experiential dimension of the spectator without the risk of 'spoilers'. In other words, this tactic reveals a lot about what we will experience and nothing about the plot of the play.

It may be an option, as the moment for curtain-up approaches, to recreate the house doctor (the *médecin de service*) gimmick inaugurated by the Grand-Guignol's greatest entrepreneur Max Maurey. Figures such as the B-movie producer William Castle kept this tradition alive in 1950s–1960s American cinema with a variety of stunts including in-costume nurses, life insurance salesmen and 'coward corners' for over-anxious spectators. Alfred Hitchcock made use of similar strategies with *Psycho*, employing uniformed security guards to ensure that audiences queued in an orderly fashion and absolutely guaranteeing that no late arrivals could gain entry. Whilst there is no evidence suggesting that actors at the rue Chaptal appeared amongst the audience in character, in a contemporary Grand-Guignol production equivalent playfulness could mean using a medical character (a doctor, nurse or both) from one of the forthcoming plays. For example, the medics from a production of *The Final Kiss* or *The Kiss of Blood* could be at the door as the audience come in, playfully giving a word of warning or a mock medical examination to selected members of the audience. Various such options exist for the plays contained in this volume in the forms of, for example, Professor Fargus from *The Man Who Killed Death* (the eccentric scientist on the lookout for interesting human specimens) or, more surprisingly, the ghost hunters in *The Haunted House* or the soldiers in *The Light in the Tomb*. This strategy can help break the security of the fourth wall. It challenges the performers to use their improvisational skills with the audience but can also help to establish character before the scripted performance starts.

In addition to performers, effects can be used. When *The Final Kiss* is the opening play in our productions we have used opium-scented incense to imbue the auditorium, an olfactory signifier of Henri's painkilling addiction. Similarly, the lighting and sound design used in the auditorium can be efficacious: in *Ghost Stories*, the auditorium featured flickering lights to create an unnerving atmosphere. To return, once again, to *Psycho*: much of its success on release was due to the 'theatrical' nature of its screenings; as well as the aforementioned guards, Hitchcock sent strict instructions to cinema managers across the US insisting on the events that should occur at the end of each screening:

> (Close) your house curtains over the screen after the end-titles of the picture, and keep the theater dark for ½ minute. During these 30 seconds of stygian blackness, the suspense of *Psycho* is indelibly engraved in the mind of the audience, later to be discussed among gaping friends and relations. You will then bring up house lights of a greenish hue, and shine spotlights of this ominous hue across the faces of your departing patrons. Never, never, never will I permit *Psycho* to be followed immediately by a short subject or newsreel. (Quoted in Rebello, 2013, 151)

Hitchcock here demands a hybridization of cinema and theatre. Although this is a particular moment in film history, the careful packaging of the event (even when the 'show' is over) offers a lesson for the contemporary Grand-Guignol practitioner: in short, Hitchcock emphasises the impact of 'post-show' as much as preshow.

Another option occasionally employed with Grand-Guignol productions has been the use of a narrator or 'master of ceremonies'. This tradition goes back to the founder of the Grand-Guignol, Oscar Méténier, and his lurid storytelling to audiences outside the theatre. In a contemporary context, an equivalent host can explain the Grand-Guignol form and set the scene for each play. In the License to Thrill horror shows in Liverpool in 2013 and 2014, different performers from the ensemble delivered a monologue between the performed one-act plays. Such devices serve to explain the Grand-Guignol form but can also establish a close link with the audience, creating a personal contact (including finding 'targets') in the popular tradition of the mountebank, showman, ringmaster or stand-up comedian. In the Grand-Guignol Laboratory we have used performers as emcees and other characters to set the scenes and build up anticipation. Their use is deliberately playful but in the overarching experience is designed to enhance the audience's focus for the main attraction: the plays themselves.

The Grand-Guignol Atmosphere and Space: Storytelling and Walkthroughs

In locating an appropriate 'mind-set' for the macabre realm of the Grand-Guignol, we have also employed a variety of games that can be used to establish a clear sense of focus and an awareness of atmosphere and environment. In 'Hum Circle', the ensemble stands in a circle and generates a low-level humming sound. Members standing opposite each other are selected (by a game coordinator) to walk slowly past each other across the circle: although the passers-by are silent, the rest of the circle increases the sound (*not* pitch) of the hum so that it peaks as the walkers pass each other. The effect can be deeply uncanny, creating an eerie ambience and aura of a subliminal malevolence. The exercise continues until all members have been a passer-by.

We have sometimes used a variety of storytelling exercises to create a sense of ensemble and the inhabitation of a space. These have included unifying themes such as:

- ghost stories and urban legends
- nightmares
- anxieties
- common or downright bizarre phobias
- uncanny experiences
- frightening experiences
- cultural experiences (particularly memorable horror films, plays or haunted attractions)

Whatever the agreed topic, sitting in a circle in a low-lit space (candlelit or torch-lit) can be highly successful in creating the right evocative 'mood'. We have sometimes used relay exercises, where the ensemble develop a story together, passing on the story and the candle. Matches can also be useful here as a way to limit the speaker's time: when the flame goes out, the next person lights a match and takes over. Jessica Swale describes a similar game used by John Arden at the Royal Court Theatre which was developed to teach writers the advantages of a minimalist approach and is now widely used as a standard exercise by practitioners in Digital Storytelling. In 'Match Point' (Swale, 2012, 64–5), participants need to tell a personal or invented story but have only the duration of the lit match to do so: when the flame is extinguished they must fall silent. As Swale observes, the participants initially have a tendency to gabble all the information they can in the time constraint. However:

> Ultimately, the most effective responses are often just a couple of select words. The players should observe how, in a certain space of time, we can communicate in an engaging manner. […] Some of the best responses I have seen involved a single word or phrase and then the player has blown out the flame themselves! (Swale, 2012, 64)

The principles of concision nurtured in Arden's game can be extremely valuable for the Grand-Guignol. The one- (occasionally two-) act structure of the Grand-Guignol is designed to be extremely efficient: Grand-Guignol plays need to 'hit the ground running' so that audiences get a sense of the scenario and setting and the gist of the narrative very quickly. These storytelling exercises can also be immensely useful when devising contemporary Grand-Guignol plays. Although a Grand-Guignol ensemble may have a team member who specializes in scriptwriting, these storytelling exercises can help a team carefully explore the Grand-Guignol formula and the location of theme, scenario, suspense, shocks and twists. Once this has been done, the story can be put to paper as a script.

Storytelling work can be developed into dynamic activities that explore the space being used. Ideally, in creating Grand-Guignol productions it is advantageous if a company has the opportunity and time to take control of their venue in order to craft an experience that can encompass the whole theatre, not just the story-world created behind the proscenium. To this end, we have found it beneficial for an ensemble to explore walkthrough work, as it can help to create atmosphere and the uncanny. This can build an *esprit de corps* as well as helping in taking ownership of a space. The ensemble (broken into groups if it is a large company) can look carefully at the venue and rehearsal space and think about how to create a walkthrough experience for rehearsal purposes. Even the most innocuous or neutral space can be turned into something uncanny, unnerving or humorous. Although the stage or performance area can be central, the creators might look at the steps, nooks and crannies of the space. Whether enacting characters from the plays they are working on or in the guise of different archetypes (from a calculated killer to the extrapolated monstrosity of zombies, ghosts or stage madmen) they can inhabit a place within the location. The performer might be instructed to maintain physical contact with the space (literally touching a wall or stair-rail) or can circulate – in clusters or as solo drifters – in a fixed pattern. A 'volunteer' guide from the group can lead the 'audience' (usually other members of the same ensemble who are perhaps developing their own walkthrough) through the space, possibly indicating or explaining what they are encountering. Of course, the guide can be suitably neo-Gothic (like Lurch, the butler from the *Addams Family*, or the in-character staff at Disney's *Haunted Mansion* rides) but we have sometimes found that having the friendliest of guides can create the most unnerving experience:

for example, impersonating an estate agent trying to 'sell' the space oblivious to the entities haunting it or a friendly warden showing some visitors the inmates of this 'special' institution. To this end, torchlight or a lit candle can be helpfully combined with a suitable soundtrack or soundscape. In this way we can explore tension, sound/silence and sudden jumps, creating the most basic of narrative experiences. The exercise can produce promenade experiences that are unnerving or humorous and frequently both. A subsequent version of this exercise can evolve into an oblique exploration of the selection of Grand-Guignol plays the team is producing, shifting the free rein of initial walkthroughs into a mapping onto the production narratives and characters. As regards this collection, examples might include the thrill-seekers in *The Haunted House* or the soldiers in *The Light in the Tomb*.

Of course, although an aspect of preshow is highly recommended, the development of a preshow *narrative* is not a prerequisite for a Grand-Guignol show, and to try deliberately to create one may risk introducing a distraction. More important for a Grand-Guignol show is the idea of the audience's building their *own* narrative as participants in a night of horror theatre. Their experience of the venue may be tacit and obscure but these exercises can create in the Grand-Guignol team an acute awareness of the potential of the venue and the audience's experience, challenging the concept that the show begins only when the audience has sat down and their chatter has dwindled towards anticipatory silence.

To return to dynamic activities in the Grand-Guignol Laboratory which focus on the relationship between the ensemble and the space, a particularly successful theatre game emerged out of a separate pedagogical project exploring digital games in the drama studio:

> The most impressive outcome of these experiments was the development of a scenario based on *Resident Evil* which we now regularly use as a rehearsal/warm-up exercise: 'The Survival Horror Game'. This theatre game requires ideally twelve participants but is easily modified. There is one 'human' (an avatar brought to life) and eleven 'zombies'. The human has a 'gun' but only ten bullets. When the game begins, the human is cast loose into the constructed environment [i.e. this can be low-lit and include constructed obstacles, artificial passageways and so forth] and attempts to survive. [...] The avatar is doomed and it is only a matter of time before death, but a mutual decision is made to stretch the time for dramatic effect. The human does not use up his or her bullets too quickly and neither do the staggering zombies swamp their victim. The result is a dramatic scenario that can be, by turns, hilarious, gruesome or genuinely unnerving. It is an innovative theatre game that has emerged from a video game and has proved extremely beneficial in developing skills

> in creating environments and moods, manipulating suspense and developing physical movements and actions. (Hand, 2005, 217)

The game has an infinite number of variations which can include using a team of survivors, still outnumbered by adversaries, who can develop a heroic narrative with each other in archetypal roles as their gruesome destiny approaches. The exercise can be repeated with different teams of survivors. The game can also be reworked to subvert a team of survivors' preplanning by introducing a surprise variation, with survivors expecting zombies but encountering other monsters such as werewolves who, in a particularly mean version, transform unexpectedly with a key word or sound just when survivors thought the game has been abandoned. The game can be rendered hilarious by the epic mock-heroism or increasing hysteria of doomed survivors, while the zombies decide when to appear and how they might work individually before becoming an amorphous power. The essential aspect of the game is the co-creation of a narrative: how pace, suspense and horror unfurl and are structured by an ensemble in dynamic collaboration.

Another consciously macabre exercise that can develop individual action while facilitating an ensemble's taking collaborative ownership of the environment is 'The Plague Game'. This game is valuable for heightening suspense, awareness and interaction. It can also be very funny. In this game (of which there are countless variations) the whole ensemble circulate, maintaining a dialogue of small talk and shaking hands before moving on. The interaction is important, even if they return to a person they have already met. However, a coin is being passed around discreetly during the handshake. When a person has passed on the coin they have contracted the 'plague' and count to thirty in their head while maintaining normal behaviour. When reaching thirty, they 'die'. The options for this are fully open: deaths might involve screaming, choking, gasping and clasping, or falling silently like a dead weight to the ground. Meanwhile, everyone else carries on as normal until everyone is dead or there is an unaffected survivor. In Clive Barker's version of 'The Plague Game', two survivors can stack the stiffened bodies into a pile (Barker, 1977, 104–5). The game promotes an ownership of the space, while developing spine-tingling, intense or downright absurd ways to die can be enormous fun.

Similarly energetic and amusing is Jessica Swale's game 'The Incredible Itch' (Swale, 2009, 10–11), in which participants suffer an itch which is taken to physical extremes until the players 'die' spectacularly. This can be facilitated by a coordinator who counts through numbers as degrees of affliction, with '1' as the commencement of the itch and '10' being death. 'The Plague Game' and 'The Incredible Itch' can be very light-hearted games, but can be easily reworked into more intense scenarios if required. In his chapter on 'Theatre and the Plague' (Artaud, 1974, 7–21) in *The*

Theatre and Its Double, Antonin Artaud provides a detailed account of the symptoms of the bubonic plague and its effects on the human body and social order. These vivid descriptions can be used, with care and responsibility, as a stimulus for physical interpretation, extrapolating from individual affliction to group interaction.

We have found some similar games to be extremely helpful when working on Grand-Guignol comedy. In rehearsals of René Berton's *Tics, or Doing the Deed* (*Après Coup! ... ou Tics*, 1908) we have often used the 'Tic Word Comedy' game, where participants engage in normal conversation but have been allocated a secret word which will instigate a bizarre tic or mannerism when uttered. Hence, the team might be asked to discuss the broad topic of sport, with individual secret words being 'football', 'Olympics' etc. Another particularly apt game when working on Grand-Guignol comedy is Jessica Swale's improvisation game 'Doctor Damage' (2012, 18–19), in which a doctor and nurse constantly misdiagnose the ailments presented by the other players. The more the examination and suggested treatment spirals out of control and into absurdity the better. As well as helping to develop Grand-Guignol comedy plays, a game such as 'Doctor Damage' can be an excellent release from playing a medical horror play, while still being medically themed.

Another game which works, as it were, on demise in reverse is Clive Barker's 'Frankenstein' game, in which the 'actors are asked to awaken at the flash of imaginary lightning that brings Frankenstein's synthetic monster to life' (Barker, 1977, 112). In this game, after life has been sparked, the participants can explore all the parts of their body and the connections between them. This can be linked into Clive Barker's 'Monster' game, in which actors 'create their own individual monster, with its own shape, its own method of locomotion and its own sound' (Barker, 1977, 114), even working towards an amalgamation with the other monsters. These games serve an important purpose for the Grand-Guignol ensemble. If 'The Plague Game' and its variants can explore ways of dying (useful for numerous Grand-Guignol plays), Barker's 'Frankenstein' and 'Monster' games can investigate ways of reviving and transforming, similarly relevant time and again in the Grand-Guignol. This can be helpful in the exploration of pace: in a Grand-Guignol production, the carefully managed build-up to 'jump' moments or the painfully slow exploitation of a suspenseful action is all-important. In production we have even artificially slowed down a sequence of violence, but have found that spectators never seem to notice if they are sufficiently 'swept up' in the unfurling horror.

In order to explore the twin themes of revival/demise and the techniques of pace and timing within narrative in the Grand-Guignol Laboratory, we often use a radically adapted script based on a classic play from the original Grand-Guignol repertoire: André de Lorde and Alfred Binet's *L'Horrible Expérience* (1909).

Grand-Guignol Laboratory Script: *The Horrific Experiment*

The Horrific Experiment
[*L'Horrible Expérience*, 1909]
André de Lorde and Alfred Binet

As well as being a classic work in the French Grand-Guignol repertoire, *L'Horrible Expérience* was also staged as *The Hand of Death* in the opening season of the London Grand Guignol in 1920, with a revival for the final season in 1922. The London production received a good deal of press coverage, its key moment of horror – the hand of the reanimated female corpse (Sybil Thorndike) rising into the air – being an evocative press photograph and irresistible target for caricaturists. In many ways, this horror play was ideally suited to the London repertoire given that its violent finale is centred on an act of strangulation, less problematic for the British stage censor than some of the more 'bloody' dénouements in the French repertoire.

De Lorde and Alfred Binet's full-length play is in two acts. It establishes the central character of Dr Charrier and his daughter Jeanne, who is in love with her fiancé, the young surgeon Jean Demare. The first act of the play establishes these relationships as well as the domestic context (which includes a characterful female servant) and the medical science discussion so favoured by the Grand-Guignol (and 'authenticated' by the professional expertise of the co-author: the psychologist and inventor of the Binet-Simon Intelligence Scale, Alfred Binet (1875–1911)). This includes a discussion of reanimation and signs of life after death. An unnamed man dressed all in black visits Charrier and recounts an experience at a guillotine execution he assisted in. He describes how the criminal gave him a terrifying look of fury while he was being prepared for the execution. After his decapitation, the corpse grabbed hold of the man and it took enormous efforts to unfasten the dead man's grip. After this dramatic signposting and careful character development, we are taken into the second act of the play. We learn that tragedy has struck and Dr Charrier's daughter – only twenty years old – has unexpectedly died of a cardiac seizure. The distraught Charrier persuades Demare to turn their extensive theoretical discussions regarding the possibility of life after traumatic death into practice and they attempt to resuscitate the corpse of Jeanne.

In this adaptation we focus on the dénouement to the play: the 'horrific experiment' of the title. This adaptation was developed primarily for the purposes of workshop activity, although the script can be performed quite viably as a short horror play in its own right. It is a particularly interesting script to work with because it is an example of a horror play that can very easily become comic. It is, in some ways, the Grand-Guignol at its most melodramatic: the heightened passion and despair of Dr Charrier clashing with the anxious voice of reason in Demare. This short play segment mixes human tragedy and desperation with 'scientific' experimentation. In addition, this set piece has tremendous Gothic potential. The action takes place on a dark and stormy night, and the presence of the dead body on the table must summon up images, for the contemporary spectator, of Frankenstein's creature on the slab, at least as popularized on screen. This is particularly the case when the dead body seems to revive, albeit over twenty years before the Universal screen version of *Frankenstein* (James Whale, 1931), with Colin Clive as Dr Frankenstein, screaming, 'It's alive!' James Whale was an actor in a brief Grand-Guignol revival in London in 1928 (himself playing the role of a re-animated corpse – or, rather, the guillotined head of a condemned man) and the heightened suspense and ironic horror of popular plays such as *The Hand of Death* must have been an influence on his subsequent film career.

In the Laboratory workshops we have frequently found that performers can slip into the mistake of rushing the script. Such an approach can seal the script's fate as comic melodrama. We have found that the solution lies in slowing ... everything ... down. The play needs to unfurl with an almost metronomic tension and control. This strategy is reminiscent of Howard Brenton's note to his play *Christie in Love* (1969):

> The play is a black sketch if played fast, and I suppose it would be quite funny if done at that pace. But I categorically forbid anyone to do so. I want it to last nearly an hour. It is written to be played very slowly. (Brenton, 1980, 26)

Brenton's play is an effective study of one of the most notorious murderers in British history: the serial killer John Reginald Christie, who targeted women in London during the 1940 and 1950s. Christie initially escaped justice when Timothy Evans, the husband of one victim, was executed in an outrageous miscarriage of justice. In contrast to *The Horrific Experiment*, Brenton's script seems *deliberately* humorous: in Scene One of the play, a Constable digs in Christie's 'garden' (a chicken-wire pen of crumpled tabloid newspapers) and recites misogynist limericks to the audience. By artificially slowing the delivery down, the 'dirty' poems are drained of irony or fast-paced comic potential (that could sweep an audience along) and seem disturbingly cold and 'calculated'.

Just as pace can be slowed, with the workshop version of *The Horrific Experiment* a decision can be taken to slow down selected *actions* artificially. To this end, de Lorde and Binet provide many detailed stage directions for a team to work from. Slowing down key moments of the piece can make it eerily compelling. This is reminiscent of the opening scene – or 'coda' – of Steven Berkoff's *The Fall of the House of Usher* (1974), in which the doctor 'walks in slow motion' in a journey which 'normally takes five minutes to cross twenty feet' (Berkoff, 1977, 88). Berkoff's neo-Expressionist, neo-Artaudian vision may not be apt for this Grand-Guignol work, but the principle is the same. Finding points to slow the action can permit nuances of character to become apparent for Dr Charrier and Demare: certainly, we have a clear sense of each character's moral agenda and emotional standpoint. By using the *unsaid* – the silent but intense gaze, the physical deportment of the characters – a great deal can be done to create an enhanced sense of meaning. Furthermore, the third character in the scene, the dead body of Jeanne, is immensely important. The eyes of the spectator can move from Dr Charrier to Demare to Jeanne. The stillness of the dead body can command the gaze of the audience (which is, after all, expecting some sign of life), not least in moments when Charrier and Demare are as still as Jeanne in the creation of a Gothic tableau. The point when Jeanne's hand movements signal reanimation can be a wonderfully eerie sequence, but it can also be deployed as a horror 'jump moment'. These approaches can be explored in detail: whether the slow graceful movement of Jeanne's hand suddenly accelerates into the death-grasp; or if her movements are consistently erratic, in keeping with the electrical current. In the Laboratory we have also explored other options, such as having the face of Jeanne turn, wide-eyed, to stare at the audience impassively yet terrifyingly. Similarly, Jeanne may emit a deathly scream or some other utterance. The options are manifold: Jeanne's revival might be agony, involuntary, maleficent or even coldly calculated. There are countless examples of reanimation in horror film, from unethical medical experimentation through to corpses awaking into zombie existence. Our cinema-savvy audiences will be familiar with many of these, which may challenge the execution of this set-piece of horror, but it can also help to open almost limitless possibilities.

In addition, this scene offers wonderful opportunities for stage design and technology. The short episode can transform a clinical scientific space into the realm of Gothic horror. The scientific experimentation seems to get out of its depth as the force of death takes over. The force of death in the scene is unseen yet inexorable, as in the film *Final Destination* (James Wong, 2000) and its numerous sequels. In order to achieve this increasingly Gothic atmosphere, a team can use the lighting (including the storm and the sudden extinguishing of the lamps), the sound (of the rain and thunder but also the electrical equipment) and visual effects (such as the window flying open). The use of lighting to create shadows on the stage was a common technique at the rue Chaptal, as was the carefully managed use of sound effects to heighten atmosphere, most famously perhaps in *Gardiens de Phare* (*The Lighthousekeepers*), where Paul Ratineau replicated the sound of seagulls pecking against the glass windows of the lighthouse in eerie anticipation of Alfred Hitchcock's 1963 horror classic *The Birds* (Pierron, 2011, 88–9). A literal 'dark' mood to the scene can help to realize the tension and atmosphere of the sequence.

In conclusion, we have found this to be a great piece to use with an ensemble to develop good handling of Grand-Guignol pace and delivery. It is a piece that can be reworked and explored in different ways, especially if it finds itself slipping into comedy. To play it for laughs is all too easy: how can we work on the play to keep an audience gripped by its tension? Sometimes we might deliberately play the script for laughs, in a fast-paced *Carry on Screaming* (Gerald Thomas, 1966) spoof version, full of hilarity and archly interpreted characters. Once that version is 'out of the system', we will concentrate on how to make the script function as horror drama. In this way, this Laboratory script can be a useful one to use during rehearsals when working on other Grand-Guignol plays, as it can fine-tune an awareness of focus, atmosphere and pace for the Grand-Guignol ensemble. These are aspects that are no less important for the Dr Charrier character, who gradually loses his mind during his crazed experiment; the morally forthright Jean, who is intimidated and lured into unethical practice; and the dead stillness of Jeanne, about to be physically resurrected.

The Horrific Experiment
[*L'Horrible Expérience*, 1909]

André de Lorde and Alfred Binet
Adapted by Richard J. Hand and Michael Wilson

Characters:
Charrier, a senior doctor
Jeanne, Charrier's daughter
Jean, a junior doctor

Scene:
Dr Charrier's surgery

Context:
Dr Charrier's daughter Jeanne has been found dead. She has died of a cardiac seizure. Her fiancé, Jean Demare, is a young surgeon and professional associate of her father. Demare found Jeanne's body and tried in vain to resuscitate her. Dr Charrier has arrived and is deeply traumatized by the death of his daughter. He mourns over the body while Demare attempts to console him …

(*Jeanne's dead body lies on a table. Dr Charrier mourns over her.*)

CHARRIER: I could almost believe that if I called out her name she would open her eyes ... (*quietly becoming more desperate*) Jeanne ... Jeanne ... my darling ... Jeanne ...

DEMARE (*leading Charrier away*): I beg you ... saying things like that, attempting to do such things won't help us in our grief.

CHARRIER (*struggles*): So what!? My 'grief' ... I don't want it to end! I want to live with it. When I lost my daughter, I lost everything. (*Goes over to the body.*) Her face. She looks so peaceful.

DEMARE: She didn't suffer ...

CHARRIER (*he looks at Demare as if he has found a little consolation*): Yes?

DEMARE: She died instantly – a cardiac seizure.

CHARRIER (*at Demare's words, he shudders and continues to tremble*): A seizure ...

DEMARE: Yes ... there's not a mark on her body.

CHARRIER (*to himself*): A seizure ...

(*Silence. Charrier looks tortured. He takes Demare's hand and looks at him strangely.*)

CHARRIER: Are we ... alone?

DEMARE (*startled*): Yes – all alone.

CHARRIER: No-one's here?

DEMARE: No-one.

CHARRIER: Did you love her? Love her with all your heart?

DEMARE: How can you ask me that?

CHARRIER: You loved my daughter and yet there you stand, resigned to her death. Just like all the others. You coward!

DEMARE: Me!?

CHARRIER: We are all cowards when it comes to ... Her.

DEMARE: Her? Who do you mean?

CHARRIER: *Death.* We all hate Death and yet we let Her do whatever She wants. No one dares lift a finger ... well, I will. I will dare ...

DEMARE (*bewildered*): What are you going to do?

CHARRIER: The experiment I always wanted to undertake – I will do it ... on my daughter!

DEMARE: On your daughter!?

CHARRIER (*moving around with energy*): We've got scissors, scalpels, sponges ... I can operate ...

DEMARE: It's impossible!

CHARRIER: Nothing's impossible. We just don't know ... we don't know anything ... we're just never brave enough to try ...

DEMARE: She's been dead for hours!

CHARRIER: I will try ...

DEMARE: We tried earlier – when I found her dead on the grass outside ...

CHARRIER: *I* wasn't there.

DEMARE: Then later, myself and two other doctors ... we all tried ... artificial respiration ... resuscitation ...

CHARRIER: We must work on the heart ...

DEMARE: It is too late.

CHARRIER: Why?

DEMARE: Her heart has stopped beating. She's dead.

CHARRIER: Maybe not. I can make her heart contract and keep that up for a few hours ... I'm sure ...

DEMARE: And then what?

CHARRIER: We will see the effect of a beating heart in a dead body ...

DEMARE: It's impossible!

CHARRIER: I'll try it.

DEMARE: The grief has made you lose your reason.

CHARRIER: I will try it. (*He moves to start work and Demare blocks him.*)

DEMARE: It's insane!

CHARRIER: You're scared!

DEMARE: I'm scared for your sanity!

CHARRIER: No! You're scared! You told me you love her and yet you're scared of her, scared of her corpse. Maybe you're not even scared – you're *disgusted* by her! (*Shoves Demare roughly.*)

DEMARE: Calm down.

CHARRIER: Get off of me! I treated you like a son – you loved my daughter ... she loved you ... *adored* you ...

DEMARE (*weak*): What are you going to do ...?

CHARRIER (*stares intensely at Demare and eventually speaks in a low tone*): You'll see ... (*Goes over to Jeanne's body.*)

DEMARE (*in terror, hardly able to speak*): What are you doing? This is terrible! What are you doing? No, Dr Charrier! No! Charrier! I beg you! (*Charrier picks up Jeanne's body and carries it to the examination table. Demare tries to restrain him.*)

CHARRIER: Let go of me!

DEMARE: No – it's impossible ... you don't really want to ...

CHARRIER: I want to carry out an experiment.

DEMARE: On your own daughter?

CHARRIER: On my daughter.

DEMARE: It's impossible.

CHARRIER: We will see.

DEMARE: No ... no ... Charrier ... don't even contemplate it ... I beg you.

CHARRIER (*oblivious to Demare*): My poor child ... we've waited too long ... (*to Demare*) Give me the scissors ... (*Demare is overwhelmed by Charrier's authority and obeys mechanically. Then Demare turns his head away, unable to watch. Charrier cuts open Jeanne's dress.*) I couldn't take immediate action when I got here ... But it doesn't matter now ... I was just overwrought earlier ... (*He folds up his sleeves and prepares to operate.*)

DEMARE (*trying to stop him*): Dr Charrier ...

CHARRIER (*vicious*): Cotton wool – at once! And the scalpel ... there ... in that tray ... We must work quickly ... I will make an incision ...

DEMARE (*assisting but unable to look*): It's horrifying ...

CHARRIER: Bring the lamp over ... (*Demare does so but is scared to look at the body.*) Why are you shaking? You're scared. Scared of what? Scared of seeing her live again? Her – my darling daughter ... my darling Jeanne ... Ah! It's so painful to think of my daughter ... Death has ruined her ... Death ruins everything She touches ... (*He operates for a while. He suddenly drops the scalpel.*) Ah!

DEMARE: What!? What is it!?

CHARRIER: Nothing, nothing, just a little blood. (*Gives Demare cotton wool dripping with blood.*)

DEMARE: Blood?

CHARRIER: Yes, I opened a vessel. There was a blood clot ...

DEMARE (*his head in hands*): It's horrible!

CHARRIER (*violently*): *It is essential to control your nerves*! (*Charrier picks up the scalpel and continues operating.*) The electrodes ... (*Demare passes them.*) We must be quick ... the flesh is beginning to decompose already ...

DEMARE: This is *immoral*!

CHARRIER: It is essential to control your nerves. Switch on the current.

DEMARE: Unethical ... futile ... (*Demare goes to the generator. Sound of electricity.*)

CHARRIER: Is the current flowing?

DEMARE: Yes ...

CHARRIER: Increase the frequency. (*Listens to Jeanne's heart.*) I'm listening to the heart ... I can't ... hear anything ... Increase the current.

DEMARE: Dr Charrier, please ...

CHARRIER: Increase it, I tell you! (*Electricity sounds louder.*) It's starting to beat ...! I am sure ... I'm sure ... increase the current! It must be ... ah! I thought I could feel her trembling ... but it's just the sound of the electricity ...

DEMARE (*horrified and sorrowful*): It is impossible to resuscitate the dead!

CHARRIER (*desperate, looking at his daughter*): We can't ... the heart is still, frozen ... it's too late ... too late ... it's over. (*Holds her head against him.*) Death has won ... She's taken my daughter ... She doesn't want us to be together anymore ... (*with rage*) Yes, Death is here! I can feel it ... touch it ... and I can't do anything against it ... Death has taken my daughter ... She's taken her away ... (*furious*) Damn you! Damn you!

(*Charrier lets her head down. Suddenly a gust of wind pounds the window and it swings open violently. As the curtains flutter in the wind, the breeze whistles through the room and the lamp goes out. The room gets darker. A long silence. Charrier and Demare run to opposite walls in their shock. All is dark. The eerie drone of the electric current can be heard. The room is lit by the blue glow of the electrical equipment. Charrier and Demare cry out in fear and then Charrier runs over to the wall next to the open window. He shudders in fear, his eyes fixed on the extinguished lamp.*)

CHARRIER (*speaking with difficulty*): Who put the lamp out? Demare, did you?

DEMARE: No – the storm ...

CHARRIER (*in terror*): Someone else is in the room ...

DEMARE: No, no ...

CHARRIER: Yes, yes ...

DEMARE: Charrier, please ...

CHARRIER: I tell you someone else is in the room, someone's over there ... in the dark ... watching us ... (*He stares over at his daughter.*)

DEMARE (*heading towards the lamp*): Calm down, I beg you ... I will relight the lamp ...

CHARRIER: No, no, don't move ... (*Pause. Suddenly staring at the corpse.*) Look ... She's reviving ...

DEMARE (*quickly turning his gaze towards the corpse illuminated by the blue light*): What?

CHARRIER (*staring at Jeanne*): Her body moved ... (*Jeanne moves very slightly.*) And now her hand ... Look at her hand! (*Very slowly, Jeanne's right hand reaches up almost automatically but with jerking movements. She tries to clasp at something invisible. Charrier remains against the wall, staring at the hand intently.*)

DEMARE: It's … it's rigor mortis setting in …

CHARRIER (*joyfully he dashes over to Jeanne*): No, no, she's coming back to life … there's no doubt about it, she's alive …

DEMARE (*trying to calm him down*): It's just the muscular contractions of rigor mortis setting in … We talked about that, remember, a few hours ago …

CHARRIER (*kisses Jeanne's hand with frenzy*): Jeanne, my darling! Jeanne! (*Just as Charrier kisses the palm of her hand, Jeanne's hand clutches Charrier's face and then slides down to his throat. Charrier falls to his knees, his face staring at the audience, and struggles.*) You're hurting me … You're too strong …

DEMARE: It's rigor mortis – and the electricity's still on! (*He rushes to the generator.*)

CHARRIER: Agh! Help me … Free me … I'm choking … (*imploring Jeanne*) Let go … you're strangling me … let me go … (*Demare dashes over and tries to free Charrier from Jeanne's grip.*)

DEMARE: I can't do it!

CHARRIER: I'm choking … (*Jeanne falls off the table on top of Charrier and they lie on the floor.*)

DEMARE: I'll have to smash the fingers … (*Demare pounds Jeanne's hands violently. Eventually he frees Charrier and pulls him away from Jeanne. Demare attempts to resuscitate Charrier for a few moments then gives up.*) Dead. (*Silence.*) Death has had Her revenge.

THE END

Games of Violence and Sensory Deprivation

There is no escaping the violence inherent in the Grand-Guignol, whether in the form of surprise attacks, bloody revenge or comic *Schadenfreude*. In this regard, it can be useful to explore more 'violent' games. However, it is inadvisable to leap into such games: a level of *trust* within the group is essential. In discussing violent theatre games, Clive Barker makes an important observation:

> Violence is relatively easy to release. Tenderness is much more difficult. […] Violence is simple to release, although it is then difficult

> to help people control it. The usual pattern is for it to be inhibited again afterwards. (Barker, 1977, 107)

What this means is that violent games must comprise a combination of *trust* and *control*. Such games must be carefully monitored and coordinated, ensuring that all processes are fair and safe. One option is to ensure that everyone gets their 'turn': this can even extend to the rehearsal of plays themselves, wherein it might be worth considering that role reversal is deployed as a strategy (as a 'welcome break') so that it is not just one actor who is enacting all the violence and another receiving it. In regard to safety, obvious measures include removing footwear and, if objects are needed, using sponge shapes, polyethylene pipe cladding or rolled-up newspapers. In an unnamed game Barker describes (Barker, 1977, 107) – which we call 'Circle Violence' – the players stand in a circle with their eyes closed and their hands outstretched behind them. Another player walks around the circle with a rolled-up newspaper and places it silently in the left or right hand of one of the people in the circle. This person then starts to chase and strike the person to the right or left, depending on which hand received the 'weapon', until the victim has completed a full circle and has retaken their place in the circle. This valuable game can build up tension and heighten senses, primarily owing to the shifts between intent listening and escaping fast.

The genre of 'Blindfold Games' is developed from violent games such as 'Circle Violence'. Very apt for this collection is the children's party game 'Blind Man's Buff' (also known as 'Blind Man's Bluff') in which a blindfolded player attempts to catch other players. The game can exploit silence and stillness but can also utilize audacious taunting and 'daring'. Other blindfold games include variations on Chinese opera set-pieces wherein two or three 'guards' are blindfolded and a 'burglar' attempts to search for treasure. This can subsequently be played in a fully sighted version where actors pretend to be in the dark and collaborate to create suspense and irony. Clive Barker describes this game in depth as 'The Fight in the Dark' (Barker, 1977, 57–61), in both sighted and blindfolded versions, and also suggests other variations. In Jessica Swale's game 'Cyclops' (2012, 62) an object is placed under a chair upon which sits a blindfolded 'Cyclops', while a sighted 'Ulysses' character(s) attempts to steal the treasure without being caught. In Anna Scher and Charles Verrall's game 'The Hunter and the Hunted' (Scher and Verrall, 1975, 24), one blindfolded person needs to navigate a space – to find an object or to escape – while another seeks to catch them. The game can also be adapted into a 'zombie' version, with survivors searching for an 'amulet' amidst staggering zombies. Similar is Patrick Goodland's 'Gladiators' game (Goodland, 1969, 62), wherein two blindfolded gladiators armed with rolled-up newspapers stalk each other in a circle of the other members of the ensemble (the duellists are like the *andabatae*, the Roman gladiators who wore helmets that rendered them sightless). When one succeeds in striking their opponent, the victim is replaced by another gladiator taken from the crowd and blindfolded.

Probably the most successful blindfold game, and the one we most frequently use in the Grand-Guignol Laboratory, is a blindfolded version of Augusto Boal's 'Vampires of Strasbourg' (Boal, 1992, 110–11). In this game, the blindfolded players are disorientated (led around the space by sighted observers), after which they must keep moving around the space with their arms folded. A coordinator chooses one victim and gently pinches them on the neck: the victim is 'vampirized', emits a burst of evil laughter and stalks other victims with arms outstretched. If they catch someone they pinch their neck and they become a vampire too. If a vampire is pinched they utter an ecstatic sigh and become humanized, folding their arms again. For variety, zombies, for example, can be used instead of vampires. The game can be as amusing as it is thrilling.

Grand-Guignol and Eroticism

The Grand-Guignol is very much a theatre for adults. It is the 'Punch and Judy theatre for grown-ups', as a translation of its French title would suggest. And, in addition to its violent themes and gruesome enactments, it was also a theatre of *eroticism*. As time went on, the Grand-Guignol did, on occasion, feature nudity, but usually its eroticism was far more subtle, with plays requiring the calculated use of seduction as a strategy to develop tension and anticipation in the audience.

The foregrounding of the erotic is immediately evident in the Grand-Guignol's repertoire of comedies: frequently these farces or romps have themes of adultery, fetishism and other sexual peccadilloes at their heart. The Grand-Guignol often takes an absolute delight in giving its audiences figures of bourgeois respectability and revealing their hypocrisy and deep-seated lusts as their pompous respectability collapses. In this collection, Régis Gignoux's *The Kama Sutra* is a case in point. Shallow middle-class propriety is seen to crack and fall apart. Likewise, in Octave Mirbeau's *The Lovers* we see the elaborate ritual gone through by a young couple in order to consummate their relationship. In such plays, the erotic needs to be a central theme: it aims for laughs, but is also designed to titillate audience members. However, eroticism also exists in the horror repertoire. Several plays – including classics such as Maurice Level's *The Final Kiss* and André de Lorde and Pierre Chaine's *Private Room Number Six* – present the audience with what could be called 'the spider and the fly' scenarios, wherein a victim is subjected to a climax of violence after gradual entrapment and slow, suspenseful manipulation – a kind of 'deadly' seduction. Sometimes eroticism in the Grand-Guignol can be far more extreme, however. In this collection, *The Haunted House* presents a jealous husband who has enslaved his wife. Other plays in the repertoire push on-stage sadism to the very limit: in a play diametrically opposed to the subtle eroticism of other plays in the repertoire, Eddy Ghilain's *Le Cercueil flottant* (*The Floating Coffin*, 1960), a woman has her nipples cut off with scissors before being burned alive, a horror graphically displayed in a production photograph reproduced by Agnès Pierron (2002, 148). Such displays can be truly horrific, but they reflect a broad cultural theme that can be detected in the Grand-Guignol and elsewhere: namely, the close relationship between sex and death. Although this 'linking of *l'amour* and *la mort* in French has become something of a cliché [there is] nonetheless in Parisian culture ... a constant interplay and exchange between the erotic and death' (Hand, 2010, 66).

Once again this takes us back to the aspect of trust in the Grand-Guignol production process. The handling of the erotic or 'seductive' element in Grand-Guignol performance needs to be managed with as much care as is needed when choreographing violence. A high level of trust between the performers is required. Among the games we have used that are helpful in exploring this is 'The Scarf Seduction Game'. In this game, in which not a word needs to be spoken, one player has a small silk scarf which they can wrap around their neck or around their wrist. Another player (or players) needs to coax the scarf away from the first player. Someone might try to snatch it off them, but the player is unlikely to let it go. More successful is a slow physical process of manipulation, coercion and persuasion, until the scarf-player relinquishes their hold on the precious object. It can be a highly sensual game, but is one that can be undertaken only when absolute trust and understanding exists within the ensemble. Although numerous permutations are possible, we have often found this game particularly useful for female characters manipulating male characters. As Karoline Gritzner writes: the 'inherent theatricality ... of seduction as a form of self-performance for another (...) can be an empowering experience especially for women' (Gritzner, 2010, 7). Many other games exploring seduction, the cherishing of fetishized objects and sensuality can be used or developed, some of which can also help develop the narrative journey of a particular play and performance. Whatever choices are made, the exercises should have clear objective purposes and be used responsibly.

The Journey of Grand-Guignol Performance

There are, doubtless, hundreds more options that can be used when developing a Grand-Guignol production. Either way, we would like to reiterate the importance of developing trust and respect in a production. In the adrenalin-fuelled roller-coaster journey of the Grand-Guignol performance the ensemble needs to take its willing audience with it on the journey, but at all times the performance needs to be totally safe. Challenging material, such as scenes of violence, might, in fact, be thoroughly melodramatic (especially when assessed out of context), but in order to take the audience to confront 'the slice of death', the journey needs to be handled with great care. A particular play may be set in a realist context and the short duration of a Grand-Guignol play requires its audience to understand the context extremely quickly. Once the audience is drawn into the narrative, the play can unfurl, usually signposting its dénouement, and the audience watches the dramatic action reveal itself at an inexorable pace. In many respects the traditional Grand-Guignol plays follow a distinct pattern in exposition that evolves from realism to melodrama, with the audience unaware of the 'join'. It can also be helpful to enhance the realism of a play with a degree of research, including speaking to willing professionals such as medics to gain authenticity in some medical-based scenes and so on (this is, after all, exactly what André de Lorde and others did as Grand-Guignol writers).

As we have already indicated, every action in the Grand-Guignol play needs to be carefully choreographed and tricks need to be mastered with the finesse of the stage magician. A scene of violence can be broken down into component parts in a manner seen in the legendary Open Theatre production *The Serpent* (1968), written by Jean-Claude van Itallie and directed by Joseph Chaikin. In the 'Kennedy-King Assassination' scene (van Itallie, 1969, 9–15), the assassination of John F. Kennedy is broken down into twelve meticulously detailed tableaux which are run in order and then in a variety of different ways – reverse, random order and so on. This type of 1960s *avant-gardist* theatre may be a world away from the Grand-Guignol, but the careful choreography of the intense scene, shifting from normality and celebration to horror and back again, is a useful way of breaking down the physical action of a violent scene. This can inculcate a sense of disciplined precision and security that is extremely valuable when portraying scenes that need to 'look' brutal and deadly.

The Grand-Guignol performer needs, as we have written elsewhere, to engage in a kind of balancing act, a careful and skilled management of opposing tensions:

> The job of the Grand Guignol actor ... has been likened to the journey of a tightrope walker, trying to keep a balance between these opposing tensions, treading the fine line that maximizes the horrific effect of the moment, by taking it to the very edge (but not transgressing it) where horror meets comedy. The opposing forces at either end of the tightrope, which keep it tense, are those of melodrama and naturalism and it is this tension that is the major preoccupation of the Grand Guignol actor. (Hand and Wilson, 2007, 45)

Similarly, in 1931 a journalist wrote of the Grand-Guignol actor that 'he does not simply live his part. He is a chronometer' (Hand and Wilson, 2002, 47). Although Grand-Guignol performers might immerse themselves in a role in a psychological way, much more than that is needed (albeit full-blown Method Acting is probably to be avoided): the actor is a chronometer, a timepiece, working with metronomic precision, judiciously balancing action, character and the relationship with the audience.

The Grand-Guignol is a theatre of decisions carefully managed to achieve maximum effect. Just as an actor/director/team considers how to unfurl their playful night of horrors as a whole, they need to consider all specific moments to optimise the event. In our 2009 touring production of *Horror and Laughter: A Night at the Grand-Guignol* we included *The Kiss of Blood* as the final play in the *douche écossaise*. In developing the finale of the play, we made an important decision which would have repercussions for all on stage:

> As in other places in the Grand-Guignol, when Hélène bursts into manic laughter we are witnessing a character become a (stage) lunatic. However, in production this was expanded so that *all* the characters descended into individual insanities. Although Antonin Artaud never mentions the Grand-Guignol in his writing, his concepts of cruelty and plague in the theatre were contemporaneous with it. Using Artaud-based workshops in rehearsal was a welcome shift away from exploring naturalism and melodrama. We were able to locate individual 'madnesses': Hélène finds the delirium of her ecstatic triumph; Joubert collapses into suppliant degeneration; the super-rational and egotistical Leduc is rendered into traumatic shock; and Volguine is frozen in introverted and appalled horror. The world has gone mad: all reason has unravelled. (Hand, 2013, 155)

Another key area in decision-making is the concept of the fourth wall. We have already outlined how this can be explored in a preshow, but it can also be built into a play itself. In the rare and invaluable footage of a Grand-Guignol performance presented in *Ecco* (1965), we see the actor suddenly stare directly at the audience. We have analysed this sequence in depth (Hand and Wilson, 2002, 35–7), but what is important in this context is the decision that is implicit: when a Grand-Guignol actor looks into the eyes of the audience it is a bold performance statement from which there is no turning back and so it is a decision that has to be taken with the utmost care and calculation.

Other decisions are similarly calculated in order to maximize the desired effect and impact. In our 2002–03 touring production of *The Ultimate Torture* we replaced D'Hémelin's scripted revolver with a blood-emitting knife, partly because we had recently acquired this excellent bespoke prop from Davenports magic shop in London and wanted to put it into action, but also because we wanted to explore the dynamics of the climactic scene with a blade as opposed to a gunshot, which allows for a much slower and more measured unravelling of the play's final moments. We had used a stage gun in the violent finale of the 2000 premiere of Joseph Conrad's Grand Guignol play *Laughing Anne* (1920) and it seemed an ideal opportunity to explore 'something different'.

The fact that the Grand-Guignol is a form of popular culture that inhabits the world of horror means that there are many possibilities for the contemporary ensemble to utilize in the creation of horror plays. Although the Grand-Guignol is an example of ultra-realist horror, as verified by the evidence of its congealing stage blood and the verisimilitude of its eye gouging, acid attacks and decapitations, for the modern audience a night of Grand-Guignol can often echo the neo-Gothic and more familiar iconography of film, especially the horror or thriller genres. For example, in locating a production concept and paradigm for the aforementioned *Laughing Anne* production, a structure broadly parallel with *Taxi Driver* (Martin Scorsese, 1976) was discovered and the violent gun-toting dénouement to the film was used as inspiration and allusion (see Hand, 2001). The use of cinema in this way can be helpful in performing Grand-Guignol for contemporary audiences. This was an acutely important issue in the *Horror and Laughter: A Night at the Grand-Guignol* production, as it was commissioned for the 2009 Abertoir Horror Festival, an event traditionally dominated by horror movies. In order to negotiate the 'lost' historic form of Grand-Guignol popular horror performance and to find contemporaneous 'equivalents' for an audience predominantly of film fans, the production of *The Kiss of Blood* located an overarching principle influenced by a specific horror film:

> *The Kiss of Blood* is a script which is, as it were, in two halves. The first half is set in Leduc's surgery with all the wipe-clean paraphernalia and hierarchy of the medical world. The second half takes us to Joubert's home and it is within this domain that we are led to the dénouement of horror, retribution and madness. In our design principal, we kept the first half as white as possible: the lighting; the uniforms worn by the medical staff; the equipment they used; and the section of skull the surgeon removed from the doomed patient's head. By the same token, when we get to Joubert's house, the theme was oppressively gothic: dark coloured clothes and props; and subdued, brooding lighting which left the corners of the stage in oblivion. The inspiration for this was taken from Alfred Hitchcock's *Psycho*, essentially the juxtaposition between the mundane, brightly lit world of the modern office, freeway and shower room tiles and the gothic world of the Bates mansion where we witness the profound horror and madness of its occupant. There is also an equivalent construction

> of abject females in *Psycho* and *The Kiss of Blood*: Norman Bates lives with the oppressive fantasy figure of his mother and believes her to be 'real', Joubert beholds his corporeal wife as a fantasy figure. (Hand, 2013, 156)

We must emphasise that we could have approached this production in countless different ways. What we would recommend, however, is the establishment of strong character and interaction: the dynamic of the performers' constructed characters and their dramatic conflict are key to any Grand-Guignol production. To this end, work on the balance between character, pacing and tension – and how this (and hence the audience) can be manipulated – is invaluable. To help us explore this in the Grand-Guignol Laboratory we have often used an adapted script of *The Lottery of Death*.

Grand-Guignol Laboratory Script: *The Lottery of Death*

The Lottery of Death or Seven Crimes in the Barber's Chair
[*La Loterie de la Mort ou Sept crimes dans un Fauteuil*, 1957]
Eddy Ghilain and Pierre Larroque

Rather like *The Horrific Experiment*, this Laboratory script is also performable as a short play in its own right: the audience can understand the situation not least because the script utilizes such a large amount of backstory. Eddy Ghilain and Pierre Larroque's *The Lottery of Death* is a play from the twilight years of the Grand-Guignol. In this heightened tale of vengeance, a cuckolded husband – Victor Foulon – was incarcerated in a lunatic asylum. After escaping with a psychopathic sidekick and stealing the identity of a dead man, the two take over a barbershop and use it to exact revenge on Foulon's adulterous wife and all her lovers. The play is set on Bastille Day, the noise and commotion on the city streets distracting from the horrors being perpetrated in the barbershop. Although the original play is longer, with more characters 'framing' the central drama, we have streamlined the narrative, plot and action for three performers. This is a very 'male' play in terms of cast, but we frequently adapt the script for an all-female group of actors (relocating the play to a hairdressers) and find it works equally well.

For many readers and audiences the fact that this horror play is set in a barbershop immediately summons up the legend of Sweeney Todd. A fascinating example of an urban legend and part of London folklore, Sweeney Todd first appeared in the anonymously authored 'penny dreadful' series *A String of Pearls* (1846–47), although figures such as Peter Haining have insisted that the events are based on a true story. The success of the serial swiftly led to dramatizations such as George Dibdin Pitt's hugely popular 1847 stage melodrama and numerous others, while in the twentieth century and beyond the 'demon barber of Fleet Street' has been interpreted on screen by a surprisingly diverse range of actors. As Richard J. Hand and Mary Traynor write:

> *Sweeney Todd* presents a fascinating and probably unique story in terms of its origin, legacy and cultural reinvention. (...) Sweeney Todd has become an icon of horror: not like Transylvanian icons, the fantasy horrors of Frankenstein, Dracula and the Wolfman made so popular in Universal movies; Sweeney Todd is a horror icon of the 'possible' and as such has joined the sepulchral pantheon inhabited by Jack the Ripper or Norman Bates. (Hand and Traynor, 2011, 190)

The notion of 'possible' horror lies at the heart of the Grand-Guignol and, in this respect, the demon barber and his equally diabolical neighbour, the baker Mrs Lovett (who disposes of Todd's victims in her popular meat pies), would seem ideal material for the 'Theatre of Horror'. However, the very British legend of Sweeney Todd was a staple of Victorian melodrama, a very different world of heightened horrors to that of the Parisian Grand-Guignol. Moreover, the story was so popular that it did not belong in the modern horrors of the Grand-Guignol. When the Grand Guignol was running in London between 1920 and 1922 one might have expected a Sweeney Todd-esque tale in the repertoire, but this new theatre of thrills consciously avoided anything too obviously reminiscent of Victorian melodrama. This is despite the fact that one of the screenwriters behind Tod Slaughter's film version of *Sweeney Todd: The Demon Barber of Fleet Street* (Georg King, 1936) was none other than H.F. Maltby, the most prolific playwright in London's Grand Guignol. Although the London Grand Guignol did not stage a version of Sweeney Todd, the 1920s audience did get *Shepherd's Pie*, a play about cannibalism which was, significantly, a comedy (it is noteworthy that its title gives away its central black joke and, as such, is a precursor to one of the funniest lines in Stephen Sondheim's *Sweeney Todd* musical play (1979): "we have some shepherd's pie peppered/With actual shepherd on top!"). *Shepherd's Pie* was itself a translation of *Bloomfield et Cie* (*Bloomfield and Co.*), a 1906 Grand-Guignol comedy by Léon Frapié and Georges Fabri.

Although so strongly associated with British culture, it is highly ironic that the legend of Sweeney Todd seems most likely to be *French* in origin. As Robert L. Mack explains, a 1612 publication by Jacques du Breuil contains:

> ... what is very possibly the earliest published account of the story of a barber who murders his customers, and whose cellar is connected to the premises of a nearby 'patissier' or pastry-cook, who then makes use of the bodies of victims by turning them into meat pies. (Mack, 2007, 337)

The location of the crimes was a building known as the 'Marmousets' in Paris, but further evolutions of the tale place the murderous barber and baker in the Rue de la Harpe. Like Sweeney Todd, the Rue de la Harpe murders have been contested both as urban legend and as true history. Either way, it is fascinating to consider that Sweeney Todd – a horror icon so synonymous with London – is likely to be Parisian.

Whatever the derivation of Sweeney Todd, a barbershop is an irresistible setting for a horror play, and Ghilain and Larroque's 1957 play finally exploited this for the Grand-Guignol. This French take on Sweeney Todd is familiar and gruesome, but the difference is that, in the French context, we witness crimes of passion: revenge for adultery. This is a stark contrast to Todd and Mrs Lovett, the diabolical but very British shopkeepers, who relish the money. Interestingly, Christopher Bond's reworking of the story in the play *Sweeney Todd, The Demon Barber of Fleet Street* (1973) – the source for Stephen Sondheim's musical (in turn adapted to the screen by Tim Burton in 2007) – introduces a revenge theme: Todd a man much wronged and, initially, commanding our sympathy.

The barbershop or hairdressers make for a fantastic visual setting on stage and screen. The horror potential of a situation so familiar yet, in theory, so perilous has been used, very memorably, in a number of films. The classic of early British cinema *A Cottage on Dartmoor* (Anthony Asquith, 1929) exploits the danger of the barbershop, the central character being an insanely jealous barber. In one of the most memorable episodes in the masterpiece of horror-comedy *Theatre of Blood* (Douglas Hickox, 1973), Edward Lionheart (Vincent Price) masquerades as a hairdresser and murders one of his critics (Coral Browne) by electrocuting her with customized hair-curlers. Barbershops as suspense locations have also featured on television: *The Alfred Hitchcock Hour* episode 'Return of Verge Likens' (5 October 1964) is set in a small mountain town in the US in which a young man (a very young Peter Fonda) vows to kill the man who murdered his father; having trapped his victim in the barber chair he gradually reveals who he is as he shaves the man with a cutthroat razor. The film's pacing and close-ups exploit the tensions of the victim and his vengeful nemesis and, at the end, when the sheriff breaks open the door he finds the victim is dead ... but from a heart attack.

In many ways, the adaptation we have provided here can find itself between *Theatre of Blood* and 'Return of Verge Likens'. The scene has a perverse humour to it, especially to be found in the sidekick Leon. As well as Leon's antics and the heavy-handed exposition and explanations offered in the dialogue, however, the scene is exceptionally useful in developing a sense of dramatic tension: the murder of Jean at the end of the play is clearly inevitable, but the journey there is a fascinating one. The play establishes three powerful characters in the vengeful *tormentor*, the murderous *sidekick* and the hapless *victim*. Because of this, we have always found the adaptation to be immensely useful in Grand-Guignol rehearsal and training, as it allows a vivid exploration of both the triangular relationship and the place of very bleak humour within the mounting tension. As with *The Horrific Experiment*, the performers can play with character, pacing and tension and explore the control of humour, building up the pressure and apparently letting it abate before the gruesome end.

As well as being an excellent exercise for performers and the management of a horror narrative, the script affords interesting technical opportunities, such as the closing of the blinds – a moment which should transform the mood as radically as it transforms the lighting. Likewise, the central prop of the barbershop chair affords a range of opportunities. For example, does the audience see the bloody murder of Jean full-on or do the killers swivel the chair away from the audience and turn it back to show the gory aftermath? How does the victim enact his demise? The focus of the killing is on his throat, but the actor might use feet and hands to convey the death, not least to distract from the stage-blood trick being conducted in the area of the neck, as a syringe or packet of blood concealed behind the victim's collar or on the killer's blade oozes its contents.

The Lottery of Death
or Seven Crimes in the Barber's Chair
[*La Loterie de la Mort ou Sept crimes dans un Fauteuil*, 1957]

Eddy Ghilain and Pierre Larroque
Adapted by Richard J. Hand and Michael Wilson

Characters:
Jean Garnier, a customer
Leon, the Barber's assistant
The Barber (Victor Foulon)

Scene:
A Barbershop on Bastille Day

(Leon is by the barber's chair and sets out the combs and scissors etc. The Barber stands at the side, partly obscured. The shop door opens and Jean Garnier enters.)

LEON: Good evening, sir. Please sit down. We'll be with you in a minute.

JEAN: Um … my name's Jean Garnier. I received an invitation to come here today. I'm rather late, but I have been extremely busy today –

LEON: We would've waited even longer for you before locking up and going home!

JEAN: I hope I haven't kept you *too* long.

LEON: Oh, I'm in no rush.

(Leon helps Jean out of his coat. Jean sits down. He still has not noticed the Barber.)

JEAN *(leaning forward in the seat)*: So, are you the new owner?

LEON: No! That'd be Mr Noirmoutier. I'm just his assistant. If you'd like to sit back in the chair …

BARBER: I'm the new owner. Let me be at your service, Mr Garnier. *(In a swift, mechanical movement Leon and the Barber tie Jean into the straitjacket attached to the chair.)*

JEAN: What? What are you doing? *(Jean struggles and they tie him more firmly.)*

BARBER: There's no point struggling. You're securely fastened by the straitjacket. And no one can get out of one of those! I should know.

JEAN: You're … You're a lunatic?

BARBER: Yes.

JEAN: Oh just stop this stupid joke, will you. Release me – at once!

BARBER: Don't even ask. *(He moves around so Jean can see his face clearly.)* Look at me closely, Garnier. You haven't seen me in five long years. I've lost quite a bit of weight. I've shaved off my beard. But all the same – look at me.

JEAN: Who are you?

BARBER: Think about it. Just try. Don't you think I bear a resemblance to a certain Victor Foulon?

JEAN: The husband of Lisa Foulon?

BARBER: Yes. Well …?

JEAN: You do look a bit like him … But Victor Foulon is dead.

BARBER *(mocking)*: Yes?

JEAN: Yes, he died horribly. A car struck him, and his head was crushed.

BARBER: Really?

JEAN: Lisa identified the body.

BARBER: And you drove her to the morgue to identify it.

JEAN: Who told you?

BARBER: My late wife.

JEAN: What? You ... You really are Foulon? Your wife's dead?

BARBER: Yes, I've been a widower for about a week now. But before the soul of that whore was sent packing to Hell, she made a confession to me.

JEAN: Where is ...

BARBER: Upstairs. She's up there right now.

LEON: It's so hot, Mr Foulon. I can hardly breath!

BARBER: Leon, from now on call me Victor. We've finished our little bit of acting. Let's introduce ourselves: Leon Crouet, formerly a barber before he lost his mind. Eight years in a padded cell in an asylum in St Egeve. And me, I'm Lisa Foulon's cheated husband, ex-lunatic and *apparently* deceased.

LEON (*laughing*): We escaped together last month, didn't we, Victor!

BARBER: For eight years they didn't let him have anything sharper than a toothpick – you can imagine how much he missed his scissors ... his razor blades ...

LEON: It was my idea to steal a straitjacket. Good idea, eh, Victor!

JEAN (*panicking*): What do you want?

BARBER: I want to settle our debts.

JEAN: Explain – explain to me!

BARBER: Explanations? I've got so many. Ah, it's been such hard work to get you in my trap. I've spent years planning this moment.

JEAN: You're mad!

BARBER: Officially, yes. To get rid of her husband Lisa had me locked up in a loony bin. Five years! I was there for five years! I spent five years with complete lunatics when I wasn't insane myself. Can you imagine that? No, you can't. But now it's what will save me. I can slit the throat of anyone I want – and they won't be able to cut off my head on the guillotine!

LEON: Me neither – it's a piece of cake.

BARBER: The worst is yet to come – they will lock me up again. (*Sniggers.*) But not for a long time. And then ... very slowly ... I will become normal and sane again. The doctors don't have a clue! (*Demented laughter.*) Ha, ha! And the proof that I'm sane will be when I 'come to terms' with what I've done, when I face up to how I embarked on this lottery of death which has led me to all my wife's lovers. And I'll get them all – I will get them all! All of them ...! You're the last on the list, Garnier.

JEAN (*choking with fear*): The last?

BARBER: Yes, it's your turn now. Anything I can get you? A final cigarette?

LEON: A little bottle of eau de Cologne? Something for the weekend?

JEAN: Okay, listen. Tell me what you want. How much?

BARBER: Money? No. I want your skin. (*Leon sharpens a razor.*)

JEAN (*suddenly screams*): Help! Murder! (*Victor turns on the radio and a loud Viennese waltz plays. Leon dances with the razor. Jean faints.*)

BARBER: He's passed out.

LEON: Let's take advantage of it. (*Moves the razor towards Jean.*)

BARBER: No! I'm in charge. I'll wake him up – close the blinds.

(*Leon closes the blinds and the room darkens. The Barber dabs some eau de Cologne on a handkerchief and puts it on Jean's neck and ears then begins to wake him up.*)

BARBER: Is that better?

JEAN: How long are you going to torture me?

BARBER: I've got all the time in the world to cut your throat. Instead, I think I'll just make a fuss of you. Won't that be nice?

JEAN (*hopefully*): You've changed your mind –

BARBER: I didn't say that. I will decide what to do with you … when we get bored.

JEAN: Why have you closed the blinds? Why?

BARBER: So that we're not disturbed. Anyone passing on the street might have seen what's going on in here. (*Silence.*) If you've got anything to say – say it now!

JEAN: I beg you … can't you see that you've blown everything out of all proportion –

BARBER: Out of proportion!? If someone put you in an asylum for five years –

JEAN: I didn't put you there!

BARBER (*violent*): Yes! Yes you did! It was *because* of you! You screwed my wife and you were jealous when she slept with me again, her own husband!

JEAN: I assure you –

BARBER: No! Lisa told me before I … (*Gestures slicing throat.*) It was you who gave her the idea to get me locked up.

JEAN: If you hadn't been mentally ill no one would've –

BARBER: Mentally ill? I was mad with love. That's why I put up with all her affairs, before you. Like a cretin, I always forgave her and it drove me crazy … And it was you who showed me that to forgive all of that I must have been mad!

JEAN: I can't remember anything …

BARBER: Anything!

JEAN: It's all so long ago. Ancient history. Shortly after you were certified my affair with Lisa ended.

BARBER: So why did you go with her to identify my body?

JEAN: I went with her ... Maybe I'd recognize him ... you ... from memory ...

BARBER: So you recognized me from distant memory, eh?

JEAN: I really thought it was you –

BARBER: You were so desperate to see me dead – it was a wish come true.

JEAN: Who was the body?

BARBER: Some tramp. We found him run over the night we escaped.

LEON: It was such a stroke of luck. It let us get away with everything.

BARBER: He was about my size and weight. He had papers in the name of 'Noirmoutier'. I gave him my things, took his ID, and I was truly free!

LEON: We smashed his skull in with a paving stone. And his fingers. Destroyed his fingerprints! Foulon was dead – long live Noirmoutier!

BARBER: And once I was 'buried' I could wander around without fear of being stopped or recognized by the police. So now you know everything. Farewell Jean! (*Leon approaches with the razor.*)

JEAN: No! No! Wait – I'll tell you who had you locked up!

LEON: We don't care! (*Leon grabs Jean's hair roughly and puts the razor below his chin.*)

BARBER: You've got some names for me?

JEAN: Dr Darfells signed the papers.

BARBER: So what?

JEAN: He did it for Lisa – he was her lover!

LEON (*sadistic joy*): Another one!

BARBER: Thank you, Garnier. We'll have a little chat with him. Go on, Leon. (*Leon presses the razor to Jean's throat.*)

JEAN: Wait! Wait!

BARBER: Stop, Leon.

JEAN: A doctor can't certify someone without the signature of a district official.

BARBER: What was his name?

JEAN: Arthur Brouer. He was also involved with Lisa ... So have some pity on me ... you can see who was really to blame.

BARBER: Who was to blame? Lust was to blame.

LEON: Don't worry, I'm good with the razor – it'll all be over in just a moment.

JEAN (*struggling*): Help! Help! Help!

(*Leon checks the razor, then swiftly and proficiently slices Jean's throat open. Jean's eyes reveal absolute horror. Blood squirts out of the wound. Leon and the Barber watch him die with fascination. Leon sits down, content. The music of the Bastille Day celebrations is heard and the Barber slowly begins to dance and Leon joins in.*)

BARBER (*singing*): Oh happy, happy day, that's what I said!
The lovers of my wife will be dead, dead, dead!

THE END

Concluding Note

In sharing some of our experiences in working with students in the studio on Grand-Guignol performance, our intention has not been to establish any kind of orthodoxy of Grand-Guignol practice. Different contemporary Grand-Guignol practitioners and companies have developed their own ways of working (for example, Vigor Mortis's development of the concept of the 'actor-prestidigitator') that offer new and experimental approaches and there is much that we can learn from the current generation of Grand-Guignol innovators. Our own experiments, based largely upon the modification of well-tested theatre games and textual work, will, we hope, inspire others to innovate for themselves and devise and develop new ways of working with this endlessly fascinating genre.

A Gallery of Production Photographs from the Grand-Guignol Laboratory

1 Suspense

A moment of measured, intense focus, as the celebrated surgeon Professor Leduc (Nikolai Ribnikov) examines the injured hand of M. Joubert (Paul Owens) with a nuanced professional concern in Aragny and Neilson's *The Kiss of Blood* (2009). Joubert has presented himself in quietly contained agony, but the surgeon's focus begins to shift as he attempts to ascertain whether the injury is in the patient's hand – or in his head. The meticulously paced and studied naturalism of this early scene in the play stands in contrast to its melodramatic finale. (Collection Hand and Wilson)

2 **Despair**

The Passion of Bornin: in a moment redolent of a religious composition the agonized screams of the injured and dying Bornin (Rob Ryan) contrast with the silence of Clément (Bo Channon), who kneels in calm supplication, as if administering the last rites, in de Lorde and Morel's *The Ultimate Torture* (2002). Kerdrec (Rhys Bishop) tensely struggles to hold his composure, as he comforts his dying comrade. The solidarity and heroism of the besieged survivors will soon descend into chaos and self-destructive insanity as they realise their terrible fate. (Collection Hand and Wilson)

3 Ecstasy

At the finale of Aragny and Neilson's *The Kiss of Blood* (2009), the deranged Hélène (Sabrina Dickens) watches her annihilated husband chop off his own hand for her. Having pretended to be a ghost, Hélène is unleashed into visceral physicality: she has torn off her spectral veil and laughs in ecstatic triumph, revelling in orgasmic joy as she literally savours the sweet taste of her bloody revenge. (Collection Hand and Wilson)

4 The Two Masks of the Grand-Guignol

Morgan Thomas, as David, lets his naturalistic mask momentarily slip to reveal a hint of sardonic melodrama in Noël Coward's comedy *The Better Half* (2008). Meanwhile Alice (Ruth Majeed), sat at her dressing table, looks on with barely concealed venom. This image illustrates the tightrope journey of the Grand-Guignol between naturalism and melodrama, but also the underlying sinister potential of Grand-Guignol comedy and its close relationship with horror. (Collection Hand and Wilson)

5 Dark Laughter

Rather than an instrument of terror, that revered symbol of the French Revolution, the guillotine, is used here for comedic effect in Héros and Abric's sex farce *Chop-Chop!* (2002). The philanderer and adulterer Lecardon (Rob Ryan), trapped in the museum exhibit by his insatiably adventurous mistress, resigns himself to his moment of public humiliation with a wry smile. (Collection Hand and Wilson)

6 **Fury**

Rather than starve to death or stoop to self-destruction, Clément (Bo Channon) decides to confront the unseen doom that surrounds him and his comrades in de Lorde and Morel's *The Ultimate Torture* (2002). At this point, the tightly coiled tension established in the play finally breaks and the slow build-up of terror is unleashed into an energetic and defiant fury. (Collection Hand and Wilson)

7 **Madness**

In the final moments of de Lorde and Morel's *The Ultimate Torture* (2002), the previously resolute consul D'Hémelin (Michael Wilson) finally loses both his mind and his daughter (Amy Humpage) in the face of the marauding Boxers. The tension within the body of D'Hémelin not only allows for a controlled manipulation of the stage-blood syringe concealed within the knife, but along with the staring, bulging eyes, is used to signify a violent insanity. This physical stylization is further emphasised by the careful use of the victim's arms in a typically melodramatic pose that frames and accentuates the knife. (Collection Hand and Wilson)

8 Eye-Catching Publicity

The programme cover for *Horror and Laughter: A Night at the Grand-Guignol*, a touring production commissioned for the 2009 Abertoir Horror Festival, Aberystwyth. A slightly modified version was used for the production's poster. This startling and mordantly playful design by Gareth Hughes captures the populist thrill-ride of the Grand-Guignol, giving the viewer an all-important 'health warning' which provides some clues as to what the audience will witness during the show. (Collection Hand and Wilson)

SECTION III
Prefaces and Plays

THE GRAND-GUIGNOL LABORATORY

The work of the Grand-Guignol Laboratory is ongoing and the authors are very keen to know if anyone in theatre companies, drama groups, educational environments etc. makes use of the material in this book for practical workshop investigation.

The authors would be delighted if anyone undertaking such work would contact them via the publishers to let them know about the experience of using this book as a way to undertake experiments and research into Grand-Guignol.

FIRST PROGRAMME

The Haunted House
Kama Sutra
Blind Man's Buff
The Light in the Tomb

Preface

This first programme brings together four plays: two from the pre-First World War *Belle Époque* and two from the inter-war period. *La Maison hantée* (*The Haunted House*), by Marc Bonis-Charancle, was premiered in 1903 and is an early example of the emerging Grand-Guignol horror aesthetic under Max Maurey (1866–1947), who ran the theatre from 1898 until 1914.

Kama Soutra, ou Il ne faut pas jouer avec le feu (*The Kama Sutra or Never Play with Fire ...*), by Régis Gignoux, first played at the rue Chaptal in 1922 and is a typical Grand-Guignol sex farce, redolent of *Après Coup ... ou Tics* (*Tics ... or Doing the Deed*, 1908) in its satire on bourgeois morality and sense of decency. One cannot imagine a translation of the play being passed by the Lord Chamberlain for public performance at London's Grand Guignol (1920–22), given the censor's abhorrence of anything that was deemed sexually dubious or morally distasteful – *Save the Mark* (Wilfred Harris's adaptation of Marcel Nancey and Jean Manoussy's 1916 comedy *La Ventouse*), for example, was refused a licence for London's Grand Guignol in 1920 because of its depiction of a love-bite acquired through an adulterous encounter! Likewise, the third play in this programme, *Blind Man's Buff*, by Charles Hellem and Pol d'Estoc, an adaptation of their 1907 Grand-Guignol horror *Aveugle!*, was refused a licence in 1921 on grounds of public decency.

The final play, René Berton's *The Light in the Tomb/Gott mit uns!* is set in the trenches of the First World War and was first produced in 1928, ten years after the guns fell silent and the same year as R.C. Sherriff's *Journey's End* premiered in London. Both of the inter-war plays in this first programme, both staged in the 1920s, reflect different aspects of post-First World War culture, rather than the pre-Second World war culture that can often be found in the plays of the 1930s. Here we have both a coming to terms with the horrors of trench warfare and, in *Kama Sutra*, the post-war social and sexual decadence of the Roaring Twenties and the Jazz Age.

Marc Bonis-Charancle was a prolific writer of one-act plays whose writings for the Grand-Guignol included the drama *Les Loups* (*The Wolves*,

1899) and the comedy *Les Oubliettes* (*The Dungeons*, 1899), described in the Ondet publication as a 'satire judiciaire', or judicial satire (1903, 2). Bonis-Charancle was primarily a writer of comedies, but his short dramas included the plays *Jacques* (1903) and *L'Espion* (*The Spy*, 1903), which were both set during the Franco-Prussian War of 1870, and *L'Outrage* (*The Outrage*, 1902), which was, the Ondet publication of *La Maison hantée* reveals, 'interdit par la Censure' (1903, 2) and had to be performed at the Pigallele (sic) Theatre in private. Aside from short plays, Bonis-Charancle also wrote for opera, including as librettist for Émile Bonnamy's opera *Le néophyte* (*The Novice*, 1904).

In many respects, *The Haunted House*, Bonis-Charancle's short horror play from 1903, is a fascinating summation of the Grand-Guignol horror genre. The play dabbles in the conventions of the seemingly supernatural and neo-Gothic, only to locate true horror in something terrifyingly *real*. The play has tremendous potential for suspense and atmosphere in its pacing and scenography. Interwoven with this is a sense of sardonic humour, notably at the expense of the bourgeois 'thrill-seekers' who have broken into the seemingly abandoned house.

The play begins with all the signifiers of a haunted house yarn: a dilapidated mansion in which is a group of uninvited visitors with lit candles. The story unfurls with suspense and atmosphere: the bravado (of the male intruders) and the nervousness (of the female intruders) building with playful tension. The macabre history of the house and the continuing rumours surrounding it seem to be setting the scene for a supernatural manifestation. When the night reaches the witching hour and the clock chimes midnight a manifestation does occur and – in a classic archetype of Gothic cliché – a door swings open very slowly. The appearance of Fulbert, the rightful occupant of the house, initially defuses the supernatural, although, in performance, the uncanny aspect to the strange house-owner could be exploited further. However, just when the supernatural is fully refuted, the *real* horror begins. The incarceration of the emaciated and ragged Genevieve is a shocking spectacle and realization. All the same, a production might always keep Genevieve's innocence in the balance – is she, as Fulbert claims, dangerously insane?

As well as the Gothic detail of its setting and atmosphere, Bonis-Charancle's play also draws on the Gothic literary trope of the 'madwoman in the attic', most famously associated with Bertha Mason – the wife of Edward Rochester – in Charlotte Brontë's *Jane Eyre* (1847). The theme is critically explored in Sandra Gilbert and Susan Gubar's *The Madwoman in the Attic: The Woman Writer and the Nineteenth-Century Literary Imagination* (1979), which examines the juxtaposition in female Victorian literature between what could be called the 'angel in the house' and the 'madwoman in the attic'. We could argue that, in Bonis-Charancle's play, Fulbert's love for his angelic Genevieve turns to paranoid hatred as he tries to contain and tame his 'unruly' wife. Alongside the use of the 'madwoman' trope, the tragic figure of the immured Genevieve brings to mind Sophocles' Antigone or Edgar Allan Poe's Madeline Usher. Although they could not be more different – Antigone a martyr who made a principled stand and Madeline prematurely buried by her brother – like Genevieve they are victims of male authority. Compared to the horror of Fulbert – the real lunatic in the house – the bourgeois housebreakers seem the picture of decency and normality. Yet, the play can even be troubling in that aspect, not least in terms of the Lawyer who strictly forbade his wife to attend because of her fragile sensibility. The oppression of women takes many forms, perhaps.

In terms of the horror genre, *The Haunted House* shows us a warped domestic setting like those of the *Texas Chain Saw Massacre* (Tobe Hooper, 1974) or Stephen King's tale of incarceration, *Misery* (1987). The play is even reminiscent, in its brutal entrapment of a woman, of the 'torture porn' genre. It is a precursor to the true story of Joseph Fritzl who, in 2008, was revealed to have kept his daughter incarcerated and sexually abused in the basement of his house. Similarly, it finds echoes in the Columbian case of Arcedio Alvarez who, in 2009, was discovered to have imprisoned and sexually abused his own daughter for twenty-five years. These were hideous crimes but have sparked creative interpretations such as Emma Donoghue's *Room* (2010), which is based on the Fritzl case and captures the unimaginable horrors of the experience.

By contrast, sex (or, rather, bourgeois sexual morality) lies at the heart of Gignoux's comedy *Kama Sutra*. Régis Gignoux (1878–1931) was born in Lyon and moved to Paris in around 1910, where he began a career as a theatre critic before becoming a playwright and novelist. Gignoux's novels were mainly written in collaboration with Roland Dorgelès, author of the celebrated First World War autobiographical novel *Les croix de bois* (*Wooden Crosses*, 1919). Indeed, one of Gignoux and Dorgelès' co-written novels is also a war-themed work: *La machine à finir la guerre* (*The Machine that will End the War*, 1917): in contrast to the poignancy of *Les croix de bois*, *La machine à finir la guerre* is a satirical comedy in which an inventor develops a machine that can end war immediately by detonating all ammunition within a 100-kilometre range simultaneously. The bitter satire of the novel lies in the fact that no one in any position of power (whether military, industrial or political) is interested in this ingenious invention. It makes for an interesting comparison with St. John Ervine's *Progress*, which is included in our Second Programme here. The comedic aspect to *La machine à finir la guerre* is reflected in Régis Gignoux's career as a playwright. His play *Le Fruit Vert* (*Green Fruit*, 1924), co-authored with Jacques Théry and performed at the Théâtre des Variétés in Paris (the theatre which Max Maurey ran from 1914 after leaving the Grand-Guignol), was adapted to the screen on a few occasions, including as the Hollywood comedy *Between Us Girls* (Henry Koster, 1942).

Gignoux wrote a number of comedies for the Grand-Guignol, including *Le monde renversé* (*The World Turned Upside Down*, 1925), *Le cheval de cirque* (*The Circus Horse*, 1930) and *Le prof' d'anglais* (*The English Teacher*, 1930). *Kama Sutra or Never Play with Fire* ..., is Grand-Guignol farce at its risqué, titillating best. It is a play which turns the common Grand-Guignol theme of Orientalism into sex comedy. In this play, a bourgeois family encounters a copy of *The Kama Sutra of Vatsyayana*, the sacred Hindu text. Although it remains most famous in the West as a guide to sexual intercourse, much of the text is about pleasure and the harmony of relationships more broadly. Of course, a Grand-Guignol comedy is going to focus on the sexual synonymity of the Sanskrit text. As much as being a suggestive erotic comedy, however, Gignoux also targets the bourgeoisie for his laughs. The Béroutte family may be very respectable to all appearances but a more uninhibited dimension lies bubbling beneath the surface. In a horror play, it is madness and shocking violence that lies beneath the hollow surface of the comfortable world: in Gignoux's comedy it is eroticism and sex drive. Gignoux delights in satirizing the 'decent' family: the individual morality and religious faith that Mrs Béroutte declares is the only thing that can protect modern society proves woefully inadequate. The play also offers numerous delightful satirical jokes, such as when Marcelle assumes that, because the *Kama Sutra* is an Indian text, it must have been written by Rudyard Kipling.

Blind Man's Buff is presented here as an example from the London Grand Guignol, although it was never performed. In 1921, the London Grand Guignol producer José Levy sent an English version of Charles Hellem and Pol d'Estoc's 1907 play *Aveugle!* to the Lord Chamberlain's Office seeking approval for performance at the Little Theatre. The script held in the Lord Chamberlain's archive reveals evidence of the censor's blue pencil, above all in the final three pages of the script, where the violent dénouement is excised. However, although it looks as if amendments and modifications are being demanded, ultimately the play was banned for public performance.

The adaptation retains the French setting of the play, which is a cruel tale of a young deaf mute visiting an institute for the blind. When the blind inmates suspect a thief in their midst they trap and mutilate the young man. It is a sustained tale of uncompromising dramatic irony that is exacerbated by the use of the name of a children's game for the English title and the fact that the violent dénouement to the play is described in the stage directions as a 'horrible blind man's buff'. The play has interesting parallels with other plays from the Grand-Guignol repertoire. Lucien Descaves' *Atelier d'aveugles* (*Workshop for the Blind*, 1911) is set in a workshop of blind men and was successfully performed as *Seven Blind Men* in the London Grand Guignol in 1921. In Descaves' play, the blind labourers in a brush-making workshop complain about their working conditions. In his panic, their boss locks them inside and goes to the police. The blind men think that the building is on fire and in their desperation to escape one falls to his death from a window and another is stabbed to death. Other themes in *Blind Man's Buff*, such as vitriol – the character of Estaguer having been attacked with acid by a woman – are familiar from Maurice Level's *Le Baiser dans la nuit* (*The Final Kiss*, 1912). In terms of its structure and pace, the play is as inexorable as André de Lorde and Alfred Binet's *Un Crime dans une maison de fous* (*A Crime in the Madhouse*, 1925): from the moment the deaf mute Daniel enters the stage in the latter half of the play, we can sense that he is doomed. All that remains is to see what – and how terrible – his fate will be. The play walks a tightrope that balances between grotesque irony, tragic nihilism and even mordant farce.

The destruction of the eye is a favourite atrocity in the Grand-Guignol.[1] Arguably, the illusion of blinding is easier to manage than other forms of mutilation and dismemberment, and yet it has the potential to be extremely shocking. In addition, the blinding motif in the Grand-Guignol has a symbolic resonance in relation to Freud, who associates the terror of eye injury or going blind with castration (Hand and Wilson, 2002, 198–9). In fact, the theme of the blind in drama extends back to Sophocles' *Oedipus Rex*, and the blinding of Gloucester in Shakespeare's *King Lear* is a powerful emblem of the degeneracy and despair of the kingdom. Nearer in time to the Grand-Guignol, *Les aveugles* (*The Blind*, 1890) is one of the most famous plays by the Belgian playwright Maurice Maeterlinck. In this masterpiece of Symbolist theatre a group of blind people are lost in a forest while on a day out. A work of delicate lyricism and irony, *Les aveugles* is a metaphor of the powerlessness of the human condition. The use of blind characters can often be found in the thriller genre. In Frederick Knott's *Wait Until Dark* (1966), successfully adapted to the screen in Terence Young's film starring Audrey Hepburn in 1967, a young blind woman is besieged in her apartment by gangsters and uses her ability to navigate the total darkness, to outwit her tormentors by cutting the electricity. The plotline returns in *See No Evil* (Richard Fleischer, 1971), in which Mia Farrow plays a blind woman tormented by a pursuer in a country house. In the British television series *Thriller* (1973–76) blindness features as a theme several times, including in episodes called 'The Eyes Have It' (1973), in which a terrorist group infiltrates an institute for the blind, and 'The Next Voice You See' (1975), in which the victim of a ferocious attack hears the voice of a man who blinded him and killed his wife.

[1] As a counterpoint here, we might also consider *Les Yeux sans visage (Eyes Without a Face)*, a stage version of Georges Franju's controversial 1960 horror film of the same name based upon Jean Redon's novel, which played in the final season at the rue Chaptal in 1962. Having been horrifically facially disfigured in a car accident, Christiane Génessier, the daughter of a renowned surgeon, lives behind a mask. It is the contrast of her expressive eyes with the expressionless mask that provides one of the enduring and haunting images of the film.

Of course, *Blind Man's Buff* combines blind characters with a deaf one. The theme of the blind encountering the deaf recurs in Grand-Guignol writer Maurice Level's short story 'La Nuit et le Silence' ('Night and Silence', 1922), a horror tale about a deaf man and his blind brother. The scenario is also echoed in US horror radio with Robert Newman's radical adaptation of Poe's 'The Tell-Tale Heart' (*Inner Sanctum Mysteries*, August 3, 1941), in which Boris Karloff plays a deaf man who cohabits with a blind man (Everett Sloane), with horrific consequences. The same theme of two men, one deaf, one blind, even receives comic treatment in the film *See No Evil, Hear No Evil* (Arthur Hiller, 1989).

René Berton's *Gott mit uns!* was performed later in 1928, the same year as his play *L'Homme qui a tué la mort* (*The Man Who Killed Death*), included in the 'Third Programme' of this book, was staged, but the two plays could not be more different in setting. *Gott mit uns!*, set on the front line of combat, is remarkable as an example of the Grand-Guignol looking directly at the First World War. The title is, of course, German and could be translated as 'God is with us' or 'God on our side'. When Berton published the script in the theatrical magazine *La Petite Illustration* in August 1929, he retitled it *La Lumière dans le tombeau* (*The Light in the Tomb*), perhaps to restyle the script as a more consciously literary work. Undoubtedly, however, the script was published because of the positive reception the Grand-Guignol production received. Charles Méré – himself a prolific Grand-Guignol playwright – reviewed *Gott mit uns!* in *Excelsior* magazine, stating:

> The author has avoided the well-worn roads of the (Grand-Guignol) genre. He has scorned the facile techniques of horror and has opted for an effect of great emotion through more humane and, one might even say, more classical means.

Indeed, Méré likens Berton's play to Corneille and others draw parallels between it and Victor Hugo's romantic tragedy *Ruy Blas*. Writing in *Le soir*, the theatre critic Maurice Rostand praised *Gott mit uns!* as being 'a strong, powerful play which is emotionally realistic and only needs to use the truth as a way to create terror and condemn war'. For Charles-Henry, writing in *L'Eve nouvelle*, it is a play of 'perfection' which demonstrates the power of theatre inasmuch as Berton captures the reality of battle far better than film has ever been able to (one assumes he is referring to the familiar documentation of the War as much as fiction film).

It may be a revelation to some that the Grand-Guignol chose to set plays in the First World War. Certainly, London's Grand Guignol did, with H.F. Maltby's *Person Unknown* (1921) and St John Ervine's *Progress* (1922), both outstanding examples of plays that express powerful anti-war sentiments. While Maltby and Ervine locate their plays in the aftermath of war, Berton's takes the audience back to the intensity of conflict at the front line. The action takes place in an underground bunker in the Champagne region of France towards the end of the First World War. As in other Berton plays, we see his considerable skills of characterization, offering male actors a number of rich roles ranging from the war-weary and the stoical to the delicately humorous, and encompassing a range of social class. In this regard, *Gott mit uns!* presents archetypes familiar from a range of war dramas, including full-length war plays such as R.C. Sherriff's contemporaneous *Journey's End*.

As well as the tragic and psychologically convincing figures of front-line combat on the French side, Berton also creates Hermann, a German soldier who has planted a bomb in the bunker and is not scared to die with it. Hermann is fanatical, driven by an obsessive war lust and patriotism. The original poster for the play attempts to capture this mood by showing dead and dying French soldiers surrounding a wounded German who writes 'Gott mit uns' on the wall in his own blood (see oppostie). Although the poster captures the insanity of fanaticism, Berton's play gives the audience a more complex dramatic journey by giving us Hermann's back-story: his full name is Siegfried Hermann, he is married with a wife and four children and before the War was a professor of philosophy at Leipzig University. With these facts Berton reveals that, rather than being a stereotypical 'Kraut' villain, this indoctrinated 'hero' of the 'fatherland' in fact has depth and complexity. The fact that Captain Caussade also taught philosophy (in Paris) before the War is dramatic irony, but it permits a dialogue of considerable tension as the two men debate the situation and their available options.

One of the most remarkable themes that the play presents to the contemporary audience is the idea of the suicide bomber. Although Hermann had planned to escape after planting the bomb, he turns the fact that he is captured into the opportunity to carry out an act of supreme self-sacrifice. Suicide attacks have been documented throughout the history of warfare since ancient times right through to the Japanese kamikaze pilots of the Second World War, and the phenomenon has become a key emblem of the modern, post-Cold War age, with suicide bombings during the Tamil separatist conflict in Sri Lanka as well as the use of the technique by terrorists and 'insurgents' in Iraq, Afghanistan, and elsewhere in the world. Plays that have addressed the topic include two plays about the terrorist attacks in London on 7 July 2005: Simon Stephens' *Pornography* (2007) and Bryony Lavery's *Thursday* (2013) which, in contrast to the former, makes a conscious decision not to represent the suicide bombers.

Gott mit uns! remains a play which has excellent pace and suspense combined with extremely strong characterization. The audience can be treated to a powerful drama set in a desperate situation with great opportunities for stage design, atmosphere and – in the finale – gruesome Grand-Guignol makeup. Berton permits us to 'get to know' the troops, and this enhances the claustrophobic terror of the dénouement as the bomb ticks its way to destruction. As the rave reviews of the original production made clear, this is a play that surpassed the association of the Grand-Guignol with easy 'horror' thrills, locating its dramatic horrors in the terrible reality of the recent 'War to end all wars'.

9 Poster for the premiere of René Berton's *Gott mit uns!* (*The Light in the Tomb*) at the Théâtre du Grand Guignol in 1928

The Haunted House (*La Maison hantée*, 1903)

Marc Bonis-Charancle

Characters:
Fulbert
The Lawyer
Avenel
Ravan
Genevieve
Mrs Avenel
Mrs Ravan

A large room in a dilapidated mansion. Old furniture lies around randomly. There is a variety of other items in disarray: brooms, a stepladder, boxes and empty chests. Dusty old curtains hang in front of the windows. At the back, the front door; to the right a door leading into another room.

As the play begins the Lawyer, Avenel, Mrs Avenel, Ravan and Mrs Ravan sit around a wooden table, on boxes and small barrels. On the table, there is a tablecloth and some lit candles stuck in the top of empty bottles.

RAVAN (*stoops down and tries to balance the table*): Is that any better?

MRS AVENEL: A little bit.

THE LAWYER (*to Ravan*): Don't go to too much trouble, old boy, it's simply not worth it!

AVENEL (*jovially*): This place may be derelict but there's no need for us to lower our standards! The table's just a bit wobbly on its feet, like I'll be as soon as we crack open that bottle!

RAVAN (*standing up and sitting down and taking his glass*): Yes, indeed! A drink, for god's sake! I need a drink! Don't let the sadness that seeps out of these walls get you down!

THE LAWYER (*filling the glasses*): Come on ... Come on ladies ... Don't worry yourselves!

MRS RAVAN (*standing up in fear, her voice stifled*): I think I heard something!

RAVAN: Your nerves are getting to you!

MRS RAVAN: No, I swear I did!

THE LAWYER: I have to agree with your husband – it's just your nerves! We've made the poor ladies nervous wrecks!

MRS AVENEL: Good grief ... I wish I had never come here!

AVENEL (*to his wife*): A dose of this kind of spirit will make you feel much better! (*He serves her a drink.*)

THE LAWYER: My wife wanted to come here ... I wouldn't let her.

MRS RAVAN (*agitated*): You think we might be in danger?

THE LAWYER: Not at all. But she's extremely impressionable and this little soiree might be too much for her. Not to mention all of those absurd legends which surround this house ...

MRS AVENEL: But Father Bureau has often seen lights in the windows here – he's seen them with his own two eyes!

RAVAN: Dear Father Bureau, bless him – the old drunk!

MRS RAVAN: What about old widow Cassine? When she's been around here collecting wood she's heard moans and groans!

THE LAWYER (*laughing*): Well, it's up to you if you want to believe all that nonsense! The local bumpkins are ridiculous! I see them every day in the law courts and I can never believe how backward and superstitious they are! They all talk about this as the 'haunted house' ... They say that on the stroke of midnight the doors rattle and the shutters crash open ... They've even said you can hear chains dragging across the floor boards ... What utter rubbish!

MRS AVENEL (*excitedly*): Do you think we should have armed ourselves?

THE LAWYER: With weapons? To protect us against *what*, for god's sake? Besides, there's hardly any crime round here. It's a very peaceful area, nothing ever happens here ... I know that better than anyone ... And as for ghosts ...

AVENEL (*laughing to his wife*): I think you'll find weapons aren't much cop against ghosts!

RAVAN (*very jovial, as he brandishes a bottle of champagne*): I'm well-armed now! If a ghost does turn up I'm a good shot with a champagne cork!

AVENEL (*also laughing*): Let's invite them to have a drink. We can all clink glasses and wish each other *good health*!

MRS RAVAN (*still listening*): I tell you I can definitely hear something!

RAVAN (*nervously to his wife*): What ...? Come on ...? What ...? What can you hear?

MRS RAVAN: I'm not sure ... I think it was footsteps!

THE LAWYER (*drinking and laughing*): Did you hear chains too ...? Clanking chains ...?

MRS RAVAN (*fearful*): Oh, please don't laugh! The nearer we get to midnight the more nervous I am getting! (*to Mrs Avenel*) You're much braver than I am, my dear!

MRS AVENEL: I may seem it ... But, deep down, I'm no braver than you!

AVENEL: Well, I'm really enjoying myself! This little nocturnal adventure, into this spooky house (*ironically*) with the sole intention of seeing some ghost appear, or phantoms covered in shrouds ... (*He puts a napkin on his head.*) Whoo! Whoo! Whoo!

MRS RAVAN (*uttering a scream*): Please, Mr Avenel, I beg you – please don't!

MRS AVENEL (*to her husband*): You're being ridiculous! Stop it! If you think your bad taste jokes will make us feel any better you're very much mistaken!

AVENEL: Very well! I was only trying to lighten the mood a little ... I won't do it again.

THE LAWYER (*raising his glass*): Let's drink to the health of these old rafters!

RAVAN: But why do people say this place is haunted?

THE LAWYER: Remember this old dump hasn't been lived in for over twenty-five years!

MRS AVENEL: Twenty-five years!

THE LAWYER: That's right. The house was originally occupied by a large family ... A retired army officer, his wife and their four children. His wife died. Two of his children went to seek their fortune in Africa ... The other two drowned in a tragic boating accident ... Living here all alone, one day the old military gentleman was shaving and cut his own throat.

MRS RAVAN: It sends a shiver down my spine!

THE LAWYER: The house has stood empty for three years. Nobody has fancied living here for some reason ...

AVENEL: I can see why!

THE LAWYER: An old widower bought the place but he must have been as morose as the previous owner: he didn't last long ... He was here for two years and then, one morning, the mayor received a note under his door telling him to come here. He hurried down, opened the front door and stumbled into the very room we're in now. Walking in the darkness he bumped into something – a corpse. The old man had hanged himself – right there.

RAVAN (*with a false laugh*): Well, it's certainly all very macabre!

MRS AVENEL (*alarmed*): Here ...? Right here ...?

THE LAWYER (*calmly*): Don't worry yourself ... It was a long time ago!

AVENEL: What happened next?

THE LAWYER: The old man had left a will ... He gave his fortune to the local parish: all his money and ... this house.

RAVAN: Yes, I knew that. I also know that the local community was very embarrassed by this house and it's stood here useless and unwanted ever since.

THE LAWYER (*grabs a stool and sits down*): It was for sale for years, but nobody was interested. About ten years ago, the local notary, Mr Vignet, entered into a contract over it with a client in Paris.

AVENEL: Really? (*He stands up and walks over to the fireplace.*)

THE LAWYER: Yes. It was a very strange contract. The man in Paris bought the house, but he wouldn't give his name and remained anonymous throughout the whole business. The keys were sent to the new owner, but he never visited and has since, I understand, left the country.

MRS AVENEL: If I had known all of that before, I'd never have walked through the door tonight.

MRS RAVAN: Me neither!

AVENEL (*to the Lawyer*): Surely it's all just a tall tale? (*He sits down next to the fireplace on an empty box.*)

THE LAWYER: It's entirely true. You have to understand that after a series of incidents like that, the imagination of the locals gets carried away: two suicides ... an enigmatic owner, the isolation of the house, here in the middle of the woods far from anything ... Of course, you will hear ghosts weeping and wailing! Many people have had the idea of doing what we're doing tonight ... Coming here, spending a night ... To find out the truth ...! But no one's dared to ... After all, breaking and entering is a criminal offence!

AVENEL: I'm sure the owner would have something to say about it! But, to be honest, I'm not surprised he never fancied moving in here! (*He looks around the room.*) It's so dismal!

MRS AVENEL (*standing up terrified*): Oh! No mistaking it that time! I heard a scream!

AVENEL (*shrugging his shoulders*): You're crazy!

THE LAWYER (*with a gesture*): Hush! Listen! (*Everybody stands up nervously.*) The clocks are chiming midnight ...! (*Everyone listens intently as midnight chimes a great distance away.*)

THE LAWYER: And twelve! Midnight! (*jovially*) Ladies ... Gentlemen ... as we all heard it is midnight ... The witching hour ...! And all seems quite silent to me ... The shutters aren't crashing open

… I haven't heard any moaning or the clanking of chains, and I haven't seen a single ghost …

(*At this very moment, the door on the right opens extremely slowly and Fulbert appears in the opening. Everybody stands up, the two women utter a cry of terror.*)

(*Fulbert is fifty-five years old. He has grey hair and an almost white beard, his eyes look wild and feverish and he's wearing a dressing gown.*)

FULBERT (*coldly but very calm*): What you doing here …? Who are you?

(*Everybody looks at him in fright, without reply.*)

FULBERT (*taking a step forward, as everybody recoils, he speaks with an almost alarming calmness*): I want to know who you are and what right you have to come into my house.

THE LAWYER: Please, sir …

FULBERT (*looking at each person one at a time*): You don't look like burglars … There's nothing to steal here anyway …! I must say, I'm surprised to see people like you here at this time of night … In my house!

AVENEL: I must apologize, sir, we mean no offence – we didn't even know anyone lived here!

RAVAN: Yes, we thought this house was deserted.

FULBERT (*he begins calm and speaks gently but gradually becomes more animated*): I understand …! Who can ignore all the stories that circulate about my house …? They call it the 'haunted house', don't they? I've often seen people cross themselves as they walked past my door. (*ironically*) So you decided to have a little party in the haunted house! You came hoping to see some ghosts!

THE LAWYER (*trying to be dignified*): Sir … We really are very –

FULBERT (*loudly*): Perhaps you've even placed a bet? And to satisfy your curiosity you thought nothing of forcing open my door, disrupting the solitude in which I choose to live!

THE LAWYER: We will leave at once sir, but please permit me to explain.

FULBERT (*very coldly*): I'm listening.

THE LAWYER: As you said yourself, sir, your house seems abandoned and all the locals say it's haunted … They've seen lights glimmering through the curtains …

FULBERT (*ironically*): I suppose I'm not entitled to light my house?

THE LAWYER: Of course! I didn't mean –

RAVAN: People have seen a white figure at the window!

FULBERT: And?

AVENEL: Some have heard screaming and cries of distress.

FULBERT: Total fantasy! Besides ... (*self-righteously*) No one has the right to disturb me while I'm in my own house! This is my home ... A home is meant to be sacred and no one has the right to spy on me or intrude into the solitary life that I have chosen to lead!

THE LAWYER (*firmly*): You must forgive me, sir, but I think you're going too far! If there seems to be something untoward or suspicious going on, everyone has the right to have their anxieties dispelled.

FULBERT: Oh really? On what grounds?

THE LAWYER: In the name of justice.

FULBERT (*after a hesitation, becoming a little troubled*): What do you mean ...? Justice ...?

THE LAWYER: Yes ... If there is any suspicion – or rumour – that a crime has been committed ... You see, sir, I am a lawyer and I have dedicated my life to the cause of justice.

FULBERT (*taking a step back*): You're a lawyer?

THE LAWYER: Yes, I am a lawyer. And it is because of that I feel I had the right – perhaps even the obligation – to come into your house –

FULBERT (*both fearful and furious*): But I fail to understand how any of that entitles you to break into my home! What crime do you suspect me of, exactly? (*ironically*) Do you think I've been forging bank notes?

THE LAWYER (*smiling*): No, sir, I don't ... but let me explain again. The mystery that surrounds your house has generated so many rumours it was essential to put a stop to them, to solve the mystery, as it were. Tomorrow, my friends and I will be able to tell everyone that although this house may be isolated and sinister, it does not contain evil spirits or ghosts. The spirits of the people that died in this house do not wander the corridors clanking their chains! All the superstitious locals who live around here will have nothing to gossip about any more and you yourself, sir, can get on with your life in perfect tranquility and, I absolutely assure you, in perfect security.

FULBERT (*with regained self-righteousness*): I understand what you're saying ... but will you please leave, now.

THE LAWYER: We shall go at once. Please accept our humblest apologies ...

(*Everyone prepares to leave. Suddenly, from the corridor, a piercing scream is heard followed by a burst of laughter. Everybody stands still, stunned. The two women are terrified and grab the arms of their husbands. Fulbert makes a movement towards the open door at the right. He stands in front of it threateningly. Another burst of laughter is heard.*)

FULBERT (*icily*): Will you please get out!
THE LAWYER (*hesitantly*): But ... What was that ...?
FULBERT (*violently*): Nothing that concerns you!
MRS AVENEL (*begging the Lawyer*): Please, let's go! Please, let's get out of here, I beg you!
THE LAWYER (*firmly*): No.
FULBERT: Will you please get out – all of you!

(*Singing can be heard coming from the corridor. Fulbert violently slams the door and faces everyone. A voice can be heard singing a simple rhyme. At the end of the short song, a long cry of anguish is heard.*)

FULBERT (*very aggressively*): What you waiting for?
THE LAWYER: Well, sir, you must admit that this is all rather strange ... Once again, I feel justified in demanding to know what on earth is going on here.
FULBERT (*arrogantly*): What do you mean?
THE LAWYER (*very firmly*): There are no ghosts here, but maybe something much more real ... There is clearly someone here who is in great distress and suffering terribly. I demand to know the truth!
FULBERT: And if I refuse to tell you?
THE LAWYER: Then I would know what to do.
FULBERT (*anxiously*): You'd ... You'd arrest me?
THE LAWYER: This house would be swarming with police in an instant.
FULBERT (*menacingly*): Be careful, sir ...! I have some very powerful friends and you may have cause to regret your excess of zeal ...
THE LAWYER: You can't threaten me like that! You seem to think that you're above the law ... But I can tell you now, you're not.

(*The sounds of cries get nearer to the door.*)

MRS AVENEL (*begging*): Please, let's go! I'm so scared!

(*The door bursts open violently. Genevieve enters. She is emaciated, dirty and her clothes are ragged. Her eyes are haggard and a rope is tied to her arm. Her eyes look insane as she stares at the people in the room. Fulbert rushes towards her but she escapes him and quickly moves to the group and emits a scream.*)

GENEVIEVE (*to Fulbert*): You monster! You torturer!
FULBERT (*firmly*): Genevieve!

GENEVIEVE (*to the group*): I'm free, aren't I? You've come to set me free! I cut the rope! I escaped! You rescued me? That evil man!

FULBERT (*moving towards her*): Come with me now ...

THE LAWYER (*to Fulbert*): Stop where you are!

GENEVIEVE (*to the group*): Take me away! As far away as possible!

MADAME RAVAN: The poor woman!

THE LAWYER (*to Fulbert*): I wanted to know the truth and now it's plain to see. You have held this woman hostage!

FULBERT: But she's insane – can't you see that?

GENEVIEVE: Insane? Insane! (*She laughs.*) So, I'm a mad woman, am I? (*vacantly*) I don't know any more ... (*She shows everyone the rope on her arm.*) He tied me up ... Yes ... I cut through the rope with my teeth!

THE LAWYER (*to Fulbert*): Why have you incarcerated this woman?

FULBERT (*furiously*): This woman is my wife. She's lost all sense of reason. I don't have to explain anything to you ... Even if you are a lawyer!

THE LAWYER: Don't you worry about that. You'll be seeing a judge tomorrow.

FULBERT: What?

THE LAWYER: We're going to take this woman out of here and get her to safety. (*ironically*) We're going to take you as well, sir, but you're going to go somewhere rather different.

FULBERT (*aggressively*): You're going to take me away?

GENEVIEVE: Please, get me out of here!

FULBERT (*to the Lawyer*): Please ... Sir ... You can't ... Please don't take me away from here. It's impossible! (*to Genevieve very gently*) Genevieve?

GENEVIEVE (*with hatred*): Torturer!

THE LAWYER: Did you hear that? Torturer. You have been slowly killing this woman just like you have killed all sense of reason in your head!

GENEVIEVE (*vacantly*): Yes, he has been killing me ... He has been killing me! (*to Fulbert*) You coward!

THE LAWYER: To hold someone against their will is a serious crime ... You have the right to defend yourself in court, of course ... But rest assured, this poor woman will be kept far away from you!

FULBERT (*aggressively*): No! You can't take me away! (*pleading*) If you knew the truth ...

THE LAWYER: Do you seriously think you can justify yourself?

FULBERT (*solemn*): Please let me speak! If you let me speak, you will understand. You said that she's a poor woman? But I've suffered too, please have pity on me! I have suffered like a damned soul! This woman ... This woman that I married ... (*He raises his hands to his face.*) Yes ... fifteen years ago! My god, has it been so long? Fifteen years! You won't believe how beautiful she once was ... Everyone who saw her fell in love with her!

GENEVIEVE: He tried to kill me!

FULBERT (*overwhelmed*): We were so happy ... So very happy! And then she became ill ... She was so ill, she nearly died ... Oh, why didn't death take her? And when she recovered, she was never the same again ... The illness completely changed her ... She was no longer the Genevieve I once knew, a woman so pure, so dignified, so chaste ... (*becoming sombre*) She deceived me ... She pretended that she loved me, she told me that she loved me ... And I believed her, in spite of everything, I believed that she did still love me. (*full of hate*) Then everything became clear for all to see ... She no longer tried to hide her behaviour ... she humiliated me! I wanted to leave her ... Divorce her ... But I couldn't do it, because I still loved her so much! The doctors told me it was just because of the illness and her behaviour would change ... Oh, how she fooled me and everyone ... She became more and more brazen, under my very nose, in our own home ... in our own bed ... She relished in torturing me ... ridiculing me ... the one man who adored her! Perhaps I should have killed her. It would have been a relief for me ... and for her! Twenty times I grabbed her throat and squeezed it with my hands ... (*overwhelmed*) But I always let go of her ... I didn't want to hurt her ... I couldn't! (*He collapses onto a stool.*) So ... we left Paris ... I brought her here ... Ten years ... It must be ten years now ... I've guarded her, protected her here! And here she is mine once again ... *all mine*!

LAWYER: You imprisoned her.

FULBERT: You talk to me of imprisonment? But I was a prisoner too! I've suffered too! The gaoler is more tortured than the prisoner! At night, I creep out and search around for food ... I do everything as quietly as I can to be sure that I am never seen ... (*becoming overwhelmed again*) We live away from the world, waiting for death to set us free ... (*gently*) We've been waiting so long! (*He points at Genevieve.*) Look at what's become of us! Our bodies and our souls are wasting away! (*He stands up.*) Please go, I beg you. Forget all about tonight, forget about this tragedy that you've uncovered.

GENEVIEVE (*to the other women*): Look, I cut through the rope with my teeth ... My mouth is bleeding!

THE LAWYER (*gently to Fulbert*): Perhaps you are worthy of some pity … But you have lived so long like this, you have clearly lost your sense of right and wrong. (*firmly*) *But I have not.*

FULBERT (*anxiously*): What are you going to do?

THE LAWYER: I told you. We're going to set this woman free …

FULBERT (*with fury*): Set her free! Set her free! So she can carry on with her disgusting debauchery? She'll be lost without me! And I can't let that happen! You hear me? I would never let that happen! (*He runs into the group, which scatters away from him, and tries to seize Genevieve, who escapes him.*) She's my wife and my lover! (*very violently*) She belongs to me, you understand? And you won't take her from me! Who are you anyway? Perhaps you are just burglars! You've broken in like thieves! Go away! Off with you!

(*Genevieve moves towards the others but Fulbert stops her.*)

GENEVIEVE (*begging*): Set me free, please!

FULBERT (*laughing like a lunatic*): Set you free? Oh no, my dear!

(*He grabs a knife from the table and stabs Genevieve again and again with a wild jerky motion. Genevieve collapses to the ground. The women scream in terror. Mrs Avenel screams out 'Murder! Murder!' Mrs Ravan faints. The Lawyer kneels down next to Genevieve. Mr Avenel and Mr Ravan seize hold of Fulbert from behind.*)

FULBERT (*screaming and making wild gestures*): Set her free now, why don't you! No you can't, can you!? She's mine now … *Mine forever*!

THE END

The Kama Sutra or Never Play with Fire … (*Kama Soutra, ou Il ne faut pas jouer avec le feu*, 1922)

A comedy in one act by Régis Gignoux

Characters:
Mrs Béroutte, 43 years old
Mr Béroutte, 45 years old
Jean, their son, 17 years old
Marcelle, their niece, 16 years old
Mrs Vermeuil, 29 years old
Antonia, maidservant, 20 years old

The dining room of a house in the country. Ten o'clock in the morning. At the back, a French window opens onto a sunny garden. To the right and the left are doors: one leading to Mr Béroutte's study and the other to the kitchen. As well as dining room furniture there is a sofa with cushions centre stage.

Mr Béroutte reads a newspaper. He is rather untidy, enjoying a lazy morning in the countryside. Mrs Béroutte uses a duster to clean the objects on a dresser.

MRS BÉROUTTE (*finding dust*): Oh! Oh! It's obscene!

BÉROUTTE (*carries on reading*): Obscene … obscene …

MRS BÉROUTTE: It's always the same!

BÉROUTTE: Always the same …

MRS BÉROUTTE: This is beyond negligence …

BÉROUTTE: Negligence … negligence …

MRS BÉROUTTE (*looking at her husband*): This is done on purpose!

BÉROUTTE: No. The government is paralysed by the mistakes of the previous administration.

MRS BÉROUTTE: What …?

BÉROUTTE: That's why they've had to grovel to the bloody English.

MRS BÉROUTTE: The English? (*She understands and flicks her husband with the duster.*) I was talking about Antonia. She's getting more and more lazy, the little slut!

BÉROUTTE: Sack her.

MRS BÉROUTTE: Oh, I suppose you'll find me another one! There are simply *dozens* of maidservants willing to move to the country, hmm!

BÉROUTTE: Well, keep her until the end of the summer holidays.

MRS BÉROUTTE: So be it. But I'll tell you something she certainly *won't* be doing again ... (*Béroutte returns to his newspaper.*) What she did last night .... (*From the garden the happy voices of teenagers playing tennis can be heard: "15–30 ... 30-all ... 30–40 ... Game!"*) Oh, the children are so annoying! As soon as they wake up they're out playing tennis! (*changes her tone to be confidential*) Last night, Antonia was outside the barn larking around with the farmer's son until ten o'clock ...

BÉROUTTE: At least she was *outside* the barn – I wouldn't worry about it. (*Returns to his newspaper.*)

MRS BÉROUTTE: You! Things have to smack you in the face before you'll even notice them! I need to send Antonia over to the farm this morning. Just wait and see how long it takes her ...! (*Goes to the door and calls out.*) Antonia! (*Béroutte shrugs his shoulders. Enter Antonia, an attractive and cheerful young woman.*)

MRS BÉROUTTE (*brandishing the duster*): An excellent job of the dusting, I must say.

ANTONIA: I didn't have time, madam. Master Jean and Miss Marcelle had breakfast at half past seven and after that I ...

MRS BÉROUTTE: Spare me the details ... Have you been to the farm to get the beans for dinner? No. What are you waiting for!

ANTONIA: Very good, madam. (*Before leaving, Antonia wipes the dresser with her apron.*)

MRS BÉROUTTE (*giving Antonia a push*): Get a move on!

ANTONIA: Yes, madam. (*Exit.*)

MRS BÉROUTTE: You see, give that girl an inch and ... (*She goes to the door.*) I've got my eye on you, my girl!

BÉROUTTE (*desperate to read in peace*): I know, why don't you follow her and see what she gets up to! Off you go, before it's too late ...

MRS BÉROUTTE: Why don't you sit in the garden?

BÉROUTTE: And get smacked in the face by a tennis ball? (*Voices outside: "15-love ... 15-all ..."*) Listen to that!

JEAN AND MARCELLE (*in the garden*): 30–15 … 30–30 … 30–40 … *Game*!

MRS BÉROUTTE (*tearing the newspaper out of Béroutte's hands*): You don't want to spoil their fun, do you? That would be ridiculous. There they are – a nice young man and a nice young lady who only want to run and jump and leap around, far too busy to get into any mischief …! I've been watching them. Trust me: they're like bosom pals!

BÉROUTTE: That's alright then.

MRS BÉROUTTE: But seeing that you're so desperate to read in peace, that can easily be arranged … (*She goes over to the French window.*) Children! Can you be a little quieter, please! You don't have to behave like a couple of lunatics! There's no need to shout and scream so much! You're distracting father from his newspaper … (*She returns to Béroutte and hands back his newspaper.*) You see? As easy as that … They'll be quiet now and you can read in peace … You've got everything you need now … You should be content now … Go on, then … What are you waiting for …? Read … *Read*! (*Exit.*)

(*Béroutte settles down with his newspaper, but Jean and Marcelle enter in tennis clothes and come either side of the sofa where Béroutte is sat.*)

JEAN (*coming from the right*): Is everything alright, dad?

BÉROUTTE (*irritated*): Yes, perfectly.

MARCELLE (*coming from the left*): Morning, Uncle Jules! Did you sleep well?

BÉROUTTE (*kissing Marcelle*): Very well, thank you, my dear.

JEAN: You didn't mind us playing tennis, did you, dad?

BÉROUTTE: Not at all … but maybe play a little more gently, more gracefully … You're exhausting Marcelle.

MARCELLE: No he isn't, Uncle Jules, I'm fine …

BÉROUTTE: Well … off you go … Have a great game, but nice and gentle, eh …?

JEAN: Very well, dad … (*to Marcelle with exaggerated gentleness*) Are you up to any more, my dear?

MARCELLE (*same ironic tone*): Alright then, but please be gentle with me … (*They exit.*)

BÉROUTTE (*finally getting to read his newspaper*): 'The President has declared to the English government that France is willing to move forward in a spirit of conciliation as befits the friendship between the two nations …'

MRS BÉROUTTE (*runs in and, ripping the newspaper from his hands, speaks with a constricted voice*): Jules. Are you the father of this household? Yes or no.

BÉROUTTE: What?

MRS BÉROUTTE: Do you safeguard the virtue of your son and protect the innocence of your sister's daughter?

BÉROUTTE: What *are* you talking about?

MRS BÉROUTTE (*brandishing a book from behind her back*): Look what I found in Antonia's bedroom.

BÉROUTTE: What? A book.

MRS BÉROUTTE: What sort of book, hmm?

BÉROUTTE: Does it have words in it?

MRS BÉROUTTE (*handing it over to Béroutte*): Ha! You won't be in such a frivolous mood when you clap eyes on this!

BÉROUTTE (*opens the book*): Oh ... Oh ...! OH ...!

MRS BÉROUTTE: Have you ever seen such *filth*!?

BÉROUTTE (*reading the tile page*): *The Kama Sutra: the Hindu Manual of Erotology* ... (*to Mrs Béroutte*) Erotology!?

MRS BÉROUTTE: Hindu! Hindu!

BÉROUTTE (*consulting the book and turning it on every angle*): Oh! The illustrations ...! Look at the engravings!

MRS BÉROUTTE (*snatching the book from him*): I think you've seen enough!

BÉROUTTE: But it's my duty to see what we're dealing with here.

MRS BÉROUTTE: Huh! I *knew* you'd be interested in this!

BÉROUTTE (*taking back his newspaper and returning the book*): Just leave me to my newspaper – *please*!

MRS BÉROUTTE: Is that it? Is that all you're going to do about it? And it isn't just the *Kama Sutra*, oh no ... There's more than that! (*Reading out the table of contents.*) As well as the *Kama Sutra* there are "Succulent Selections from *Gamiani*", "Fantasies of a Flagellator", "Confessions of a Footwear Fetishist" ...! (*Brandishing the volume to Béroutte with the utmost disgust.*) Such filth! Such disgusting filth under a maidservant's mattress!

BÉROUTTE: Wherever did she get hold of something like that?

MRS BÉROUTTE: From the snake-pit she came from!

BÉROUTTE: I thought she came to us from the Sisters of the Deliverance.

MRS BÉROUTTE: Yes, you're right ...! Oh, the hypocrisy ...! Obviously you won't stand for her being under our roof for another minute ...

BÉROUTTE: Of course not ...! But on what grounds can we dismiss her ...? You can't exactly say that you were rooting around under her mattress, now can you ...?

MRS BÉROUTTE: Do I need to justify my actions to a shameless hussy!?

BÉROUTTE: But what if she asks for her book back?

MRS BÉROUTTE: Ha! I'd tell her to complain to the police – if she dare! Look out, here come the children … Hide the book!

BÉROUTTE (*leaping up*): Hide it – where!? (*He tries to squeeze it into his pocket but as Jean and Marcelle come in he hides it behind his back.*)

MRS BÉROUTTE: Why have you come in so soon, children? Surely you can't have finished playing?

JEAN: Dad doesn't want us getting tired out.

BÉROUTTE: A strapping lad like you? Tired? What nonsense!

MRS BÉROUTTE: Off you go! Give those balls a jolly good whacking, eh! Better than sitting around twiddling your thumbs! Off you go! (*to Marcelle*) I can't stand children who don't know what to do with themselves.

MARCELLE: Auntie … Are you sure I can't give you a hand with anything?

MRS BÉROUTTE: No help needed – at all. Off you go and play …! Show my son what you're made of, my dear! Give him a terrific run for his money!

JEAN (*to Marcelle as they near the garden*): What's with them?

MARCELLE: I don't know but your father was trying to hide something …

JEAN: A surprise …? A little gift …? We'll see later, no doubt …

BÉROUTTE AND MRS BÉROUTTE: *Will you go and play tennis*! (*Jean and Marcelle exit.*)

BÉROUTTE (*producing the book*): I think they very nearly saw it …

MRS BÉROUTTE: I think we got away with it … But you must hide that horror as quickly as you can.

BÉROUTTE: Where?

MRS BÉROUTTE: Upstairs, in the cupboard where you keep your revolver … Have you got the key?

BÉROUTTE (*leaving rapidly*): Yes …!

MRS BÉROUTTE: No! Wait! Throw it in the pond.

BÉROUTTE: Won't it float?

MRS BÉROUTTE: Tie it to a stone.

BÉROUTTE: If the string breaks it'll come back to haunt us!

MRS BÉROUTTE: Burn it! Burn it in the stove!

BÉROUTTE: That's the best idea … (*He speeds over to the kitchen and opens the door but recoils, clutching the book to his chest.*) Antonia is in the kitchen!

MRS BÉROUTTE: She's back already?

BÉROUTTE: The farmer's son must've brought her back quickly.

MRS BÉROUTTE (*anxious*): Do you think she suspects something ...?

BÉROUTTE: So what? We'll be showing her the door anyway.

MRS BÉROUTTE: Hold on! A woman who can read that sort of filth is capable of anything!

BÉROUTTE: You think we shouldn't say anything about the book?

MRS BÉROUTTE: That would be wisest ...

BÉROUTTE: What shall I do with it?

MRS BÉROUTTE: Hide it in your pocket.

BÉROUTTE (*trying again*): It's too big!

MRS BÉROUTTE (*staring at the kitchen door*) Look out! Here she comes ...!

BÉROUTTE: Where should I hide it? Ah! The sofa! (*He hides the book under a cushion as quick as he can. At that moment, Jean, who has been lurking by the French window and spying on his father, slips away. Enter Antonia.*)

ANTONIA (*very simply and formally*): Can I have my book back please, madam?

MRS BÉROUTTE (*very sweetly*): Antonia, my dear girl, I haven't seen any book ...

ANTONIA: I think you have, madam.

MRS BÉROUTTE: No, Antonia, not at all.

ANTONIA: I am sure that madam must have taken my book.

MRS BÉROUTTE (*even more sweetly*): My dear, dear Antonia, I haven't left this spot, have I, Jules? Ask him yourself ...

BÉROUTTE: She's been right here. All the time.

MRS BÉROUTTE: I have been right here all the time you were out ... How quickly you returned from the farm ...! Marvellous! Thank you so much, Antonia ...!

ANTONIA: Well, what on earth has happened to my book? Maybe Master Jean ... (*She heads towards the garden.*)

MRS BÉROUTTE (*stopping Antonia*): Jean ...!? You must be crazy!

ANTONIA: Madam. I had my book last night ... I know I did ... (*She takes a step towards the sofa.*)

BÉROUTTE: Well, it's not on the sofa, that's for sure! (*He sits down.*)

MRS BÉROUTTE (*coming to the rescue*): A book on the sofa? The very idea! Ha ha!

ANTONIA (*desperate*): But where can it be ...? It's not in the kitchen and the farmer's wife didn't have it.

BÉROUTTE: The farmer's wife?

ANTONIA: Yes, sir, I often lend it to her ... (*Béroutte and Mrs Béroutte glance at each other, appalled.*) So that she can check on the amount of milk, butter and beans.

MRS BÉROUTTE (*suddenly arrogant*): Oh! You mean your cookbook?

ANTONIA (*nonchalantly*): Yes, madam.

MRS BÉROUTTE (*severely*): And you've no idea where you've put it? You're a disgrace, my girl! Totally disorganized!

ANTONIA: But madam …

MRS BÉROUTTE: Totally disorganized! (*to Béroutte*) That's why everything gets lost in this house! Sheets, linen, bedcovers … (*to Antonia*) Last Saturday, two more dishcloths went missing! If I made you pay for everything that went missing you'd think twice before *stealing*!

ANTONIA: Madam! How dare you!

MRS BÉROUTTE (*viciously*): Insolence now, is it? Not under my roof, my girl … That's the final straw …! You can pack your bags!

ANTONIA: Madam!

MRS BÉROUTTE: I'm going to find your book myself, I'll find your cookbook and then we'll throw you out … (*She pushes Antonia and turns to whisper urgently to her husband.*) Don't leave me alone with her! (*Exit Antonia, Mrs Béroutte and Béroutte. When they have left, Jean appears at the French window and comes in.*)

JEAN: They've gone … (*Marcelle appears.*)

MARCELLE: What were they were hiding?

JEAN (*goes over to the sofa*): Something in the sofa. (*He feels around and pulls out a book.*) Huh! It's just a book.

MARCELLE (*disappointed*): Tch! (*She turns away.*)

JEAN (*reading the title page*): *The Kama Sutra.*

MARCELLE (*laughs innocently*): What's that?

JEAN: *The Hindu Manual of Erotology.*

MARCELLE: Erotology? What on earth is that?

JEAN: Um … Ha ha … a Greek word. *Eros*: love. *Logos*: science. Hindu erotology. The Hindu science of love.

MARCELLE: Hindu love? Is it by Rudyard Kipling?

JEAN (*sitting down and putting the book on a cushion*): No, I don't think so … I'm not sure who wrote it … Ah! Look, there are some illustrations …. Oh! OH! (*He shuts the book.*)

MARCELLE: Let me see …

JEAN: No …

MARCELLE: Why ever not …?

JEAN: It's not the sort of thing you should see.

MARCELLE: Oh, it's something personal is it?

JEAN: Yes … that's right.

MARCELLE: Maybe you should put it back where you found it.

JEAN: Yes, good idea. (*He puts the book back under the cushion but remains on the sofa. Marcelle heads out.*) Are you going somewhere?

MARCELLE: I'm going up to my bedroom.

JEAN: What's the matter? You're not sulking, are you?

MARCELLE (*at the door*): Don't be so rude! I'm just going to my bedroom.

JEAN: We could wait for the post to arrive ... together.

MARCELLE: In a while ... You're going to stay here?

JEAN (*slightly embarrassed*): Yes ...

MARCELLE (*coming over to him*): You're going to look at that *Kama Sutra* thing while I'm out, aren't you?

JEAN: Of course not.

MARCELLE: Liar!

JEAN: What do you mean 'liar'?

MARCELLE: I can see you're dying to have a little peak.

JEAN: Me?

MARCELLE (*staring him in the eyes*): Yes, you.

JEAN: Well ... So are you. (*He pulls the book out.*)

MARCELLE: If you're going to look at it – so am I!

JEAN: Let's just flick through it. (*He opens the book.*)

MARCELLE (*leaning over his shoulder*): Let me see ...

JEAN: Oh no, don't look!

MARCELLE (*bending over him to see*): Oh, come on ... what is it?

JEAN: It's a ... (*Suddenly hides the page with his hand.*) No ... No ... Don't look!

MARCELLE (*pulling his hand away*): Oh ... (*Her voice tensing a little.*) Different ways of ... kissing ... (*Suddenly there is a distant noise: Jean and Marcelle separate quickly and Jean rapidly hides the book.*)

JEAN: Someone's coming!

MARCELLE (*by the French window and returning to Jean*): No ... It's nothing ... No-one there ... You were really scared, weren't you?

JEAN (*taking hold of her hand*): Yes ... But feel my heart now ... It's as steady as a rock ... (*He sighs.*)

MARCELLE: So it is ... (*She takes his hand and puts it on her breast, keeping her hand on his chest all the time.*) Feel mine ... It's just the opposite to yours ...

JEAN: Oh, Marcelle! How fast your heart is beating ... It's beating so fast ...

MARCELLE: Hands off, now!

JEAN: But, Marcelle! It's beating so fast ...

MARCELLE (*gently pushing him away*): That'll do, Jean ... You do make me laugh sometimes ... What on earth has got into you ...?

JEAN: I've no idea ... I can hardly breathe ... I'm all in a sweat

... I feel like crying and at the same time I want to hold you ... (*He takes her in his arms.*)

MARCELLE (*wriggling away from him*): Let go, Jean ... Stop being a naughty boy ...

JEAN: Don't you ... like me, Marcelle ...?

MARCELLE (*lovingly*): Oh, Jean, you know I do!

JEAN: Show me then ... Kiss me ...

MARCELLE: No, no, we mustn't ... We mustn't ... (*A noise behind the door makes them both leap in shock.*)

JEAN: Quick! Outside now!

MARCELLE: Yes ... Yes ... Quickly! (*They run out into the garden.*)

(*Mrs Béroutte wears a hat and carries an umbrella; Mrs Vermeuil holds a little prayer book.*)

MRS VERMEUIL: It's disgraceful! Totally disgraceful! I cannot believe what you have told me ... Having heard what you've been through this morning I would never have troubled you ... I just thought I'd pay a little visit to my dear friend and neighbour after Mass ...

MRS BÉROUTTE: Think nothing of it ... Please, sit down ... There's a few minutes until the bus arrives ...

MRS VERMEUIL: As I was saying, the grocer opposite the village hall could probably find you a new maid better than the butcher could ... You must also have a word with the lady who runs the post office: she found an excellent maidservant for Mrs Tary.

MRS BÉROUTTE: Thank you so much for the advice ... Oh! My dear friend ... Imagine if everyone found such poisonous things in their houses!

MRS VERMEUIL: It's disgraceful! Totally disgraceful ...! Imagine if your son or niece found something like that ...

MRS BÉROUTTE (*going over to the sofa in a panic*): You've got me worried now ...! Oh, thank god, it's under there ...

MRS VERMEUIL (*unconvincingly indifferent*): Ah ... That disgraceful book is *there* is it ...?

MRS BÉROUTTE (*placing her hand on the cushion*): Underneath this cushion.

MRS VERMEUIL: Guard it with the utmost vigilance.

MRS BÉROUTTE: I'll have to have everything disinfected ...! I sent her packing alright! You know, the little harlot didn't even dare ask me for her final wages ...

MRS VERMEUIL: Did she ask for her book?

MRS BÉROUTTE (*pulling the book out*): Here it is! Horror of horrors!

MRS VERMEUIL: It's quite a pretty volume ... Nicely bound ...

MRS BÉROUTTE: The pictures inside are neither pretty nor nice!

MRS VERMEUIL: It's disgraceful! Totally disgraceful ...!

MRS BÉROUTTE (*tucking it back under the cushion*): We're going to incinerate it.

MRS VERMEUIL (*disappointed*): Oh. (*changing her tone*) Quite right too ...! Where on earth can people get hold of a disgusting book like that, anyway?

MRS BÉROUTTE: In Paris, obviously.

MRS VERMEUIL: Don't the police protect us from this sort of thing?

MRS BÉROUTTE: Huh! Not anymore they don't. Our individual sense of morality and our religious faith is the only thing that protects us in this day and age ...

MRS VERMEUIL: It's disgraceful! Totally disgraceful ...!

MRS BÉROUTTE: Here comes my husband. (*Enter Béroutte.*)

BÉROUTTE: Ah! Good morning, Mrs Vermeuil ... My wife has told you ...?

MRS VERMEUIL: I have heard the full story ... It's disgraceful! Totally disgraceful ...!

BÉROUTTE: You can say that again! (*to Mrs Béroutte*) The charabanc from the farm is here. The farmer has collected Antonia's trunk and will take it straight to the station.

MRS BÉROUTTE (*standing up*): I don't want to see that girl again. (*to Mrs Vermeuil*) I'd give her such a thrashing! Anyway, I must catch the bus. Goodbye. (*to Béroutte*) The farmer's wife will prepare lunch ... Marcelle will lay the table ... But before you call her in, incinerate that loathsome book. (*She pulls out the book and hands it to her husband. She exits into the garden.*)

BÉROUTTE (*calling after her*): Yes, yes ... right away ... Good luck finding a servant ...

MRS BÉROUTTE (*re-entering*): Burn it! *Burn it!* (*She exits.*)

MRS VERMEUIL: I've never seen Mrs Béroutte in such a state.

BÉROUTTE: She's lost her head ... The trouble is ... She's left me with this book ... And everyone spies on you around here ... And my wife hasn't realized that I can't get to the stove now because the farmer's wife is preparing lunch ...

MRS VERMEUIL: I thought as much ...

BÉROUTTE: And you know what the gossip is like around here ... The farmer's wife will tell everyone that when my wife went out I destroyed some compromising papers ...

MRS VERMEUIL: Your love letters, for instance ...

BÉROUTTE (*stupefied*): Yes ... love letters ...! Oh my God ...!

MRS VERMEUIL (*very friendly*): Why don't I help you – I can dispose of the book at my house.

BÉROUTTE: Oh, I wouldn't dream of letting you take this shocking book with you …

MRS VERMEUIL: Look … I'm a grown woman. I'm twenty-nine, you know.

BÉROUTTE: Twenty-nine? No! I would never have guessed! Only the innocent look young …

MRS VERMEUIL: Flatterer …! I've been married too, you know … I know what is what.

BÉROUTTE: But you can't possibly imagine …

MRS VERMEUIL: What? *The Kama Sutra*. It's a sacred and religious Hindu text …

BÉROUTTE (*cheerfully*): But it isn't just *The Kama Sutra*! It's a right assortment … (*Shows her the volume.*) You see, 'Succulent Selections from *Gamiani*' – to be fair, it's actually beautifully written …

MRS VERMEUIL: Really? Some genuine authors write these horrors … well, er, perhaps we should say *fantasies*, just like there are some fine artists who do the artwork?

BÉROUTTE: *Gamiani* is by Alfred de Musset.

MRS VERMEUIL: Alfred de Musset …!? Would you believe it! I love his work! (*She reaches out for the book.*) Since de Musset is in it …

BÉROUTTE: I must warn you that the illustrations are rather explicit even if, believe it or not, some of them have been done by a truly great artist: Fragonard …

MRS VERMEUIL (*taking hold of his arm*): Aren't you able to stand back and make an objective judgement? Can't you see the perfection of the design? The talent of the artist …? Can't you make an informed aesthetic appraisal, pure and simple …?

BÉROUTTE: Pure and simple? Not exactly the phrase I'd use! Er … no … no … I feel like this book is stuck to me …! It's like a curse!

MRS VERMEUIL: Really?

BÉROUTTE: Ever since my wife made this wonderful discovery, I feel like Baggessen.

MRS VERMEUIL: Baggessen?

BÉROUTTE: The juggler – "the plate-smasher" …? Oh, of course … You wouldn't have seen him … You're far too young and you've never been to the Folies-Bergère … When he'd finished smashing plates, Baggessen would come on with a sheet of paper that he couldn't shake off … (*Béroutte mimes with the book.*) When he freed his right hand, the paper would stick to his left hand, then his elbow, his knee, under his foot … everywhere … No matter how much he stamped on it, shook it, leaped up and down, he could never shake it off ...

MRS VERMEUIL (*moving closer to him*): That sounds hilarious ... What happened at the end ...?

BÉROUTTE: I can't quite remember ... I think he staggered off-stage with the paper still stuck to him.

MRS VERMEUIL (*taking the book delicately*): He just needed someone to do this ...

BÉROUTTE: But whoever did that would be stuck themselves ... You see, you've got it now ... *You're* stuck with it!

MRS VERMEUIL (*seductively*): Why don't you come and take it off me ...

BÉROUTTE: No, you keep it ... That's really quite funny – it's all yours now!

MRS VERMEUIL: Well ... I'm not in the least scared ... Look ... (*She opens the book, gasps, and slams it shut. She looks at Béroutte, smiles and then opens the book again.*) Yes ... Oh ...! Oh ...! That's *monstrous*! (*Slams it shut.*) I see what you mean ...

BÉROUTTE: What did I tell you?

MRS VERMEUIL (*opens the book again*): Let me see ... What's this ...? Ah! The school of love ... That's a fascinating concept ... So there are schools of love in India ...? (*Silence.*) What a marvellous country ...

BÉROUTTE (*beginning to lean against Mrs Vermeuil*): I've always dreamed of visiting India ...

MRS VERMEUIL (*gazing at the book*): Look ... What a wonderful engraving this one is ... An Indian gentleman ... Is that right?

BÉROUTTE (*looking closely at the picture*): Yes ... A handsome Indian gentleman ...

MRS VERMEUIL: Have you seen Indian people before ...?

BÉROUTTE: Not naked I haven't.

MRS VERMEUIL (*leaning back heavily against Béroutte*): I must say the men are very handsome and obviously extremely *ardent* ...

BÉROUTTE (*in determination*): Yes ... Yes ... And with irresistible temptations like that or like *that* ... (*He quickly kisses her on the lips and they fall flat and roll on the sofa.*)

MRS VERMEUIL (*almost swooning as she collects herself*): Oh! It's disgraceful! Totally disgraceful ...!

BÉROUTTE (*stunned by his actions*): Yes. (*He is stung by passion once again and throws himself at her feet.*) How beautiful you are ... You're so beautiful ...!

MRS VERMEUIL (*standing up*): But, darling, someone might see us ...

BÉROUTTE (*taking hold of her*): Quick ... Into my study ...

MRS VERMEUIL (*reaching for the book*): Let's take the Hindus with us, shall we?

BÉROUTTE (*refusing to let her go*): But I am Indian ... I am *your* Indian ... (*They exit and slam the door behind them. In the garden we hear the voice of Mrs Béroutte.*)

(*Mrs Béroutte appears like an angel dragging Adam and Eve out of Paradise. She clutches Jean and Marcelle by the wrist. They are both flushed and dishevelled, and look extremely sheepish, having been caught* in flagrante delicto *by Mrs Béroutte.*)

MRS BÉROUTTE: You naughty children! You naughty, little children! I'm going to tell him exactly how I found you. (*To Marcelle, letting her go.*) Wait for me right here, you little hussy! (*Pushing Jean towards the door of the study.*) As for you, you filthy pervert, you are going to see your poor father ... You are going right in to see him now! (*She opens the study door, looks inside and shuts it quickly.*) Ah! Him as well ...!? Am I the only person who has not been reading the bloody *Kama Sutra*!?

The End

Blind Man's Buff
(1921)

Charles Hellem and Pol d'Estoc

Characters:
Darlet, director of the workshops, 55
Durand, journalist, 40
Maria, 40
Daniel, a deaf mute, 19
Huguet, head clerk, blind
Brichet, porter
Estaguer, workman
Rougemar, workman
Marten, workman
Ballot, workman
Raquier, workman
Verlin, workman
Martinot, workman
Anne Verlie, work woman
Men and Women workers

The action takes place in an establishment for the blind situated in the suburbs of a big city.

SCENE: *The Director's Office – the back of the stage is almost entirely taken up by enormous bay windows, in the centre of which is a glass door – the door gives on to a corridor which extends the length of the bay windows and leads to the various workshops of the blind. At left a desk, at right, a bookcase. Hanging on the walls, at about a man's height, are geographical cards for the blind in stucco or cardboard, uniformly white, in frames without glass – The Administrator's notices are picked out with drawing pins – Framed diplomas with medals – Fixed to left wall, also at a man's height, a clock with glass. At L. a window – between the window and left back, behind the desk, a nest of drawers, with a bust on top. Armchair, chairs, etc.*

During the whole of the act, workmen and women, all blind, pass at intervals along the corridor, behind the bay windows – Some carry brooms, some baskets, chairs, etc. – They all walk with the same phantom-like step – their hands in front of them feeling where they are going – Some have bandages over one eye – some over both – others wear glasses. They are in their working clothes – leather aprons, grey smocks or shirts, corduroy waistcoats etc. The women, black blouses, or blue aprons or overalls.

Time, 4 p.m. a winter's afternoon – it is commencing to get dark.

On rise of curtain, Darlet, the Director, is discovered writing at his desk – a pause – then Huguet knocks at the glass door.

DARLET: Come in, Huguet.

(*Huguet enters, and although blind moves with a certain ease – he carries a little bag filled with money.*)

HUGUET: I've brought the money for the men's pay, monsieur.
DARLET (*continuing to write*): Good – just put it down on the desk.
HUGUET: There it is, monsieur.
DARLET: Did you agree the figure? Was my total correct?
HUGUET (*bringing out a paper from his pocket and putting it on his chest – he figures with his fingers the special writing for the blind*): I made it 1926 francs and 65 centimes.
DARLET (*after checking with his papers*): 1926 francs 65 centimes – quite correct. I hope you took care that they didn't pass you off any bad coins this time – we don't want a repetition of last Saturday.
HUGUET: I hope not, monsieur. I've checked it all very carefully.

(*Brichet knocks on the door.*)

DARLET: Come in – Well, what is it Brichet?
BRICHET: There's a gentleman downstairs who wishes to see you, monsieur.
DARLET: Did he give you his name?
BRICHET: Yes, monsieur – Monsieur Durand.
DARLET: Ah! Durand – Ask him to come up.
BRICHET: Yes, monsieur. (*He exits.*)
HUGUET: Estaguer is hanging about, waiting to see you too, Monsieur.
DARLET: Oh, he's always taking up one's time with his complaints … What's his trouble now, I wonder?
HUGUET: I don't know exactly – the same old story I expect – something about his work – too much to do.

DARLET: Work! – why, he doesn't know the meaning of the word. He's about the worst man we've got in the place unfortunately. I've tried him at everything. The only thing he ever succeeds in doing is causing trouble.

HUGUET: I know, m'sieur. He's a bad tempered brute. Only yesterday he had no end of a row with Raquier and half strangled him.

DARLET: He's getting too dangerous and I shall have to get rid of him.

HUGUET: The sooner the better, m'sieur. Last Saturday as he was leaving the workshop, after having been paid, someone waylaid and robbed him. Ever since then he's become worse and worse – nobody dare speak to him.

DARLET: He does not suspect any of his fellow workers?

HUGUET: Goodness knows – he accuses everybody. To tell you the truth, since they have put up that casual ward near here, this neighbourhood has become infested with all sorts of bad characters; everyone is complaining about it, and since Estaguer has been attacked, all our workmen are terrified out of their lives. They think everyone they knock up against is a thief – it makes them more suspicious than ever.

DARLET: I'll have a word with them when they are all up here for their pay.

HUGUET: I wish you would, monsieur, they will listen to you. (*After feeling for the time on his watch with his fingers.*) You won't be ready to pay them until six, monsieur, will you?

DARLET: No, don't let them come up before then.

HUGUET: Right, monsieur, I will have the bell rung as usual at six o'clock. (*He makes as if to exit.*)

DARLET (*calling him back*): Ah, just a minute, Huguet, I was forgetting. I am expecting two people here shortly – a young man and his mother – as soon as they arrive, send them up to me.

HUGUET: Certainly, monsieur.

(*Darlet, alone, takes the bag of money which Huguet has placed on his desk, and puts it in a drawer, locking it up – seeing Durand appear behind the glass door, he rises, goes to the door, opens it and greets him.*)

DARLET: Good evening, my dear Durand. It is good to see you again, but what brings you out into these wilds?

DURAND (*shaking hands*): I am delighted to see you too, but surely you got my letter telling you I was coming?

DARLET: Oh, of course, I remember now. You've come to see me in your professional capacity – an interview – eh?

DURAND: Precisely.

DARLET: Come along, then. (*Pointing to chair.*) Sit down and fire ahead. (*Darlet sits at his desk – Durand on a chair opposite him.*)

DURAND: Well, you see people are beginning to talk about the wonderful things you have been doing in this establishment of yours, and my paper is frightfully keen on getting full details first hand ... What goes on in what you are pleased to call your House without Windows should make excellent copy for a fine article.

DARLET: I shall be very glad to tell you all I can.

DURAND: You have been experimenting in these workshops with those unfortunate people who, through blindness or any other physical defect, are unable to earn an honest living in the ordinary way. You arrange the work of your various inmates in such a manner that, what one man is lacking, another supplies, and the two together, form, so to speak, a complete whole. Isn't that so?

DARLET: You have expressed it exactly. All large cities have their workshops for the blind, but this idea of mine of helping the blind and the maimed to help each other, is unique, and I find it intensely interesting.

DURAND: And have you obtained good results so far?

DARLET: Really splendid. At the present moment, for instance, I have here a poor devil who hasn't any arms.

DURAND: Oh!

DARLET: They were crushed in a printing machine and had to be amputated. Well, we give him employment here.

DURAND: In what capacity?

DARLET: Well, I give him my rough notes for all the unimportant correspondence, which is very heavy, and he dictates them to the typist, who is blind.

DURAND: Otherwise, of course, there would be nothing left for him to do but beg in the streets.

DARLET: Then again, I have a young girl who hasn't any legs. She was smashed up in a tramway accident.

DURAND: Horrible!

DARLET: She keeps all the books of the various workshops, and translates the accounts made out in Braille into ordinary figures ... She lives quite near here, in one of the tenement buildings I have had built, and a couple of blind men fetch her every morning and sit her down at her desk.

DURAND: In Braille ...

DARLET: Yes, that is the name of the special writing invented for the blind – where the figures are written by means of these 'points in relief' by the cashier, who is blind, and then passed to her.

DURAND: It is really wonderful work you are doing – an absolute benefit to humanity ... Tell me, these maimed and mutilated people, do you find they suffer very much, having to mix with the others in the workshops?

DARLET: Far less than they would under other conditions, for here they are not seen.

DURAND: That is true. I can understand that. They must feel that they are not being looked at with eyes of horror, perhaps disgust.

DARLET: You must not forget that, hitherto, with the exception of myself, everyone here has been blind ... everyone.

DURAND: You mean to say you are the only person in control here who can see?

DARLET: The only one. My clerk, secretary, the cashier, porters, the workmen, all are blind – every one of them – as in many blind institutions.

DURAND: How many have you altogether?

DARLET: A hundred and eighteen – men and women – spread amongst the various workshops.

DURAND: And all blind?

DARLET: All of them ...

DURAND: You may well call it the House without Windows.

DARLET (*pointing behind the bay window at workman who passes carrying a basket*): See that one going along the corridor ... He is an extremely skilled workman, there is no one equal to him in the whole shop.

DURAND: What's his speciality?

DARLET: He is a basket maker, and possesses a most extraordinary delicate touch, and able to do extremely fine work. When I give him someone who can see to assist him to put the bands of colour around the base of his baskets – or could colour them with paint – the two together will be able to turn out some wonderful work, and they will sell very well, too.

DURAND: I suppose you will use one of your maimed or mutilated to help him?

DARLET: No. In this case we need somebody with special taste and a perfect sense of colour. But I think I have found some one who will just answer my purpose – a deaf mute.

DURAND: A deaf mute? Good gracious! That's an extraordinary idea.

DARLET: Oh, it will be a long and difficult experiment ... Just think – a deaf mute and a blind man ... it will be almost impossible to make them understand each other.

DURAND: Why not? You have already been able to do such marvellous things ... those that you have already told me about.

DARLET: Ah – yes – a deaf mute and a blind man ... just think, they have absolutely nothing in common – no point of contact.

DURAND (*after a moment's reflection*): What do you mean, I don't quite understand ...

DARLET: Well, look! Here are two persons who must remain absolute strangers to each other, even though living side by side ... there is absolutely nothing but the sense of touch, that can help them to realize that there is anyone near them ...

DURAND: Yes ... you are right – quite right ... It is a very curious combination.

DARLET: One might almost say, that a blind man is to a deaf mute, what a bird must be to a fish.

DURAND: Ah! Most extraordinary ... I should never have realized it. I can quite see that under the circumstances, your difficulties will be enormous.

DARLET: I don't despair, however, that I shall eventually make the pair of them, a very useful combination ...

(*Estaguer knocks – Durand makes a movement as if to go, but Darlet, wishing him to assist at an interesting visit, by a gesture makes him sit down again.*)

Come in!

(*Estaguer enters, closes the door after him and advances – Darlet, with a gesture, imposes silence on Durand, whose presence Estaguer ignores.*)

What do you want, Estaguer? You know very well I do not like being disturbed in my office.

ESTAGUER (*very loud, and in gruff tones*): I want to shift over to another workshop, monsieur.

DARLET: That will be the third time you have changed in two months.

ESTAGUER: The foreman doesn't like me – he is always up against me ... I am sick of this basket making.

DARLET: It was just the same when you were in the brush department.

ESTAGUER: I tell you I don't want to stop there any longer.

DARLET: Where do you want me to put you, then?

ESTAGUER: I don't know – and I damn well don't care.

DARLET: Look here, Estaguer, you know where I shall put you if you go on like this. I shall put you out altogether. That is what I shall do with you.

ESTAGUER (*between his teeth*): I don't care what the hell you do with me!

DARLET: Why can't you behave yourself like the others? I hear you were fighting again yesterday.

ESTAGUER: Oh, they have gone and told you that already, have they? It doesn't take long for somebody to go sneaking to you.

DARLET: Of course, they told me. It is my business to know everything that goes on here.

ESTAGUER: Oh yes, I know, I am always in the wrong. If there is bad work done in the workshop, who is blamed for it – Estaguer. If there is any argument, or any trouble, it is always me who is wrong. It is me who gets punished. It was Raquier who started it last night, and besides – I don't care – I've had enough of it ... (*he gesticulates wildly*) I am sick of this kind of life, and I warn you, Monsieur Darlet, I won't put up with it. I won't be brow beaten and sat upon by everyone. Do you hear? Just let me get hold of him for once. Let me catch him, and then you will see something ...

DARLET: Who are you talking about?

ESTAGUER: Why, the man who knocked me down and robbed me, after I had been paid last Saturday night. I had only just left here – only a hundred yards away ... (*breaking out*) Oh, monsieur, to rob a poor blind man ... he half killed me.

DARLET: Do you know who it was? Do you suspect anyone?

ESTAGUER: Ah! I am not quite sure, but I shall find out. Whoever it was, he robbed me of all my money and my watch too ... My God! When I do get him, he won't have much chance of robbing anyone else, I can tell you ... (*Takes a knife out of his pocket.*)

DARLET: Just shut that knife up and put it back in your pocket. If you would take my advice and go straight home when you have finished here, instead of hanging about in disreputable drinking booths with all the rogues and vagabonds in the neighbourhood, this would never have happened to you.

ESTAGUER: Rogues and vagabonds, indeed! I know who did me in. I know who it was!

DARLET: Well, since you know who it is, tell me, and I shall see that justice is done, and that the man is properly punished.

ESTAGUER: Justice ... Justice! Don't talk to me of justice! It's a bit too thick ... Was it justice who acquitted Maria Goudet, and let her go Scot free?

DARLET: Maria Goudet? I don't know what you mean. Who is she?

ESTAGUER: The blasted woman who did this. (*Showing his face burnt by vitriol.*) Ah ... the ... the ...

DARLET: Now then, Estaguer, that's quite enough. You are forgetting yourself.

ESTAGUER: Ah ...! Good God! When you think that at one time I could see like the rest of you ...

DARLET: I tell you this is quite enough, Estaguer. Leave the room. I won't have you coming in here making a scene. You know that very well.

ESTAGUER: I am not even allowed to speak now. I tell you, I won't stick it.

DARLET: Clear out, will you – and quickly.

ESTAGUER: You wait ... one of these days I'll get my own back. Just let me catch one of you, and I'll show you what I'll do ... Swines, all of you! (*Exit Estaguer.*)

DURAND (*after a pause*): What an awful face! How did it happen?

DARLET: A young girl he had seduced and deserted when she was going to have a baby, threw some vitriol at him.

DURAND: It's a terrible punishment. And the woman – was she acquitted?

DARLET: Yes. He has lost his eyes and probably his reason. He seems to be getting worse and worse. You can see for yourself that he is not quite all there ... There is always trouble with him in the workshop, and as he is a strong, hefty man, he becomes dangerous at times. He is cruel too. The other day he strangled a cat that he found eating from his plate. I am afraid we'll have to get rid of him.

DURAND: What will he do?

DARLET: I have asked for him to be transferred into an asylum. Fortunately, all my men are not like him.

DURAND (*rising*): Well, I think you are doing wonderful work, Darlet, and I can assure you that I shall do all I can to obtain for you public support and sympathy.

DARLET: Well, I think we are doing something to alleviate the sufferings of the world.

DURAND: You have given me some excellent copy, and I hope to be able to write an article worthy of the subject. I will send you a proof so that you can judge for yourself.

DARLET: It is very good of you, and whatever help you and your paper can give me will be greatly appreciated.

DURAND: Au revoir, then, my dear Darlet.

DARLET: Good night – good night ... if you want any more details, you have only to ask me.

(*Darlet accompanies Durand to the door and they shake hands – EXIT Durand. Maria and Daniel are seen entering through the corridor.*)

DARLET: Ah, come in – come in. So this is your son?

MARIA: Yes, monsieur.

DARLET: So you have at last decided to bring him.

MARIA: Ah ... monsieur ... if you only knew how it will hurt me to part with him. It will be the first time he has ever left me.

DARLET: But, my good woman, you cannot let a young man like that grow up without some sort of employment. How old is he?

MARIA: Nineteen.

DARLET: What's his name?

MARIA: Daniel, monsieur – Daniel Goudet.

DARLET: Daniel Goudet?

MARIA: Yes, monsieur.

DARLET: H'm ... And you have never had him taught anything?

MARIA: No, m'sieur.

DARLET: Has he never attended a deaf and dumb school?

MARIA: I was too frightened to leave him out of my care, in case anything might happen to him.

DARLET: And has he never been apprenticed to any trade?

MARIA: Oh no, m'sieur. I could not bear the thought of his being laughed at, or poked fun at, by any of the other boys.

DARLET: But why should they poke fun at him?

MARIA: With his terrible infirmity ...

DARLET: So you have to keep him yourself?

MARIA: Yes, m'sieur.

DARLET: You haven't too much money to spare, I can see. Come now, if he can earn a little money for himself, it would help you, wouldn't it?

MARIA: Of course, m'sieur. It is very hard for a woman like me to earn enough to keep both of us.

DARLET: You are a widow, then?

MARIA (*embarrassed*): Yes ... no ... I mean ... he never knew his father ...

DARLET: I understand.

MARIA: What kind of work would you give him to do? If only there were something in the painting line ... I think you saw some of the beautiful pictures he has done.

DARLET: Exactly ... Here he would be most useful to my poor blind people, for after all, he can see. (*Then, looking at him.*) He looks quite intelligent.

MARIA: Oh yes, m'sieur, I can answer for that. He can understand everything I say to him by watching the movements of my lips. You will find him a really good and intelligent boy, m'sieur, quiet and painstaking. Aren't you, Daniel? (*Daniel nods his head.*) Is it not terrible, m'sieur, a fine boy like that. (*She wipes her eyes with her handkerchief – Daniel approaches her and kisses her.*)

DARLET: Come now, you mustn't upset yourself. He will be very happy here, and we shall take every care of him.

MARIA: Oh yes, m'sieur, you promise me that you will look after him?

DARLET: Of course, of course. And you will find the work will occupy his mind, and make him far happier – and you can always come and see him.

MARIA: Ah! … you will let me come and see him?

DARLET: Of course, especially at first, when he won't be too busy.

MARIA: What will you give him to do?

DARLET: Nothing very hard, I assure you. We'll put him to sort out the various colours for the sides of the baskets we make here. You see that won't be very difficult, and he'll be able to make use of his taste for colour.

MARIA: Ah! you are very good, m'sieur, and I am very grateful. So he will be working with the blind in their workshops?

DARLET: Yes, certainly. Would you like me to show you over them? You will see there is nothing very dreadful there.

MARIA: Thank you very much, m'sieur. Would you mind if I went with you first, alone? I should prefer it.

DARLET: Why don't you want him to come too? Are you frightened it may upset him?

MARIA: All those poor faces with eyes that gaze at you, and yet cannot see. It must be a terrible –

DARLET: He will have to see them though, sooner or later, and I want him to start next Monday morning. I shall expect him then.

MARIA: Yes, m'sieur, he shall be here, I promise you, but in the meantime, I should be able to make him understand in my way, and explain to him what I have seen, and what he will have to do. It will help me to make things a bit easier for him.

DARLET: Very well, then. Come with me now. He can wait here for you.

MARIA: Certainly. (*To Daniel with a special articulation of the lips and a gesture accompanying each word.*) Wait for me here, Daniel. I am going out for a minute with monsieur, but I'm coming back … Yes … yes … I'm coming back … (*Daniel makes a sign with his head 'Yes, yes'.*)

(*Daniel alone, looks all over the room. He is interested in the cards and notices stuck on the wall – approaches them and examines each one intently – goes from one to the other – then looks through the window. His steps on the parquet floor make quite a loud noise, but he himself, of course, cannot hear it.*)

(*Huguet knocks behind the glass door; receiving no reply,*

knocks again, then ENTERS – Daniel, who has his back turned, does not see him – Huguet hears the noise of Daniel turning.)

HUGUET: Monsieur Darlet ... (*A pause.*) Monsieur Darlet ... who's there ...? Who's there? (*Noise of Daniel who turns his back to Huguet.*) It isn't Monsieur Darlet ... Who else can it be then? (*louder*) Monsieur Darlet, are you not well? (*At this moment Brichet comes into the corridor.*)

HUGUET (*continues*): M'sieur Darlet ... (*uneasy*) Why don't you answer?

BRICHET (*entering*): M'sieur Darlet is asking for you, Huguet.

HUGUET: Yes, but he doesn't answer ...

BRICHET: Oh, M'sieur Darlet is not in there, he is in the chair workshop.

HUGUET: Are you sure?

BRICHET: Of course I'm sure. I have just left him.

HUGUET: But there is someone in his office.

BRICHET: Who?

HUGUET: I don't know ... they don't reply.

BRICHET: You must have made a mistake ... There cannot be.

HUGUET: I tell you there is someone in there ... I distinctly heard ... I know I am right.

(*At this moment Daniel turns round and walks a few steps – he perceives with astonishment Brichet and Huguet who are talking together at the door in undertones.*)

HUGUET: There ... there ... don't you hear?

BRICHET: You are right. (*Aloud.*) Who is there? (*A pause.*) Why don't you answer? (*Pause.*) Who is there? (*Pause.*) Say something, won't you?

HUGUET: Who are you? What are you doing in there?

BRICHET (*after listening and hearing nothing – in a low voice*): He's hiding.

HUGUET (*in an undertone to Brichet*): And the money for the men's pay on the guvnor's desk.

(*Daniel takes a few steps towards them.*)

BRICHET (*in a loud voice*): You can't escape – you won't leave this room anyhow.

HUGUET: Let's keep guard by the door.

(*Daniel, very astonished, stops.*)

BRICHET (*in the doorway*): You won't say who you are. Very well. You won't get out of here.

HUGUET: What's your game? Nothing honest, I'll be bound.

(Daniel, who now understands that something strange is happening, shows distress.)

HUGUET: Call m'sieur Darlet – go on – shout out for him – get him here as quickly as possible whilst I guard the door.

BRICHET *(going a little way down the corridor)*: M'sieur Darlet … M'sieur Darlet … *(Rougemar enters.)*

ROUGEMAR: What is it? What's the matter?

HUGUET: There's a thief in the guvnor's office.

ROUGEMAR: A thief!

BRICHET: Yes! he's hiding somewhere, and we can't get him to speak.

HUGUET: We both heard him in there, distinctly.

BRICHET: Call for help, Roumegar – call the men – we mustn't let him escape.

ROUGEMAR *(in the corridor)*: Help – help – Marten – Ballot – Raquier – help – Verlin – Martinot – Estaguer – help!

HUGUET: M'sieur Darlet – Help quick – M'sieur Darlet.

ROUGEMAR: Stop, thief – help – help –

(Estaguer, Marten, Ballot, Raquier, Verlin, Martinot, and Anna all appear.)

VERLIN: What's happening?

MARTINOT: What is it?

MARTEN: What's the matter?

ROUGEMAR: A thief!

VERLIN: A thief!

MARTEN: Where is he?

HUGUET: There – in the guv'nor's office.

BRICHET: He must have come in through the window.

HUGUET: He was after the money for the wages.

BALLOT: We must keep him here, until M'sieur Darlet arrives.

MARTINOT: Yes, rather.

MARTIN: He mustn't get away.

VERLIN: If we guard this door he can't possibly escape.

RAQUIER: M'sieur Darlet – M'sieur Darlet – Help – help!

ESTAGUER: I'll kill the dog – if I can only get hold of him – let me pass.

ALL: Yes – yes – let's go in.

HUGUET: Be careful – he may be armed …

(They enter with great caution, keeping on their guard.)

MARTINOT: Yes, take care.

VERLIN *(to Anna who is holding him by the arm)*: You stay here.

ANNA: Ah! I am frightened!

ESTAGUER: Frightened – pooh! Only let me get hold of the swine – I'll show you.

BALLOT: Yes, let's seize him, boys.

ESTAGUER: Wait till I get my fingers round your neck – I'll teach you to rob honest blind men.

RAQUIER: There he is!

BALLOT: Yes – yes – there!

HUGUET: Careful now – take care.

ANNA: I'm frightened – I'm frightened.

HUGUET (*who is still barring the door*): One of you go and find M'sieur Darlet – quickly – quickly –

BRICHET: He's in the chair-making department.

HUGUET: And see that all the doors are locked downstairs so that he can't escape.

ESTAGUER: Let me get hold of him – he won't have much chance to escape – blast him ...

(*The blind feeling their way with their hands slowly advance – along the walls and around the furniture – Sometimes whilst searching they get hold of each other by mistake.*)

MARTEN: Ah ... I've got him.

BALLOT (*frightened – being seized by Marten*): It is me – Marten – it is me.

RAQUIER: Ah ...!

VERLIN: There he is – no!

MARTINOT (*clutching someone*): Who is it?

RAQUIER: It's Raquier – Raquier – you fool!

MARTINOT: Ah! Raquier!

MARTEN (*seized also*): Ah – let me go – let me go!

VERLIN: This way – this way –

ESTAGUER: Where are you hiding, damn you! Let me get at you, you dirty thief!

ANNA: Ah! my God! my God!

HUGUET (*at the desk*): The money which I left on the desk has disappeared.

(*Daniel now understands the horror of the situation – he holds out his hands in vain and in the impossibility of making himself understood – half mad with fear he makes supplicating gestures as if by a miracle his pantomime might be understood – With mad fear showing in his eyes, tracked and surrounded by all those arms, he escapes from the nearest blind man, touches another, and knocks up against a third, escapes his grasp – But gradually the circle gets smaller – he tries to run away but Rougemar and Brichet push him back into the room.*)

ROUGEMAR: Here he is – he's trying to get away.
BRICHET: Yes, I felt him – I touched him …
MARTEN: Don't let him get away.
ESTAGUER: No – no – he mustn't leave the room.

(*Seeing that flight is impossible Daniel falls on his knees supplicating – at the moment Raquier, who is armed with a knife and is on the defensive, knocks up against Estaguer and wounds him.*)

ESTAGUER (*with a shriek*): By God – he's stabbed me – the filthy hound – he's struck me with his knife.

(*The horrible blind man's buff continues, amidst Estaguer's groans, the hard breathing of the blind, and the continual shock of their knocking up against the furniture.*)

HUGUET (*at the door*): M'sieur Darlet – M'sieur Darlet – whatever could have happened to him – why doesn't he come? (*Suddenly shouting to someone off stage.*) Ah! ring the alarm bell somebody – ring the bell – he'll understand then and he'll come – ring – ring.
ESTAGUER (*staggering upon Daniel*): Ah – this time – I've got you. I've got you …

(*He struggles with Daniel and they roll on the floor together – at the noise of the struggle the blind come nearer.*)

ESTAGUER: Ah! the swine – he's bitten me – hell – just you wait a minute – here – help me some of you – I've got him safe enough – there's nothing to be afraid of … Here – take hold of his arms and legs – there – hold him down – I've got him too.

(*The blind are all around Daniel holding him down by the arms and legs – he is absolutely powerless – the bell is clanging loudly.*)

BALLOT: We've got him right enough now.
VERLIN: Hold him.
RAQUIER: Don't worry – I shan't let go of him.
MARTEN: That's right – hang on to him tight.
VERLIN: Thief!
MARTINOT: Skunk!
RAQUIER: Perhaps now you'll open your mouth and say something.
ESTAGUER: Don't let him move – you just wait – I'll show you.
HUGUET: Hold him tight! M'sieur Darlet will soon be here.
ESTAGUER: You thief – you dirty thief – I'll teach you to rob the blind – Ah – ah – so it was you stole my money and my watch, was

it? Ah ah – well now it's my turn – tit for tat eh? – Where are your eyes, eh? Where are they? (*He feels all over Daniel's face with his hands, then having found them, he gouges them out with a quick movement of his thumbs.*) There – there – now you're the same as us – there's no difference between us now – You won't be able to steal any more, will you? There you are! Now you can go …

(*In his agony Daniel struggles with the human mass holding him and gets away – he puts his hands to his face and gives vent to uncanny noises of pain and terror.*)

DARLET (*off stage*): What's the matter? What does all this mean, Huguet?

HUGUET (*to the blind*): Here's M'sieur Darlet at last.

BRICHET: The boss. (*Darlet and Maria enter.*)

HUGUET: We've caught a thief in your office, m'sieur.

DARLET (*pushing his way through the blind men at the door and realizing the horrible situation*): Good God! What have you done! What have you done!

MARIA (*rushing to Daniel who is rolling on the floor in agony*): My boy – my boy – what have they done to you – (*Looking up.*) Oh, you brutes – you brutes – you inhuman brutes … (*Recognizing with stupefaction and horror Estaguer amongst the blind.*) Estaguer – here … Ah – God – ! (*to Darlet*) He is his father!

(*The bell is still clanging.*)

CURTAIN

The Light in the Tomb/Gott mit uns! (*La Lumière dans le tombeau/ Gott mit uns!*, 1928)

René Berton

Characters:
Captain Caussade (45)
Hermann (35) a German soldier
Private De Manzac (40)
Corporal Barnaby (40)
Private Laussel (45)
Voice of the Commandant (50)

The action takes place in the Champagne region of France near the end of the First World War.

The scene presents an abandoned cave system carved out from the limestone.

At the back, to the right, is an opening in which can be seen the foot of a flight of stairs which leads outside. To the left, a passageway stretches into the darkness.

Hanging on the wall can be seen gas masks, rifles with bayonets attached, revolvers in holsters, knapsacks, helmets, and the calendar carrying this date: 28th of April, 1918. In the corner, there is a pile of empty champagne bottles and cigarette stubs. To the left, an empty stretcher is used as a make-do couch. To the rear, next to the entrance to the stairs, planks the height of a man are attached to the wall. Above can be seen graffiti scrawled in charcoal: Gott mit uns! Deutschland über alles! Tomorrow Paris! Some small barrels serve as stools, empty tea chests as tables. On one of the latter is a field telephone. The scene is lit by two candles mounted in the empty champagne bottles.

Act One

As the curtain rises, Manzac is resting on the stretcher, both hands behind his neck, smoking a pipe. Laussel sits on one of the chests, writing a letter. Suddenly, in the distance, we hear a shell whistling before it hits the ground and explodes.

MANZAC (*without moving*): Ah, one of the big ones ... Still, blew up a long way from us ... (*The telephone rings. Manzac goes and answers it.*) Hello ...? Yes ... A 240 blasted thirty metres ahead of the frontline ... No damage ... Good. (*He hangs up the receiver, makes a note in a ledger. He lies back down on his camp-bed.*)

LAUSSEL (*putting down his pen*): There! All done ...! Oh, I forgot to put the date ... (*He turns to Manzac.*) What's the date ...? (*Manzac doesn't move.*) You asleep Manzac ...? What day is it?

MANZAC: I'm afraid I don't know, mate, and what's more I couldn't give a toss. What does it matter if it's March or December let alone if today is a Monday or a Saturday? I try not to think about time any more – and I'm much happier for it. I don't even know how old I am any more!

LAUSSEL: You're kidding!

MANZAC: Back in 1914, I was 36 years old ... And now I couldn't tell you if I was 40, 50, or 100! I don't have the faintest idea.

LAUSSEL (*laughing*): ... I think you're pulling my leg ...! You honestly mean you don't know what year it is!?

MANZAC: Well, I think this is Year Four of the War, but I can't be certain.

LAUSSEL: You always have to be different, don't you? Why can't you just come out and say it's 1918?

MANZAC: Because, Laussel, my old mate, I think that since 1914 a new epoch has begun. Just as people talked about before and after Jesus Christ, now we talk about before or after the War.

LAUSSEL: You know, you might well be right.

MANZAC: Anyway, if you just look over there there's a calendar that the Krauts left behind.

LAUSSEL: So there is! (*He goes over and looks at the date.*) 28th of April ... (*He writes the date down on the letter and puts it in the envelope.*) This'll keep her happy.

MANZAC: You've written to your bird, eh?

LAUSSEL: My bird? (*He heaves his shoulders.*) Actually, it's to my poor old mum. She's moved to Paris to run my business and look after my two kids while I'm away ... I'm a widower, you see.

MANZAC: Sorry, Laussel, I didn't know ... (*Pause.*) I'm sorry for your mother.

LAUSSEL: Why did you say that?

MANZAC: The poor woman must be suffering terribly knowing that her son is in the front line.

LAUSSEL: You're right! That's why I write as often as I can, to keep her happy. (*With a heavy sigh of resignation.*) I'll keep writing, until someone has to do it for me. I love her so much, the poor old dear! Yes, she's had her share of suffering ...

MANZAC: I think suffering is how mothers have done their bit for the war effort.

LAUSSEL: Have you still got a mother?

MANZAC: No ... I've got no one. I'm all alone in the world. Probably explains why I no longer give a toss! The day I disappear, no one will cry for me ... No one, except perhaps my drinking buddies in the bars in Montmartre, who will miss all the booze I used to buy them ... And all the gambling dens ... I was the best bloody customer they ever had!

LAUSSEL: You know, you've only been in the company a month ... I don't know anything about you ... What did you do before the War?

MANZAC: Nothing.

LAUSSEL: That wasn't too demanding then!

MANZAC: Oh, it was backbreaking! Laussel, you've got no idea how hard you must work night and day to ensure you don't have to do a thing.

LAUSSEL: Lucky you could afford to live like that! Did you have an inheritance or something?

MANZAC: I got the money my parents left me and I spent it carefully.

LAUSSEL: I find it amazing that someone with some money and the right kind of family background didn't sort out a cushy little number away from the front line when the War began.

MANZAC: I did just that ... I did have a cushy little number.

LAUSSEL: And you threw it all away ...!? What an idiot! God, if I was in your place ...!

MANZAC: If you were in my place you would have done exactly the same thing ... When the mobilization began, I stayed behind at the regiment's headquarters.

LAUSSEL: It's funny that you're just a regular private like me. With your name and breeding, you're officer material, you are. At least two stripes on your shoulder!

MANZAC: They asked me – but I said no ... Me, an officer ...? That'd be too much responsibility! I can kill or be killed, no problem. But I couldn't command others to do it ... Not me ... I just wouldn't be able to do it ...

LAUSSEL: Maybe you're right. (*He picks up a book from a chest.*) You reading this?

MANZAC: No – it's the Captain's.

LAUSSEL (*reads out the title*): *Plato: The Banquet.* Must be a cookery book.

MANZAC (*sniggers*): Could be!

LAUSSEL (*flicks through pages*): Blimey! What gobbledegook is this ...!? Is it in Hebrew or something ...?

MANZAC: No – it's Greek.

LAUSSEL: How come he knows Greek!? At least they're on our side, I suppose ... What did he do in civilian life?

MANZAC: I think he taught philosophy at some college in Paris.

LAUSSEL: Philosophy? Now there's a fine job for you! Still, doesn't hide the fact that he's a decent bloke.

MANZAC: Too right – he's the best!

LAUSSEL: The man has no fear!

MANZAC: He was tremendous in the battle yesterday.

LAUSSEL: Yes, he was! Remember how that bitch of a machine gunner started showering us with bullets ...? Everyone fell to the ground and daren't move ... Not him, no – he kept advancing ... Then we all got up and followed him; and we took that bastard gunner out!

VOICE OF BARNABY (*calling cheerfully down the stairway*): I say! I'm looking for the eighth guard! Are you there!?

LAUSSEL (*cheerily calling back*): All present and correct, sir! Please come down and join us!

MANZAC: Who's that?

LAUSSEL: You don't recognize that voice ...? It's Corporal Barnaby back from leave.

(*Corporal Barnaby enters, stumbling down the stairs. He is dressed in a brand new uniform with a little bunch of wild flowers attached to the lapel of his greatcoat. He carries three haversacks bursting with bottles.*)

BARNABY: You call these stairs? The least they could do is install a lift! So dark down here ...! I've nearly broken my bloody neck ten times! Why on earth can't the servants light the gas ...! Hello, chaps. (*Shakes their hands.*) But where is everyone ...? Bernard, Martin, Desvignes ...? (*Manzac and Laussel lower their heads.*) Clamsés ...? Oh no ...

LAUSSEL: I'm afraid so ... In the last attack ... Bernard has disappeared. Martin was decapitated by a bomb blast: we buried him, but we couldn't find his head ... Desvignes was shot in the guts. It took him two hours to die. He was calling for his mother ... his kids ... his wife ... It was horrible!

BARNABY: Poor bleeders!

LAUSSEL: That's what fate has in store for all of us ...! (*Pounds fists in rage.*) Oh, if I could get hold of the bastards that started this war!

BARNABY: So, this is all that remains of my squad?

MANZAC: Yes.

BARNABY: Oh well, never mind ...! What fun ...! (*He looks around him.*) So, this is to be our new home ...? The pinnacle of comfort! Every kind of luxury: chairs, tables ... (*Pointing at the stretcher.*) The chaise longue ... (*Pointing at the planks hammered onto the wall.*) There's even woodwork in Louis the 16th style.

MANZAC (*pointing at the telephone*): A telephone ...

LAUSSEL (*holding up his water flask and gas mask*): Pure water ... And gas in every room!

BARNABY: Tell me, chaps, is this place infested with lice?

LAUSSEL: No, I haven't found any on me ...! But Manzac over there is covered in them ... Look at him: he's laughing about it, the idiot!

MANZAC (*laughing*): I'm just happy to be alive! As for the lice, I think they're good company, it passes the time looking for them.

BARNABY: Well every man needs his pleasures ...! (*Pointing at the graffiti on the wall.*) Seriously, boys, I think you should scrub off that filthy writing!

MANZAC: Why? I think they're a very nice feature. They give our home a bit of local colour.

BARNABY: How long have you been down here?

MANZAC (*looking at his watch*): Exactly thirty-six hours.

LAUSSEL: But I must let you know ... We made an attack yesterday morning, at dawn, and we pushed the Boche back from their front line. We found this abandoned cave. The locals used to store their champagne here. It's nice and secluded.

BARNABY: Judging by the empty bottles and all the cigarettes, I'm sure the last residents had quite a hangover. I'm amazed the officers didn't take over this one. It's a perfect headquarters!

MANZAC: Yes, you'd think that wouldn't you, but at the last moment they decided against it. The colonel said it was too much of a bunker away from the action. He preferred a base a little less 'buried' than this shelter. What they did put in here was a telephone so that they can transmit orders and tell me exactly where and when the enemy is attacking and I can write it down.

BARNABY (*pointing to the passageway on the left*): Where does that lead?

LAUSSEL: Nowhere. After three metres there's just a wall.

BARNABY (*still looking down the passageway*): You've put our beds in there.

MANZAC: Yes. Our bedrooms are over there, and here is our dining room!

BARNABY: Well sheltered from bomb blasts if nothing else.

LAUSSEL: That's right – we're at least six metres underground here.

BARNABY: Well, that's something to put us at ease then.

MANZAC: Yes, for the time being. Our Teutonic friends will no doubt have something up their sleeves to disturb the peace ...

LAUSSEL: Sometimes the bigger blasts get through to us ... My goodness, you should have heard them yesterday!

BARNABY: Far from here?

MANZAC: About 300 metres – at the most.

LAUSSEL: Unfortunately, as you've seen, the shelter opens towards the front. We have to be careful when going in or out. But once inside, it's as safe as houses!

BARNABY: That's good news.

LAUSSEL (*pointing at the flowers Barnaby has on his lapel*): Did you pop into a florist's ...? Thinking of sweet-talking the ladies round here?

BARNABY: I picked them up on the way here. The fields are blooming with them just back there.

LAUSSEL: You're joking!

BARNABY: No, I'm not ... Believe it or not, it's springtime.

MANZAC (*shaking his head with a wistful smile*) Ah, spring ...

LAUSSEL (*looking at the calendar*): It is April after all ...

BARNABY (*looking at the flowers*): They're nothing much, but they're beautiful and it freshens the heart just to look at them. (*He gives them to Laussel.*) Come on, put these in some water. They'll be a little ray of sunshine in this crypt. (*Laussel raises the flowers to his lips and then puts them in some water poured from his water flask. The two men watch him do this, smiling broadly, as if he's doing something extremely important.*) For a moment there I was lying on the grass, in the shade of a tree. Sitting beneath a tree, eating and drinking and thinking of having a picnic with a group of beautiful ladies in the Bois de Boulogne ... What a wonderful daydream ...

MANZAC: Don't stop! Picnics on the grass!

BARNABY: Yes ... Now I'm plucking dandelions! (*Silence.*)

LAUSSEL: So tell me, how's the weather out there? Is it beautiful?

BARNABY: Yes, it's wonderful ...! The sky is blue, as blue as the sea, and the sun is blinding, dazzling like a firework! The air smells so sweet it puts fire in your blood as if you were drunk! For a moment when I was out there, I opened up my greatcoat and let the wind blow against my skin ... Oh God, it felt so good to stand in the sunlight, to feel the joy of the sunshine and the sky, only thinking of the goodness of life ... Life, life ...

LAUSSEL (*disheartened*): Yes ... and for four years we've crawled in the earth like worms! Breathing foul air and poisonous gas! Instead of thinking about life, we've been only able to think of death ...

MANZAC (*phlegmatically*): That's war!

LAUSSEL: All curses on it! The war will never end!

MANZAC (*wanting to change the subject, he turns to Barnaby and admires his outfit*): Your uniform looks good!

BARNABY (*turning around on his heels to let them admire it*): Yes? You think this is pretty good ...?

LAUSSEL: The peak of fashion!

BARNABY: I freshened up my wardrobe while I was on leave. I was pretty ashamed of what I was wearing. It's amazing how quickly you get through clothes in this part of the world!

LAUSSEL (*looking at his own uniform, covered in mud*): You can say that again!

BARNABY: All the same, I've brought my old rags back with me, I'm sure they'll do another turn.

MANZAC: Tell me, Corporal, what's new in Paris? The women are as pretty and as frisky as ever!?

BARNABY: These days women have other things to worry about than their looks: they're working. My wife's working in a factory making shells. The poor woman! She slaves away as much as any man.

LAUSSEL (*roars with laughter and jostles Barnaby*): I guess you had chance to exchange a couple of words with your missus while you were home!?

BARNABY (*laughs*): I should be so lucky!

MANZAC: So these days, women are France's most valuable workforce?

BARNABY (*heaves a sigh*): I'm afraid so ... This is a terrible time for married men ...

MANZAC: But we have to accept it … there are so many jobs to fill!

LAUSSEL: They should be off breeding a new generation of soldiers for the next war to end all wars!

MANZAC: I guess life goes on as usual for civilians.

BARNABY: No – it's no honeymoon for the Parisians, I promise you. Nearly every night, German aeroplanes fly over and drop two or three hundred kilos of explosives. When any of that hits a house, there's not a thing left … That's not to mention the Big Berthas …

MANZAC: Yes, the Big Berthas – you've got to admire them!

LAUSSEL: What crap are you talking now? Do you really think it's 'admirable' to bombard defenceless towns, killing women and children?

MANZAC: No … I think it's despicable. But what I do think is admirable is that the mind of a man worked out how to make cannons that can shoot from miles and miles away and hit their target with complete accuracy.

BARNABY: Yes, a job well done there, I suppose …

LAUSSEL (*pulls out of his pockets the letter he had been writing*): You know I'm worried it's no longer safe in Paris … I think I'll put something in this letter to my mother telling her to close the shop and take the children out of the city. (*He opens up the letter and starts to write.*) Bad news for the locals on Rue Bergère, they'll have to buy their cheese and butter elsewhere.

BARNABY (*a shiver runs through him*): You have a shop on Rue Bergère?

LAUSSEL: Yes … Number four … My apartment is there too … Why do you ask? You know the area?

BARNABY (*forcing himself to laugh*): A little bit … I used to know a young lady who lived around there …

LAUSSEL (*bursts out laughing*): God bless you Barnaby! (*He continues to write.*)

BARNABY (*aside to Manzac, whispering in his ear*): Last night there was a massive blast on Rue Bergère. It was at that end of the street … eighteen people were killed.

MANZAC (*terrified*): Oh my god … His mother, his kids …? (*Barnaby passes his hand across his throat then shrugs.*) Oh, the poor bastards …

LAUSSEL (*standing up and putting away the letter*): There, all done! Now I can rest easy. At least I'll get to see the poor old dear one more time!

BARNABY (*talking aside to Manzac*): Not a word, eh? He'll hear the terrible news soon enough … (*He is suddenly very jovial and slaps his hand on his haversack.*) Good news lads, I've brought back a little something for us! (*He begins to empty one of the bags.*) First of all, here's some booze to give us some Dutch courage during the next attack ... And here's another bottle of something made from the finest vines, far better than all that champagne rubbish we drink round here which is like Epsom salts for stomach ache.

LAUSSEL: I quite agree, mate! Champagne is overrated – it only makes you fart. Give me a good strong red any day, that's proper booze!

(*Barnaby opens a bottle, fills three cups and they toast each other.*)

BARNABY: To your very good health, gentlemen! (*He raises his glass.*) To absent friends.

LAUSSEL: And to us soon to join them!

MANZAC: To the end of this bloody war!

BARNABY: Yes, I'll drink to that! (*They all drink. The telephone rings.*)

MANZAC (*lifting up the receiver*): Hello ... Yes, captain ... Go ahead. (*He writes.*) A delivery of munitions will be made to Depot 107 in preparation for an attack tomorrow ... Understood, captain. (*He puts down the receiver.*) Did you hear that? We'll be expecting a delivery.

BARNABY: So be it.

LAUSSEL (*furious*): Oh, this is ridiculous! We weren't fit to attack yesterday and they're going to try again tomorrow! We'll be skinned alive! They really want to make sure we never, ever leave this place ... What's the point of these ridiculous assaults where we gain fifty metres of mud and lose fifty men in the process! Tell me, *what's the point*?

MANZAC: It pushes the line forward ... Good news for the cannons ... And the munitions ...

LAUSSEL (*furiously*): Good news for coffins and graves more like!

BARNABY (*who's been listening to something else*): Shut up the pair of you!

LAUSSEL: What is it? (*Barnaby gestures for them to keep quiet. A pause. They all listen.*) Well?

BARNABY: I thought I heard a voice.

MANZAC (*bursts out laughing*): I think you're imagining things again Barnaby! You're hearing voices ...

LAUSSEL: Like Joan of Arc!

BARNABY: just shut it, will you ... I've got excellent hearing. When I used to go poaching in the woods near my home, I could hear the step of the gamekeeper a mile away ... He never caught me … Hmm, it's nothing … (*Empties a second knapsack.*) Well, chaps, what would you say to some chicken and some Perigord pâté?

MANZAC: Wonderful! It's a shame I've just had my soup – I'm really not hungry.

BARNABY: I beg your pardon? Not hungry …? Where are your manners? Besides, Private Manzac, don't you know that a French soldier is always hungry – it's his duty …! I hope this talk of a big push tomorrow hasn't made you lose your appetite?

MANZAC: No, I couldn't give a toss about that!

BARNABY: We'll survive it, you know that, don't you?

LAUSSEL: Says you!

MANZAC: Yes, we will! We always have – from the first day we started killing.

LAUSSEL (*taking a little bag that Barnaby has taken out of his knapsack and opening it*): Peanuts! Delicious!

BARNABY: My little boy slipped them into my bag at the train station … Bless him! Paid for them with his pocket money!

LAUSSEL (*daydreaming*): Peanuts … reminds me of a time before the War when me and the wife went out to a restaurant – we drank a bottle of wine and scoffed peanuts …! Those were the days …

BARNABY (*taps Laussel on the shoulder*): No time for daydreaming now! You'll eat there again one day – I promise you … Cheers! (*He drinks. A shell whistles and then blasts distantly.*) That sounded like a two-tenner!

MANZAC: It fell a distance. (*The phone rings and he picks up the receiver.*) Hello … Yes … (*He writes.*) A two-hundred and ten fell near area 107 … No damage … Good. (*He puts back the receiver.*)

LAUSSEL: Area 107? That's where the munitions are going to be delivered.

MANZAC: Yes … So what?

LAUSSEL: Don't you see …

MANZAC: You mean … How did the Krauts know that? We only heard five minutes ago ourselves!

LAUSSEL: And they were bombing in another direction before …

BARNABY: Random shelling?

LAUSSEL: Perhaps. (*We hear the whistle of two bombshells followed by two distant explosions.*) They're going in the same direction. (*We hear another whistle of the shell and then another which explode much more loudly than the early ones.*) Getting nearer …

BARNABY: Yes … (*The telephone rings.*)

MANZAC (*picks up the receiver*): Hello … (*He scribbles something down and puts down the receiver.*) They've done it, they've destroyed the depot.

BARNABY: Well it's not a disaster. We can replace munitions. Better than destroying men.

LAUSSEL: At least it means they'll have to postpone tomorrow's attack.

BARNABY: Gives us a bit more peace and quiet. It's a good life! (*He finishes the cup of wine.*)

MANZAC (*pointing at the stairs*): Someone's coming. More orders, no doubt.

(*Captain Caussade enters.*)

(*The men stand up. They salute and stand still.*)

CAPTAIN (*to Manzac*): Headquarters phoned you?

MANZAC: Yes, captain.

CAPTAIN: Is it true that depot 107 has been destroyed?

MANZAC: Yes, captain.

CAPTAIN: It's maddening …! It was only stocked an hour ago and the enemy's already destroyed it!

BARNABY: Any men there, sir?

CAPTAIN: Yes … They were still arranging the munitions …

LAUSSEL: How many …?

CAPTAIN: There are ten less men in the company … (*They lower their heads.*) The more I think about it the more I'm convinced that we must have been infiltrated … There must be someone in our ranks letting the enemy know our intentions. You will recall that this morning I telephoned the colonel that we were preparing a battery from a certain location. Five minutes later a massive bomb landed in the middle of them … There's something going on.

MANZAC: I think, captain, there's an easy explanation. We are in territory that we took over from the Bosche, they know these lines like the back of their hand, they know what they're aiming at and can do so with immense precision …

CAPTAIN: But to hit the depot just after we stocked it?

(*The whistle of the shells is heard.*)

LAUSSEL (*crying out*): Take cover, that one's for us!

(*A massive explosion. The candles are blown out and there is complete darkness. Rubble can be heard falling.*)

BARNABY AND LAUSSEL (*cursing in despair*): Damn it! We're done for now, it's caved in!

CAPTAIN: Give us some light!

LAUSSEL: Where are those bloody candles?

BARNABY: Hang on ... I've got a torch in my pocket.

(*Barnaby switches on his torch, and finds the two candles and lights them. Anxiously, the men look all around them. No one moves. Nothing has changed except that the stairway is blocked by a mass of earth and stones. Manzac is sitting down calmly smoking his pipe.*)

LAUSSEL (*rushing towards the stairway*): The stairs are blocked! We'll never get out!

CAPTAIN: The bomb's blasted the entrance.

BARNABY: Those bastards!

LAUSSEL: We've got to clear the stairs! Come on, help me. (*Barnaby and Laussel begin working on the stones.*)

BARNABY: Have you got any shovels and picks? Let's make a start with our hands!

MANZAC (*walking over*): There is nothing to be done. The stairs are completely destroyed.

CAPTAIN: Let's call for help. (*He picks up the telephone.*) Hello ... Hello ... answer me ... Hello, hello ...

MANZAC (*picks up the broken cable*): The wires were cut by the explosion.

LAUSSEL: Well, we won't be bothered now ...

BARNABY (*beginning to pace like a madman*): Oh my god, my god !

CAPTAIN: Don't worry, chaps. No one's been injured, that's the most important thing. Headquarters will know where it landed and will come to rescue us.

MANZAC (*extremely calmly*): Oh well ...

LAUSSEL: But we're going to starve to death down this hole!

BARNABY: Luckily I've got some supplies.

CAPTAIN: Food and water?

BARNABY: I've got plenty in those bags.

CAPTAIN: Thank goodness. Given the blasting the enemy's doing, our men probably won't get to us till tomorrow. (*He looks at his watch.*) It'll be night time soon ... We must keep calm and have courage ... (*They look all around them. He looks at all of them.*) You understand, lads ...? Be brave ... (*He casts an anxious glance towards Manzac.*)

LAUSSEL: Captain, are you worried they won't come to help us ...?

CAPTAIN (*forcing himself to speak with certainty*): Of course they will ... We'll be out of here tomorrow!

BARNABY: And if they don't …

CAPTAIN: We could survive days down here …

LAUSSEL (*anxious*): But any longer than that?

CAPTAIN (*staring at Laussel*): We are doing our duty … I trust none of us lack courage …

MANZAC (*smiling*): Of course not, captain.

BARNABY: Absolutely.

CAPTAIN (*looking at Laussel*): What about you?

LAUSSEL: Me, afraid? With you here, sir? Of course not, sir!

CAPTAIN (*he shakes the men's hands*): That's the spirit, boys! Has anybody got a pack of cards?

BARNABY: I do believe I have some sir, picked up when I was on leave!

CAPTAIN: Excellent! Let's play a little game then! Make ourselves at home!

LAUSSEL: Deal them out, Barnaby!

(*Barnaby shuffles the cards and deals them out, singing a song quite happily as he does so. After a few moments the other soldiers begin to join in the singing, except the captain, who watches the men, smiling. Fade to black.*)

Act Two

As the lights come up, Manzac is lying on the stretcher and Laussel is lying on the floor, both fast asleep. The Captain sits on a chair reading a book. Barnaby plays a game of patience.

BARNABY: Lost again! Oh, I've had enough of this. (*He casts down the cards angrily.*) Hey, Laussel, you asleep? (*As Laussel doesn't reply, he gives a loud clap.*)

LAUSSEL (*leaps up*): Heh … What? What is it? Have they got here yet?

BARNABY: I'm afraid not.

LAUSSEL: Then why the hell did you wake me up, you stupid idiot?

BARNABY: Because I can't get to sleep.

LAUSSEL (*standing up, he looks at his watch*): We've been stuck in this hell-hole for hours now. For God's sake, what the hell are they doing up there? This really doesn't look too good.

BARNABY: I have to agree with you.

CAPTAIN: No, lads, nothing to worry about. I've told you that they won't ignore us. They will come to help us. It's just a question of time.

LAUSSEL: Oh well, let's carry on waiting then. (*He takes his pipe out of his pocket.*) Barnaby, give me your lighter.

CAPTAIN: Are you a complete fool, Laussel? It's stifling in here and you want to poison the little air we have left with your disgusting smoke?

LAUSSEL (*he goes to the stairway and listens*): I can't hear a thing ... Barnaby, seeing that you have such good hearing, why don't you come and have a listen; perhaps you could hear something. (*Barnaby goes to the stairway and listens. Suddenly, he makes a movement with his head.*) Did you hear something? (*Barnaby gestures for silence. Laussel whispers anxiously.*) Please tell me you heard shovels and picks?

BARNABY: I certainly heard something ... It could've been digging ... But far away ... Very far away ...

LAUSSEL: They're coming to rescue us.

BARNABY: No, the sounds of digging can't be coming from up here. We'd never hear them – not through all of this.

LAUSSEL: So what? They can probably get through the staircase here.

BARNABY (*listening attentively and then walking away from the stairway*): No ... The noises ... The noises of digging are coming from *in here* ...

LAUSSEL: Coming from in here? You must be mad?

BARNABY: Shut up! (*He moves along quietly and steps over Manzac.*)

MANZAC (*sitting up*): What the hell? Where are your manners? Are you completely mad?

BARNABY: Be quiet!

MANZAC: But ...

BARNABY: For God's sake, shut up ...! Let me listen! (*Manzac stands up and watches Barnaby attentively.*) The noises have stopped ...

MANZAC (*to Laussel*): He's hearing things again!

LAUSSEL: I think there really was something this time.

BARNABY: Be quiet ... It's started again ...! (*Listening attentively, he moves towards the wall. Getting to the planks against the wall, he pulls one of the planks away and shines a torch behind it.*) My God, I thought as much! (*He steps behind the planks and disappears.*)

CAPTAIN (*watching in astonishment*): Did any of you know about that secret passage?

LAUSSEL: No ... We noticed the planks, but we never thought to look behind them. (*Suddenly a scuffle and a gunshot is heard.*)

CAPTAIN (*alarmed*): What is it! Barnaby! What is it! (*Suddenly, Barnaby comes out dragging the body of a man along the ground.*)

BARNABY: Here's our little noise maker. (*Everyone gathers around.*)

LAUSSEL: A German soldier …

BARNABY: Yes, he was trying to crawl his way out the other end of the corridor.

LAUSSEL: He's not moving …

CAPTAIN: Did you kill him?

BARNABY: I don't know … When he saw me, he shot his revolver at me. I got hold of him and hit him in the head. Not too hard though – I wanted to bring him out alive … Look he's opened his eyes.

CAPTAIN: He's waking up. (*Laussel and Barnaby lift the German up. He looks all around him. He stares at the men with contempt. Raises his chest and stares at his captors.*)

CAPTAIN: *Wie heissen Sie?*

HERRMANN: We can talk in French.

CAPTAIN: Search him. (*Manzac frisks him, discovers some papers which he gives to the Captain. The Captain reads them.*) Your name is Siegfried Herrmann and it says here you were a professor of philosophy at the University of Leipzig?

HERRMANN (*very calm*): Yes.

CAPTAIN: What are you doing down here? Does that corridor lead outside?

HERRMANN: Yes, there is a camouflaged opening. But the bomb blast destroyed the exit.

BARNABY: When I found him, he was trying to dig his way out.

CAPTAIN: How long have you been there?

HERRMANN: I've been here since everybody else left … Two days.

CAPTAIN: Alone?

HERRMANN: Alone.

CAPTAIN (*to Barnaby*): Go and look down there. (*Barnaby goes into the corridor.*)

LAUSSEL: He was left behind by his comrades by mistake – or on purpose. Alright Fritz, what were you up to? (*Herrmann replies with a scornful smile.*)

CAPTAIN: What were you doing down here? (*Barnaby comes out of the passageway with a box which he hands to the Captain.*)

BARNABY: This was at the end of the corridor.

CAPTAIN (*examining the box*): It's a field telephone … Ah, I see … You've been communicating with your officers?

HERRMANN: Yes.

LAUSSEL: Spying on us, you bastard!

HERRMANN (*remaining extremely calm*): Yes, I was spying on you … Thanks to you we were able to destroy depot 107.

CAPTAIN: You also killed 10 men in the process. (*Herrmann shrugs.*)

BARNABY: You bastard.

CAPTAIN: Silence! (*to Herrmann*) I expect your superior officers forced you to stay here to spy on us?

HERRMANN: No … When you started your assault yesterday morning we were ordered to retreat from our positions back to the second line. Our officers thought that this cave, well protected as it is, would be an obvious shelter for your headquarters and they wanted a volunteer to stay here and hide in the corridor to listen in to the commands being issued from here. I volunteered to stay behind.

CAPTAIN: Well, that was a stupid thing to do, wasn't it?

HERRMANN: I regarded it as my duty and an honour.

CAPTAIN: You must have known that the chances of getting away with it were very slim.

HERRMANN: Of course I did.

CAPTAIN: You must have known what would happen to you if you were caught? It'll be the firing squad for you.

HERRMANN: I am aware of that.

LAUSSEL: Yes, that's what's in store for you, Fritz! You'll be tied to a post and shot full of lead! That'll be your lot, mate!

CAPTAIN (*with agitation*): Will you be quiet, Laussel. There's no need to insult him, he's a prisoner now.

LAUSSEL: What?

CAPTAIN: You do not have the right. First of all, he's a captive now. Moreover, although he's an enemy he was doing his duty and we need to respect him for that … If it was one of our chaps on the other side, doing his duty for France, he'd be a hero … You see what I mean …? (*Pause.*) He'll certainly be executed, but there's no need to humiliate him.

HERRMANN (*calm and collected*): You won't execute me.

BARNABY: No, we'll let you go, of course!

HERRMANN: You will not execute me … I'm going to die the same way that you're going to die … all five of us will die buried in this tomb.

LAUSSEL: That's what you think! They're going to dig us out soon.

HERRMANN: By the time they do, it will be too late … When they pull us out of here, we'll all be dead.

BARNABY (*to Laussel*): As if it wasn't bad enough being stuck down here with a Kraut, we had to have a cynical one!

CAPTAIN: Shut up! (*to Herrman*) Are you trying to tell us something?

HERRMANN: Yes. In this bunker, this bunker from which there is no escape, a bomb has been planted.

LAUSSEL (*frightened*): A bomb!

HERRMANN: Yes, a bomb … And this bomb has a timing device which will explode at a designated moment ... (*He looks at his wristwatch.*) It won't be long now. (*Laussel and Barnaby look around themselves.*)

CAPTAIN (*with a gesture to make the men stand still*): Calm down, lads, calm down ... (*to Herrmann*) Do know where the bomb is hidden?

HERRMANN: Yes. After all, I'm the one who planted it.

CAPTAIN: Tell me where you put it.

HERRMANN (*staring the Captain in the face*): No!

CAPTAIN: Tell me where it is.

HERRMANN: No! (*Silence. Everyone looks around them.*)

CAPTAIN: Tell me! Or I will force it out of you.

HERRMANN (*with a gesture of resignation*): Go on then.

MANZAC (*shrugging his shoulders*): You do realize, captain, that this man is trying to fool us. If he'd really planted a bomb in here he'd do anything to defuse it – otherwise he'd be blown up along with us!

HERRMANN (*extremely calmly*): Yes, that's right: blown up along with all of you.

BARNABY (*with forced bravado*): Come on, Fritz! You really want us all to snuff it like this ...! That's not going to happen now, is it?

HERRMANN: You think I'm joking ...? It won't be long now until you see that I've been speaking the truth ... (*to Barnaby with a wry smile*) You're the one with such excellent hearing, aren't you? You heard me at the back of the tunnel. I am amazed that you can't hear the ticking of the mechanism, ticking and ticking towards detonation ... Ssh ... Listen ... Can't you hear the gears turning ... slowly, inexorably, gnawing away at the final moments of your life ...?

BARNABY (*listening*): Christ almighty! I can hear it, I can hear it!

LAUSSEL: Me too! (*Points to the right.*) It's over there!

BARANBY (*points left*): No! It's over there! (*They desperately search around, tapping and pressing their ears against the walls.*)

CAPTAIN: Come with me, Manzac, we'll look down the corridor. (*He speaks to the remaining men, pointing at the prisoner.*) Don't take your eyes off him for a moment!

LAUSSEL: Yes sir! (*Captain and Manzac exit. When he's alone with Barnaby, Laussel seizes Herrmann by the throat.*) Tell me where it is, damn you! I'll throttle you!

HERRMANN: I will not tell you!

LAUSSEL: That's what you think ...! Barnaby, get his hands. (*They shove him onto one of the chests and pin him down with their knees.*) Are you going to talk?

HERRMANN: No.

LAUSSEL: Very well, I'll have to force it out of you ... (*He pulls out a knife.*) You see this knife ...? It's cut many throats before, you know ... If you don't start talking, I'm going to cut out your eye ... and then, after that, I'll cut out the other one ... (*He moves the knife in front of the prisoner's eyes.*) I'm going to count to three ... If you don't start talking, I'll begin to ...

HERRMANN: Make a martyr of me: I will not talk. (*Captain and Manzac enter. They are aghast at the savage scene.*)

MANZAC (*lunges at Laussel*): You savage! Let him go!

LAUSSEL (*mad with rage*): Piss off!

CAPTAIN: Put down the knife, Laussel.

LAUSSEL (*shouting*): He'll start talking or I'll kill him!

CAPTAIN: Put it down, Laussel. That's an order.

LAUSSEL: I want to rip out his eyes!

CAPTAIN (*pulls out his revolver*): Put it down, or I'll shoot you in the head. Are we savages ...? You can see the man won't tell us anything ...!

(*Manzac takes the knife off Laussel.*)

HERRMANN: I will never talk.

LAUSSEL: If you'd just leave me alone with him, I'll get him to talk alright! (*Silence.*)

CAPTAIN (*to Barnaby*): You looked down the tunnel where we found him ... Do you think there's any way to clear the exit ...?

BARNABY: No. it's completely blocked. There's tons of earth to move and we haven't any tools we could use.

HERRMANN (*laughing*): I've got you now! There's no escape ...! All four of you will be obliterated, just as your damnable race will disappear, superseded by our superior breed! (*Continues with increasing exaltation.*) For we are the chosen race ...! (*Points at the graffiti on the walls.*) *Gott mit uns* ...! God is on our side ...! We are driving you out of this land; the hour of judgement has come and God has decided to destroy you ...! We will be victorious, despite all the mercenaries you have called to help you! Our beloved Kaiser will walk through Paris in triumph and you will meet his every demand from his throne in the Palace of Versailles!

LAUSSEL: Your beloved Kaiser might well start running in the other direction, you know!

HERRMANN (*more and more exalted*): But I have complete and utter faith in him, just as I have faith in the Lord God ...! I am absolutely certain that our nation will vanquish you and it is with joy that I give my life to my fatherland …! For the five of us entombed in here, the War is over. In a few minutes' time, my sacrifice and your execution will occur. (*Silence.*)

BARNABY: Oh, what the hell …! When the bomb goes off, it's all over …! Any day could be our last, we're probably doomed to die in the trenches. So be it. I'd rather die now and get it over with … Whatever's going to happen, nothing's going to stop me finishing my supper. (*He sits down in a corner and eats with great calm.*)

LAUSSEL: It fills me with despair. For four years we stood up to bullets and shells only to die in a wretched hole like poisoned rats!

MANZAC (*to Herrmann*): My Lord High Executioner, would you be so kind as to tell us how long we have to live …? (*Herrmann looks at his watch. Manzac looks at it too.*) It's 21:30 hours.

HERRMANN: Fifteen minutes.

MANZAC: Thank you.

HERRMANN: At 21:45 it will all be over.

MANZAC: Very well. I think I'll have a kip. (*Laughs.*) Wake me up when the bomb goes off! (*He goes over to the stretcher.*)

LAUSSEL: Barnaby, come and search with me. The bloody thing might be hidden down the corridor … If God won't help us, we'd better find it ourselves! (*They head down the corridor.*)

(*The Captain and Herrmann stare at each other in silence.*)

CAPTAIN (*very calmly*): Do you think that if the tables were turned, one of the officers of your most magnanimous Kaiser would do anything to prevent himself being 'martyred'?

HERRMANN: I have no idea.

CAPTAIN: Well, I'm a French officer. A son of that inferior race that you seek to annihilate. I did not expect to die like this – but I accept it. And I don't regard you as being the cause of my death. You see, you're a victim too. You're a victim of fate just like us. You think that you are in control of your destiny but really, you're at its mercy and it's smothered your instinct for survival … So the five of us will die because you 'will' it so … We have a lot in common, the two of us. (*Herrmann looks stunned.*) It's true. Like you, I used to teach philosophy … I wonder, in the few minutes we have left, perhaps we can engage in a little discourse. Contemplating the death that is coming to us, can you honestly say that it is a justified, a legitimate, way to die?

HERRMANN: In the few minutes you have left, it'd be better for you to say your final prayers.

CAPTAIN: No need – soldiers in battle are always in a state of grace. But tell me, *why* are we going to die?

HERRMANN: Because every man needs to do his duty, which –

CAPTAIN: ... which is to die. But why do you think it's your duty to die?

HERRMANN: Because I am a soldier. I was commanded to kill every enemy I meet. You are my enemy: I will kill you.

CAPTAIN: If we were to meet in a time of peace, would you kill me then?

HERRMANN: No, of course not. I wouldn't have the right if our nations weren't at war with each other. I wouldn't be a soldier and I wouldn't dream of killing you.

CAPTAIN: So, putting on that uniform is enough to make you lose your humanity, to turn you into a monster who will kill and kill?

HERRMANN: In the heart of a soldier there are only two passions: hatred for his enemy; and the desire to annihilate him.

CAPTAIN: But really, for a soldier the hatred of his enemy and the desire to annihilate him is justified by the danger that he faces. He knows that he must kill or be killed. But if he encounters a defenceless enemy and he kills him, is that an unjustifiable murder? Look, in here, we need no longer be enemies. We are just five human beings, made of the same stuff, we have the same desires, the same needs, we have in our hearts the same love of life and the same horror of this monstrous war and the terrible and catastrophic things that it's done to our humanity ... We're five men stuck in hell and we have a chance to rediscover our intelligence and a sense of reason and forget the horrors of the slaughter that is happening above us ... We could turn to our human conscience and for a moment we could live as human beings ... (*Herrmann lowers his head without replying. The Captain finds a photograph amongst Herrmann's papers.*) There's a photograph of a young woman and four children. It was amongst your papers ...

HERRMANN: That's my wife and children.

CAPTAIN: Before you bring death upon yourself, haven't you thought of your wife? This woman who you love and who loves you? Haven't you thought of the life that she and your children will have without you?

HERRMANN: My wife is the same race that I am. She'll understand that a husband has died for the fatherland, and my children, one day, will be filled with pride, knowing that their father was a hero.

CAPTAIN: So you think that killing four people down here will make you some sort of posthumous hero?

HERRMANN: I will also sacrifice my own life. *That* is what will make me a hero.

CAPTAIN: Are you sure about that …? At this moment, which of the two of us is really a hero? We're two men waiting to die. We are as calm as each other, we are as resigned as each other. You have evidently convinced yourself that after you die there will be another life full of joy and salvation. Whereas I am a materialist, I'm convinced that after death, there is nothing. So tell me, at this very moment, out of the two of us, who is the bravest?

HERRMANN: I will prove my courage by dying with four enemies of the fatherland.

CAPTAIN: That's a pretty poor result for such a grand sacrifice … I mean if you were killing yourself along with the generals who are running this wretched war, I would understand that and your sacrifice would perhaps be justified … But three miserable soldiers and a poor old captain, it's hard to imagine anyone more pathetic to kill in the name of your fatherland …! Their destruction hardly constitutes a moment of great heroism to inscribe your name in the history books and fill your descendants with pride! (*Silence.*)

HERRMANN (*lowers his head*): I know my fate … You will die with me in this tomb … That will be my revenge!

CAPTAIN: Ah, revenge! At last! It's no longer a hero talking, just a man …! Now I understand you …! (*Silence.*) What if I promise to let you live?

HERRMANN: That is not in your control. You are only a low ranking officer. Even if I agreed that you could let me live, your superior officers wouldn't hesitate in putting me against the wall. Spies are shown no mercy, you have already made that clear.

CAPTAIN: I could let you go and not mention any of this in my report, including the bomb. I give you my word as an officer.

HERRMANN: I don't think it's the word of an officer, I think it's the word of a man who feels the cold hand of death at his neck … Besides, why should I believe your promises, after your soldiers, those two brutes, threatened to rip my eyes out? They would stab me in the back and I would lose my moment of revenge and die alone … (*With a ferocious energy.*) No, no! You will all die with me!

(*Laussel and Barnaby come out of the hole.*)

LAUSSEL: There's nothing there …! It'll drive us all insane!

BARNABY: Have you managed to talk any reason into this crackpot, captain?

CAPTAIN (*with the dejected gesture*): No.

BARNABY: Oh God, God, God!

LAUSSEL (*he sinks down onto a stool. He takes the letter he was writing to his mother out of his pocket and looks at it for a moment. Shaking his head sadly, he puts it to his lips and murmurs*): Poor old dear!

HERRMANN: All I can do is pay tribute to your courage in the face of death. I must say, it has surprised me. I expected you to be grovelling at my feet begging to be saved ….

BARNABY: It goes to show how little you know of us. We may not be the big hero like you, but we have no fear of death.

MANZAC (*waking up*): What, are we still here? Not snuffed it yet …? Mr Executioner, you'd better go and check: I think your mechanism might be buggered.

HERRMANN (*looks at watch*): Not time yet … Six minutes to go …

MANZAC: Shame I woke up. I was having a wonderful dream – could've carried on with that one for eternity …

BARNABY (*suddenly hears something*): Ssh …! Listen …! (*Everyone listens. Distantly, digging can be heard.*)

LAUSSEL: I can really hear something … It's pickaxes! (*He runs to the staircase and listens anxiously. The blows of the pickaxes get louder. Laussel calls out in joy.*) They've rescued us …! It's not too late …!

MANZAC: Sorry, I think it might be …

HERRMANN (*looking at watch*): Five minutes …

CAPTAIN: They'll never clear the stairs in time …

HERRMANN (*laughing*): Afraid not!

CAPTAIN: We should tell them to stop … If they carry on, they might die with us …

LAUSSEL: But it's our only chance!

BARNABY: Maybe the bomb won't go off in time …

HERRMANN (*laughing*): Maybe it won't!

CAPTAIN (*animated*): No, no …! On the slim chance that it might save our lives I will not risk exposing those men to the horrific death that awaits us …

COMMANDANT (*at a distance*): Captain Caussade …? Are you there?

CAPTAIN (*calling up the stairway*): Yes, sir … I am here, with three men, but listen to me …

COMMANDANT: Is anyone injured?

CAPTAIN: No, sir, but please listen …

COMMANDANT: Have patience – we will be with you very soon! You're saved! (*The Captain moves away and, for a moment, he hesitates. His face contorts in anguish as he looks at Herrmann who is tranquil, staring at his watch.*)

HERRMANN (*implacably*): Three minutes …

CAPTAIN (*turns back to the stairway*): Sir! I beg you! Move yourself and the men away immediately …! You are in great danger!

COMMANDANT: Danger? What do you mean?

CAPTAIN: The shelter is rigged to explode, sir …! A bomb might detonate at any moment …! In the name of heaven, move yourselves away!

COMMANDANT: What are you trying to say …?

CAPTAIN: Do not expose yourself and the men to certain death …! Please, sir, you must abandon us …

COMMANDANT: Caussade, you must be joking! We won't let you die down there! We will get you out – or die trying …! Isn't that right, lads?

VOICES: Yes … Yes … (*The sound of digging doubles in tempo.*)

CAPTAIN: Oh no, the poor devils!

LAUSSEL: The brave bastards!

CAPTAIN (*to Herrmann, pointing at the stairway*): Look at that. Now *that's* heroism!

(*Herrmann stands with head bowed and then suddenly makes a resolution. He rushes towards the wall at the back, takes away the calendar and digs the blade of his knife into a gap in the wall. He pulls out a stone which has been concealing a hole. He thrusts his hand in and pulls out a metallic box which he places on the table.*)

HERRMANN: This is the bomb. (*Instinctively, the French soldiers step back. Herrmann undoes a bolt and lifts out a clockwork mechanism.*) This is the mechanism … Look, the hands are nearly at 21:45.

MANZAC (*checks his watch and laughs*): It's two minutes late!

HERRMANN: The rest of it is now harmless. (*He lobs the box into a corner.*) You can do what you want with me now.

LAUSSEL (*wipes his brow*): Bloody hell! The stress of it!

BARNABY: I thought I was going to have a heart attack!

LAUSSEL (*to Herrmann*): Oi, Fritz, you're going to be skinned alive for what you put us through!

BARNABY: Promise me he'll get a dozen bullets in him, sir. I request to be in the firing squad.

LAUSSEL: Me too. (*The pickaxes are very close now. Suddenly, a ray of light appears down the stairs.*) They're here! We're free!

COMMANDANT: Captain Caussade!

CAPTAIN (*going to the stairs*): Yes, sir …!

COMMANDANT: We've broken through to you. There's enough space for you to get out, one man at a time … We'll pass a rope down, grab hold of it and we'll help you out … Get a move on, lads! (*The end of a rope appears down the stairway.*)

LAUSSEL (*laughing as he looks at the exit*): Shall we join the gentlemen upstairs? (*The sound of a shell whistling then exploding is heard.*)

BARNABY: Yes, sounds like they're waiting for us!

COMMANDANT: Caussade …! We've tied the rope to a tree. We're going to pull back because the enemy is firing at us … Be careful when you exit … (*to his men*) Get ready to pull back, lads, keep down …!

(*In the shelter all are still, looking at the Captain and waiting for his order. After a moment, deep in thought, the Captain throws Barnaby's old uniform at the feet of the German.*)

CAPTAIN: Take this! (*Herrmann stares at him in astonishment.*) Put on that jacket – and the cap … It will enable you to slip back to your own lines … (*Herrmann picks up the cap and wears it.*)

BARNABY (*indignantly*): But, sir!

LAUSSEL (*whispers*): I can't believe it!

MANZAC (*hits Herrmann with his elbow*): Take that, you bastard! (*Herrmann is now dressed as a French soldier.*)

CAPTAIN: Now go! (*Herrmann pauses at the bottom of the stairway. He starts towards the Captain to shake his hand.*) Too late for that. (*Herrmann stiffens his back like a soldier, seizes the rope and heads out of the shelter. The Captain turns to the others.*) If you think I have made the wrong decision, if you think that my actions were unbecoming of a French officer, you have my full permission to report me to the colonel.

MANZAC: Captain, may I, on behalf of all of us, shake you by the hand? (*He does so and the others join in. Just then a shell whistles and explodes extremely close by.*)

LAUSSEL: That fell very close to the entrance … It might have got the German …!

(*We hear a loud cry, followed by a thud. Herrmann enters, tumbling backwards down the stairway. He takes a few staggering steps, his hands clasped over his face. He turns to face the audience and pulls his hands away. His face is gushing with blood and his eyes have been torn out and the left side of his head seems to be crushed. Using all his strength, he straightens his back and plucks the French cap off his head and drops it.*)

HERMANN (*flailing his arms*): *Gott … mit … uns …!* (*He collapses in a heap.*)

CAPTAIN (*to Manzac, who has gone over to Herrmann*): Dead?

MANZAC: Dead.

CAPTAIN: Attention!

(*The French soldiers all stand straight and salute.*)

THE END

SECOND PROGRAMME:

Progress
A Silk Dress
The Great Terror

Preface

This second programme presents three plays in a *douche écossaise* of two horrors interleaved with a comedy. The length of the programmes at the Théâtre du Grand-Guignol could vary from three to five plays, depending on the length of each play. In this programme, *La Grande épouvante* (*The Great Terror*) is the longest of those included in this volume and follows, relatively unusually for the Grand-Guignol, a three-act structure. As such it sits well as the final piece in a three-play evening.

St. John Ervine's anti-war play *Progress*, which opens this programme, was written for the London Grand Guignol in 1922 and played for sixty-three performances as part of the penultimate seventh series, alongside Eliot Crawshay-Williams' *The Nutcracker Suite* and André de Lorde and Charles Foleÿ's *At the Telephone*. It is given a semi-domestic setting: a middle-class, academic, bachelor environment that is disrupted by a single act of brutal violence. Mirroring the War itself, it represents the violent disruption of the stable Edwardian social order. *Une Robe de soie* (*A Silk Dress*), by Henriette Charasson, also has a domestic setting and revolves around an argument between a man and woman, each representing, in turn, a reactionary and progressive set of social and moral opinions. This time, however, the final outcome is reconciliation. It is an example of the other kind of Grand-Guignol comedy – not a farce, but a piece of gentle, even sentimental, whimsy.

Whilst the name of St. John Greer Ervine (1883–1971) may have sunk into relative obscurity, he was a well-established and highly respected man of theatre when the play opened on 3rd April 1922. Arnold Bennett described him as 'probably unequalled by any other playwright', and as combining 'great skill, fine ideals and perfect sincerity with immense popular success' (Lothian, 1922, 645). Born in Belfast, Ervine's upbringing was modest, if not poor. His father, a printer by trade and an amateur scholar of languages, died when Ervine was a boy and the family moved into his maternal grandmother's house. The young Ervine rebelled somewhat against his strict Presbyterian upbringing by developing an interest in the theatre. When he moved to London at the age of seventeen to work as an insurance clerk, he did so as a committed Fabian and in the context of the aftermath of the Boer War, which had challenged many of the assumptions of the Victorian period and 'left men face to face with the question whether those material gains for which their fathers had striven – in the world of industry or empire – were worthy or worth while' (Lothian, 1922, 645).

In 1911 Ervine's play *Mixed Marriage*, which deals with Irish sectarianism, played at the Abbey Theatre in Dublin and the following year Ervine left the insurance business to pursue a career in the theatre, principally as a writer and critic but also, for a short period, as manager of the Abbey itself. In 1914 he published his first novel, *Mrs Martin's Man*, and, later the same year, another play, *John Ferguson*, was also completed and staged in 1915 to critical acclaim. After two years fighting with the Dublin Fusiliers in France he was wounded in May 1918, resulting in the amputation of his right leg. By 1920, however, Ervine was enjoying success once more and made his first trip to the United States, where he received a favourable reception.

Ervine's relationship with London's Grand Guignol was, in the first instance, in his role as theatre critic for the *Observer*, and it was not an easy one. The once radical Ervine had become a pillar of the theatrical establishment and rounded upon Levy's experiment as immoral. Ervine's disdain was not reserved for the Grand Guignol, however; throughout the 1920s he was highly critical of the state of British theatre, which he felt had lost its seriousness, become frivolous and begun to adopt far too many continental influences. Given his loathing of the Grand Guignol, it is perhaps surprising that Ervine decided to write a play for Levy, but, in doing so, he joined the ranks of (amongst others) Régis Gignoux, Frédéric Dard and André-Paul Antoine, well-established Parisian theatre critics who also wrote for the Théâtre du Grand-Guignol in Pigalle. In addition, it should be noted that, whilst Ervine heavily criticized the plays staged at the Little Theatre, he reserved praise for the quality of acting. It was actually in the premiere of Ervine's *Jane Clegg* in Manchester in 1913 that Sybil Thorndike first made her name, so it is not inconceivable that it was out of affection and admiration for Levy's leading lady, or even in response to a personal request, that Ervine followed up his stinging attack on H.F. Maltby's *The Person Unknown* with an anti-war play of his own for the Little Theatre. After all, it would not have been the first time that personal favours had helped London's Grand Guignol on its way.

At one level the ironically titled *Progress* can be seen as part of a corpus of anti-war plays that appeared in the years immediately following the end of the First World War. However, Ervine's play is unusual in that it does not focus on the experience of the soldier himself, or the figure of the returning, wounded (and disfigured) hero, but on the wider issue of war and morality.

The play is centred on the conflict between Henry Corrie, an obsessive scientist who has just invented a weapon of mass destruction, and his sister, who is grieving the loss of her son in the War. The struggle might be portrayed as that between two extreme opposites (or, indeed, two sides of the same familial coin): the dispassionate head of Corrie against the emotional heart of his sister, Mrs Meldon. However, the relationship between them is more complex than that. Corrie's arguments may be chillingly prophetic, both anticipating the occurrence of a second world war within a generation and echoing the 'moral' arguments built up around the use of nuclear weapons in the Cold War period, but it is his sister's argument that is more reasoned and persuasive, driven as it is by her grief. In fact, it is she who essentially wins the argument by force of reason and, if anything, it is the scientist's argument that is lacking a rational and coherent basis – perhaps because, whilst Corrie is an unapologetic man of science, he is not simply driven by his search for knowledge and invention but is largely motivated by the financial gains that he stands to make by selling his new bomb to the highest bidder. Here, perhaps, we are seeing something of the old anti-capitalist Ervine coming through. As the play comes to its inevitable conclusion, we are left wondering who is really the most psychologically unstable character in the play and whether morality is determined more by our emotional response to circumstances than by our rational response.

We must remember, though, that *Progress* was Ervine's way of responding to a theatrical phenomenon that he simply couldn't ignore. In spite of his publicly voiced criticism in the pages of the *Observer*, there were too many respected pillars of the theatrical establishment involved in the project for it to be dismissed too easily. It was principally against the writing, and not the acting, that Ervine railed and he ultimately responded by demonstrating how it could, or should, be done. There is perhaps a further irony that, in producing such a carefully crafted and tightly composed script as *Progress*, he arguably created a play that is entirely consistent with the best traditions of the French theatre of horror that he seemingly so loathed. Writing in *The North American Review* a mere month after its premiere, Alice Lothian described *Progress* as a 'superb little play' and praised it thus:

> The action moves as inevitably as a Greek tragedy to its awful end, an end that, with less skill or less sincerity, might have collapsed into melodrama. There is not one superfluous word, all is restrained, compact, as finely cut and brilliant as a diamond. (Lothian, 1922, 655–6)

In 1933, long after the experiment of London's Grand Guignol had closed its doors and a new shadow had begun to loom over Europe, Jack Jouvin staged a one-off experiment at the Théâtre du Grand-Guignol, abandoning the traditional *douche écossaise* in favour of what Mme Régis Leroi, writing in *Minerva,* described as 'a collection of sketches that show us a man and a woman grappling with life, love, money, regrets and memories' (quoted in de Beauplan, 1933). The programme, entitled *Quinze Couples* (*Fifteen*

Couples), actually consisted of fourteen short one-act plays (all male/female two-handers), written by half a dozen or more different authors, divided between three acts and described variously as 'sentimental, humorous, dramatic or comic' (de Beauplan, 1933). The purpose, it seems, was to manipulate the audience's sensibilities, rather than to assault their nerves, as was usual practice at the Grand-Guignol. *A Silk Dress* was one of three one-acters written by Henriette Charasson that formed part of the evening. The others were *En Chemin de Fer* (*On the Steam Train*) and *Séparation* and all three were published later the same year in *La Petite Illustration* with an introduction by Robert de Beauplan.

Charasson (1884–1972) had been on the literary scene as a poet, critic and essayist since around 1910, but only at the beginning of the 1930s had she turned her hand to the theatre and playwriting. Her first two plays, *Le Saut du Diable* (*The Devil's Leap*) and *Les Réalitées invisibles* (*Invisible Realities*), had won her the Prix Paul Hervieu earlier in 1933 and the collaboration with Jouvin was her first since that success. These three 'simple, but poignant' plays (Sedlack, 1938, 70) appear to have been the great success of the evening at the rue Chaptal and the critics were near-unanimous in their enthusiasm for Charasson's contributions. As Robert de Beauplan says in his introduction to the plays:

> Everyone is in agreement in recognizing that in this unique contest, Mme Henriette Charasson has carried away the crown and that the three playlets of which she is the author formed the better part of the evening. (de Beauplan, 1933)

Henriette Charasson is, however, an unlikely Grand-Guignol writer. First, she was a woman and, whilst women often took prominent roles on the Grand-Guignol stage and even, from the 1940s onwards, as directors, their presence as writers was much rarer. *A Silk Dress*, then, is an interesting addition to the repertoire. Second, as a devoutly Catholic writer, Charasson might have been expected to shun any association with the theatre of horror and eroticism. Charasson's literary concerns were, according to de Beauplan, predominantly focused on 'questions that concerned women and the family' (as, indeed, can be seen in *A Silk Dress*) and it was no doubt the purpose of Jouvin's experiment in turning away from the traditional Grand-Guignol formula that persuaded her to become involved. In spite of her success, however, she never again wrote for the Théâtre du Grand-Guignol, nor did Jouvin, or any of his successors, repeat the experiment of the *Quinze Couples*. In retrospect, perhaps, *A Silk Dress* might seem to have been indulging in a slight nostalgia for the social and domestic simplicities and conventions of the *Belle Époque* at a time when more sinister forces were haunting Europe. By the following year André de Lorde and Pierre Chaine were back on the programme with *Jack L'éventreur* (*Jack the Ripper*).

Charisson's three one-acters went on to have some success as radio plays and were even translated into Italian (Sedlack, 1938, 71), whilst Henriette Charasson herself went on to make a successful career as a radio presenter (Sedlack, 1938, 72–5) and to outlive even the Théâtre du Grand-Guignol.

André de Lorde (1869–1942) was, of course, the most celebrated and prolific of all the writers who worked for the Grand-Guignol over its sixty-five-year history, and he was also one of its most prolific collaborators. Collaboration between writers was not a rarity at the Grand-Guignol and that, in itself, gives some indication of the collective working methods required to create a rapidly changing repertoire of new plays capable of satisfying the demands of the Grand-Guignol audience. In the first decade of the twentieth century de Lorde had scored a number of successes in partnership with Alfred Binet *L'obsession* (*Obsession*, 1905) and *L'Horrible Expérience* (*The Horrific Experiment*, 1909), for example), as well as *La Dernière Torture* (*The Ultimate Torture*, 1904) with Eugène Morel and *Au Rat mort, cabinet 6* (*At the Dead Rat, Private Room No. 6*[1], 1907) and *La Petite Fille* (*The Little Girl*, 1907) with Pierre Chaine. In 1915 he began a new writing partnership with Henri Bauche, with *Le Mystère de la maison noire* (*The Mystery of the Black House*), and the following year three of their plays were produced at the Grand-Guignol: *Le Château de la mort lente* (*The Castle of Slow Death*); *Le Laboratoire des hallucinations* (*The Laboratory of Hallucinations*) and *La Grande épouvante* (*The Great Terror*), all plays that the pair later published in a single volume entitled *Les Drâmes célèbres du Grand Guignol* (*Famous Plays of the Grand-Guignol*, 1924).

On the one hand, *The Great Terror* is a fine example of Grand-Guignol Orientalism: the 'East' (in this case, Egypt) as exotic, mysterious, irrational, sexual and, above all, dangerous, all seen through the lens of empire. If anything, the great fear in the play's title is the fear of 'the other', which 'appeared at the Grand-Guignol in countless variations' (Pierron, 1996). However, it is interesting that de Lorde and Bauche chose to give the play a British, rather than a French, setting, which allows them to adopt a more distanced and critical position as regards the attitudes of the members of the London colonial club where the first act takes place. It is also worth remembering that the play was written in 1917, in the midst of the First World War, in which the Great Powers of Europe and the old colonial political order, formed during the nineteenth-century race for the colonies, were fighting for their very survival.

At the beginning of the play the club members are depicted as companionable, well-mannered and courteous, if a little pompous. Even

---

1 Le Rat Mort was a famous cabaret venue located on the Place Pigalle, a short walk from the Théâtre du Grand-Guignol. It was immortalized in 1899 in a painting by Henri Toulouse-Lautrec (1864–1901).

the drunk Major Williams is able to pull himself together in the company of Miss Evelyn. However, it is their collective sense of superiority and entitlement that exposes a deeply unpleasant side to their natures, whether it is the class-ridden snobbishness that is evident in the way they treat James, the waiter, or the barely concealed racism with which they greet the Egyptian Tâni. Even the character of Frank Burton, who in the first act has a relatively benign (if rather patronizing attitude) to Tâni – it is he who wishes to propose Tâni as a club member in the first place – betrays a shocking racism in Act Two when he objects to Tâni's proposal of marriage to Evelyn on the grounds that he is 'racially inferior'. This results in a typical Grand-Guignolesque blurring of morality: on the one hand, Tâni is a manipulator, abuser and murderer; on the other, he is a victim of the British colonial sense of superiority. The Burtons, likewise, are simultaneously victims of Tâni and implicated members of the colonial establishment. The conclusion to the play could be read as an act of revenge for his earlier persecution as much as the actions of as an evil occultist. Such is the moral ambiguity introduced by de Lorde and Bauche.

The play's British setting also indicates the influence of George du Maurier's hugely successful novel of 1894, *Trilby*, which was something of a literary phenomenon at the turn of the century, spawning numerous stage adaptations and influencing works such as Gaston Leroux's *Le Fantôme de l'Opéra* (*The Phantom of the Opera*) of 1910. In addition, it introduced the world to the mesmerist Svengali, who can be seen as the inspiration for Tâni, and gave rise to numerous popular villains, such as Dr Fu Manchu, who first appeared in a novel by British writer Sax Rohmer in 1913 before eventually becoming the iconic cinema villain, as played by numerous actors including Christopher Lee in the latter half of the 1960s.

The Great Terror is probably as near as the Grand-Guignol ever got to embracing the supernatural. As a general rule, the horrors of the Grand-Guignol all occurred within an identifiable and rational world. What allowed de Lorde and Bauche to dabble in the occultism of *The Great Terror* was its Orientalism, which allowed it to be explained as one of the dark mysteries of the East. Where the play is consistent with the genre, however, is in its interest in liminal states: the moment between life and death; consciousness and unconsciousness; sanity and madness; control and abandon. As Agnès Pierron rightly asserts:

> ... what carried the Grand-Guignol to its highest level were the boundaries and thresholds it crossed: the states of consciousness altered by drugs or hypnosis, loss of consciousness, loss of control, panic: themes with which the theatre's audience could easily identify. (...) The passage from one state to another was the crux of the genre. (Pierron, 1996)

Progress
(1922)

St. John Ervine

Characters:
Henry Corrie
Hannah, the servant
Mrs Meldon

The scene of the play is laid in the study of Professor Henry Corrie in a remote village in the north of England on a spring day in the year 1919. The room is tidy enough, with the tidiness of a house dominated by a bachelor who is dominated by his work rather than by domestic comfort; and on the large table near the centre of the room there is a litter of scientific apparatus employed by Professor Corrie in the experiment in which he is now engaged. On the walls of the room are a number of diagrams, showing sections of very large bombs. There is a model of a big bomb on a stand underneath one of these diagrams. There are sectional diagrams of aeroplanes and airships to be seen, and also fairly large models of aeroplanes and airships.

Professor Henry Corrie, aged between fifty and sixty, is sitting at the centre table watching a chemical process in a large retort. He has cold, humourless eyes, and his mouth, if it were not concealed by a thickish beard, would be seen to have cruel lines about it. He does not, however, impress the casual visitor as a cruel man – indeed, he seems to be a harmless, kindly, inconsequent person, completely absorbed, of course, in his work. It is when he is angry that something of his cruelty is observable – he is inclined to utter wolfish snarls if he is thwarted or hindered in any way. But the most certain sign of his fundamentally cruel character is his absorption in his scientific work. Nothing is of greater importance to him than that, and a human being is of less consequence to him than the success of even a minor experiment.

He regards the retort very closely, muttering to himself as he does so. Sometimes his mutterings are of satisfaction, sometimes of anxiety, and once of rage that turns again to satisfaction. A knock is heard on his study door, but he does not hear it. It is repeated. He leans forward to glance more closely at the retort, and then, with a shout of pleasure, rises up and contemplates it. The knock is heard for the third time.

CORRIE (*bending over the retort and ending the experiment*): Ah, at last, at last! By Heaven, I've done it at last. (*A very loud knock on the door. He turns round in a puzzled fashion.*) Eh: Oh, oh! Come in! Come in!

(*The door opens, and an elderly servant enters.*)

SERVANT: Mrs Meldon ...

CORRIE: Yes, yes, Hannah, what is it?

HANNAH: Mrs Meldon wants to know whether you'II come downstairs to tea or have it up here?

CORRIE: Has she got back?

HANNAH: Yes, sir. She expected you to meet her at the station, sir. She waited a long time in the cold, and then got Marshall to drive her up.

CORRIE: I meant to go, but I was busy, and then I forgot. But she's quite capable of coming home by herself.

HANNAH: Yes, sir. Will you come downstairs to tea, sir, or have it up here?

CORRIE: The drawing-room's so cold! ... Tell Mrs Meldon I'II have it up here. I've news for her. Tell her I've good news for her. My experiment is ended, and it's a success.

HANNAH: Is it, sir?

CORRIE: Yes – but it's no use telling you about it. You wouldn't understand.

HANNAH: No, sir.

CORRIE: But I'm a proud man, Hannah. Perhaps you'll understand that. Go and tell Mrs Meldon.

HANNAH: Yes, sir.

CORRIE: Don't forget to tell her that my experiment is a success. Or, no! – you'd better not tell her. I'll do that myself. You're sure to make a mess of it. She'll be as pleased as I am.

HANNAH: She's not very happy to-day, sir.

CORRIE: Not happy? Why? I'm happy, aren't I?

HANNAH: Well, you see, sir, it's three years ago to-day since her son was killed in the War! ...

CORRIE (*almost forgetting his grievance*): Oh, yes, I'd forgotten that! Of course, one can't keep on thinking about these things! ...

HANNAH: She does, sir.

CORRIE: I'm sorry I didn't meet her at the station. But I had to attend to my experiment, Hannah. I wish she wouldn't dwell on Eddie's death. It's not right for the living to think so much of the dead. She's a woman, of course, and a mother – a bereaved mother. We must make allowances, Hannah. That's all. Now if I tell her about my successful experiment, how would that do?

HANNAH (*dubiously*): I don't suppose it would make her feel any worse than she is now, sir.

CORRIE: Well, tell her to come up here and have her tea with me. See? And I'll tell her about my experiment.

HANNAH: Very good, sir. (*She turns to go.*)

CORRIE: Oh! – and, Hannah, tell her I'm very sorry I couldn't meet her at the station. That'll break the ice a bit. Then when she realizes how important my work is and how much depends on it, she'll be all right.

HANNAH: Very good, sir. (*She goes towards the door. Then she stops and turns towards him.*) She really isn't happy, sir. Her nerves aren't at all right. You see, she can't forget, sir!

(*But the professor is back at his table, intently regarding his experiment, and, except for a grunt, he does not reply. Hannah goes out. The professor makes some calculations on paper, and then sits back in his chair regarding them with delight. His manifestations of joy are interrupted by the entrance of his sister, Mrs Meldon, aged about forty-three. She is dressed in black, partly because she is a widow, but chiefly because of her son's death. She is a sensitive-looking woman, now plainly suffering deeply from her memories, but her nervous sensibilities give her a strength on occasions which is hardly credible. She is not a fretful, complaining woman who behaves as if she were the only person in the world who had suffered a bereavement, and when, in the course of the play, she speaks of her loss she does so with grave and beautiful dignity.*)

MRS MELDON: Henry!

CORRIE: Eh? (*Turning.*) Oh, my dear Charlotte, I'm sorry I did not meet you at the station! ...

MRS MELDON (*seating herself by the fire*): It doesn't matter, Henry. Only

I thought you were coming – you said you would – and I waited a long time in the cold! …

CORRIE: Yes, I'm sorry about that, but, you see, I was busy, Charlotte. I've succeeded at last. I've got just exactly what I wanted, Charlotte. Absolutely *the* thing. This will bring fame and fortune to me. I shall be rich now, but more than that, I shall be famous. My name will live forever. When I saw how well the experiment was going, I said to myself, 'Charlotte won't really expect me to meet her just when everything's going so right, and after all, she's a grown-up woman and she knows the way home as well as I do!' So I didn't go. I stayed here and did my work. I knew you'd understand. And it's a success, Charlotte, the greatest and most wonderful success I've ever had.

MRS MELDON: Oh, yes.

CORRIE (*dashed*): Well, you don't seem very excited about it.

MRS MELDON: Of course, I'm glad it's a success, Henry, whatever it is, but, you see, you've never told me anything about it.

CORRIE: No, that's true. I've always believed in keeping secrets to myself. Tell no one anything until you are obliged to, that's my principle. No one knows that I have been working at this thing – except myself. The secret of successful invention, Charlotte, is reticence! But now, I can tell you what it is. The component parts are still my secret and will remain such until I can get a binding offer from some government! …

MRS MELDON: Government! Is it a government matter?

CORRIE: I should think it is. I shall offer it first to the British Government, of course, but if they won't pay my price, I'll offer it to somebody else. Too many inventors have been let down by the British Government, Charlotte. But they will not let me down. No. I can take care of myself. But then, when they hear what my invention is, they'll jump at it.

MRS MELDON: Will they?

CORRIE: Of course they will, though you're quite justified in feeling sceptical about them. It was very hard to get them to use tanks in the War – very hard. These cavalry generals had to be forced to use them. They ought to be horse-knackers, instead of soldiers. And tin hats, too! Look what a time it was before that damned War Office could be persuaded to use 'em! … But I'm sorry, Charlotte. I ought not to be talking about the War to you – especially to-day.

MRS MELDON: I don't mind, Henry. And, after all, the War Office isn't the War!

CORRIE: No, that's true.

MRS MELDON: What is your invention, Henry?

CORRIE: Ah, Charlotte! There's something interesting to talk about. (*Hannah enters with a tea-tray.*)

HANNAH: Here's the tea, sir.

CORRIE: Damn! Oh, all right! Put it down there! (*Hannah arranges the tea-tray in front of Mrs Meldon. The professor, meantime, is back at his table and his retorts and his formulae. Now and again he exclaims to himself.*)

MRS MELDON: Has everything been all right, Hannah?

HANNAH: Yes, ma'am. Gage, the gardener, brought up the wreath you ordered for the War Memorial, ma'am. I've got it in the kitchen now. Shall I fetch it for you?

MRS MELDON: Yes, do, please, Hannah.

(*And then Hannah, having finished with the tea-table, goes out.*)

MRS MELDON: Come and have your tea, Henry!

CORRIE: All right! (*But he does not stir.*)

MRS MELDON: Come along, Henry!

CORRIE: Eh? Oh, all right! In a minute!

MRS MELDON: Your tea will get cold if you don't come now!

CORRIE (*getting up and coming to the tea-table*): Oh, how women do fuss! Your sex is most extraordinary, Charlotte. Always willing to break off things for other things. No application. No concentration. No capacity for complete, impersonal devotion. That's why no women have ever been great artists or scientists. Because they will not forsake everything and follow – well, whatever it is they ought to be following!

(*Hannah returns, carrying a bunch of flowers to which a label is attached.*)

HANNAH: Here it is, ma'am.

CORRIE: What's that?

MRS MELDON (*taking the flowers from Hannah*): I ordered it from Gage to put on the War Memorial. It's for Eddie! ...

CORRIE: Oh, yes, yes!

MRS MELDON: I shall take it down there after tea. Will you come with me?

CORRIE: I'd like to, of course, but I really must finish up these things.

MRS MELDON: Very well, Henry. (*to Hannah*) Thank you, Hannah. I'll keep the flowers here.

(*Exit Hannah.*)

MRS MELDON (*to her brother*): They're very beautiful, aren't they, Henry?

CORRIE: Oh, yes! Quite nice! You know, Charlotte, this invention of mine –

MRS MELDON: Will you have some more tea, Henry?

CORRIE (*vaguely*): Oh-h-h-h! (*then definitely*) Yes. Half a cup! (*He hands the cup to her, and she fills it and returns it to him while the following speeches are uttered.*)

CORRIE: I was saying this invention of mine will revolutionize warfare.

MRS MELDON: Will it abolish warfare?

CORRIE: Abolish war! ... My dear Charlotte, don't be childish!

MRS MELDON: I'm very interested in that subject. It seems to me more important than anything else in the world, Henry. You don't realize how deeply women like me feel about this ... this organized butchery of boys. Look at me! I had a husband and a son when the War began. I had neither when it was over. I am a most lonely woman ... cruelly alone! ...

CORRIE (*a little annoyed by what seems to him sentimental harping on one string*): I know, of course, that the War hit you very badly, Charlotte – what with Eddie being killed and Tom taking his death so badly! ...

MRS MELDON: Tom died of a broken heart, Henry. That may sound sentimental and unscientific to you, but it's true. I sometimes wonder why I was not granted the mercy of death – why I should be compelled to live on alone! ...

CORRIE: Oh, come, come, Charlotte! Not alone! No, no, not alone! You're happy enough with me, aren't you? Your only brother! ...

MRS MELDON: You're not a very good substitute for a son, Henry!

CORRIE: Well, no, I suppose not, but, still, there's no need for despair. Let me tell you about my invention. (*He puts his cup down and prepares to explain.*)

MRS MELDON: Will you have some more tea?

CORRIE: No, thanks! Now, Charlotte, when I say that war ought to be revolutionized, I mean that it ought to be made more expeditious. The war we've just had lasted for a ridiculous period. Five years – or nearly five years. Perfectly preposterous. It ought not to have lasted more than five weeks.

MRS MELDON: Have you invented a means of restricting the duration of wars?

CORRIE: Well – yes, I think you might put it like that. What the combatants ought to aim at, in war, is to get the first blow in so hard that the other side immediately succumbs to it.

MRS MELDON: I see.

CORRIE: That means that the weapons of war must be made immeasurably more horrible and devastating than they now are.

MRS MELDON: More horrible! Is that possible?

CORRIE: Yes. Oh, yes! We haven't yet reached the limits of horror in war! Oh, dear me, no!

MRS MELDON: My son was nineteen, Henry, and he was killed in a fight of which he knew very little. That seems to me a horrible thing!

CORRIE: Oh, a mother's feelings, of course, but look at the matter from a broad point of view. Put your own feelings aside! …

MRS MELDON: I can't do that, Henry. The whole war for me comes down to this one thing, that my son, a boy new from school, was taken away from me, just when his life was beginning to open out, and killed. I'm not a clever woman, Henry. I can only feel things as they touch me and mine. Eddie was my only son, my darling, my heart's joy I expected so much from him – and he's gone, and there's nothing … nothing … nothing!

CORRIE (*being very gentle with her*): Yes, I know, Charlotte, but you really ought not to dwell too much on your sorrow. It isn't good for you. You ought to take a broad point of view. Imagine yourself a statesman! …

MRS MELDON: If Eddie had been a statesman, he would not have gone to the war. He would have compelled some other person to go.

CORRIE: Oh, now, don't be bitter, Charlotte; don't be bitter!

MRS MELDON: My dear Henry, I'm beyond being bitter. Do you know what I discovered to-day?

CORRIE: No.

MRS MELDON: You know I've never really known how Eddie died. I found out to-day.

CORRIE: I wish you wouldn't think so much about it.

MRS MELDON (*with sudden passion*): I must think about it. I can't help thinking about it! … I met a young man in town to-day who had been in the same battalion as Eddie, and he told me about it. Poor lad, it slipped out before he realized that I hadn't known before! …

CORRIE: People oughtn't to talk so much about the War. Much better forget about it!

MRS MELDON (*recovering herself*): You remember the C.O. of the battalion wrote to me and said that Eddie had been killed by a piece of shell and that he had been buried behind the line somewhere?

CORRIE: Yes, I remember.

MRS MELDON: That comforted me very much. It made things easier to think that he wasn't ... mutilated ... that even when he was killed he was still my dear and beautiful boy ... a soldier, buried by soldiers, in a soldier's grave! ... But he wasn't buried, Henry!

CORRIE: Wasn't buried?

MRS MELDON: No. There was nothing to bury. The shell came and ... and ... there was nothing. (*They are silent for a moment or two.*) Don't you think *that* is horrible, Henry? There was no decency in his death! ... Oh, my God! My God! You tell me to take a broad point of view about that! My son! ... They'd been in a little, shallow trench, Eddie and his men, sitting there for eight days and nights, waiting and waiting and waiting; and then a shell came right into the middle of a group of them and destroyed them ... utterly destroyed them. Five of them ... nothing left ... nothing left!

(*She sits back in her chair and both of them are silent. Then the professor goes to his table and sits down before his papers and retorts.*)

MRS MELDON: What is your invention, Henry?

CORRIE: Oh, I think we'd better not talk about it! You're upset! That chap ought not to have told you about Eddie.

MRS MELDON: He thought I knew. What is your invention?

CORRIE: I'll tell you another time.

MRS MELDON: I'd like to know now. Something to make war more expeditious! To end it quickly!

CORRIE (*swinging round to her*): Really, Charlotte, this is a most humanitarian invention. I don't believe, mind you, that wars will ever end. No. We're altogether too pugnacious, we human beings. So the only thing to do then is to make war so horrible that no nation will engage in one unless absolutely driven to it. That's where I come in. I'm going to make war horrible, *really* horrible!

MRS MELDON: Yes.

CORRIE: I've got something here, Charlotte ... the formula for a bomb that will make war not only stupendously horrible, but will end it almost as quickly as it began.

MRS MELDON: On that table? (*She rises and goes to him.*)

CORRIE: Yes. I've made tests and I've worked out the formula with mathematical precision, and I've discovered a combination of gases and explosives that will obliterate thousands at once. Thousands!

MRS MELDON: Thousands?

CORRIE: Yes.

MRS MELDON: Obliterate them ... just like Eddie.

CORRIE: Oh, my dear Charlotte, you really must not be so morbid. We've got to deal with the world of fact, and if this country is going to maintain her position in the world, she will have to use every device she can employ to keep her there. I consider that I'm performing a highly patriotic act in offering this discovery to my country. Now, listen! By means of my formula, we can make a bomb, a big bomb, not one of those little footling things the Germans used to drop on London, but an enormous bomb, full of corrosive gas, which will be dropped from a powerful aeroplane or airship – that has to be settled yet – but it's not really my job. Now, when the next war breaks out! ...

MRS MELDON: The next war?

CORRIE: Yes, I should say we'd have another in twenty or thirty years, wouldn't you? Not more than fifty, anyhow. Well, when it comes, our ultimatum will consist of a number of airships or aeroplanes dropping these big bombs on the country with which we're at war – just in the way the Japanese declared war on the Russians by blowing their ships to pieces. Only ours will be much more effective than that. The Japs only sank a few ships. We'll utterly obliterate whole cities ... perhaps a whole nation.

MRS MELDON: Yes.

CORRIE: When this bomb falls, the explosion will devastate a wide tract of the district in which it falls, and at the same time will release a powerful, spreading gas, without colour or smell, which will spread over a wide area and poison every person who inhales it. They won't know that they've inhaled it until they see their bodies rotting. And nothing will save them then! With a single bomb we could wipe out the population of a city as big as Manchester. Single bomb, Charlotte!

MRS MELDON: But that would mean everybody – men and women and children.

CORRIE: Oh, yes. After all, nowadays, there is no logical distinction between a civilian and a soldier. What's the difference between the girl who makes munitions and the man who uses them in the trenches? You know, Charlotte, it's a terrific thought, to think that I can sit here at this table, with a formula written out on those sheets of paper which will enable a few men to go up into the air and wipe out a whole city. And I'm the only man in the world who knows how to do it.

MRS MELDON: Aren't there men like you in other countries using their brains for the same purpose?

CORRIE: Yes, but I don't imagine anyone will discover as powerful a weapon as this. If I had made this discovery in 1914, the War would have been over before the end of that year, and there probably wouldn't be any Germans left now. They'd be an extinct race.

MRS MELDON: Perhaps an enemy of this country might make a similar discovery, Henry, and use it on us.

CORRIE: We'll have to take the risk of that. Anyhow, my discovery will be available to our people, and if a war does come along, we've only got to get our bomb dropped on them before they get theirs dropped on us, and the trick's done.

MRS MELDON: I suppose it was someone like you who invented the kind of shell that destroyed Eddie ... that obliterated him!

CORRIE (*rising and patting her on the shoulder*): Now, now, don't go back to that subject, Charlotte. Come over here by the fire, and try and take a more cheerful view of life.

MRS MELDON: Cheerful view! My dear Henry, I sometimes wonder whether, in spite of your cleverness, you aren't really the stupidest man on earth.

CORRIE: Oh, come!

MRS MELDON: I'm not clever. It seems odd that I should be your sister, a quite ordinary, commonplace woman, with nothing in my life but my love for my husband and my son. But when I hear you telling me to take a broad statesmanlike view of my son being blown to pieces, I begin to think that you're a fool, Henry – just a dull, unimaginative, bloodless fool. And when you ask me to rejoice because you've invented a bomb that will destroy a whole city in a few minutes, I think you're ... you're mad – wickedly, horribly mad.

CORRIE: My dear Charlotte! ...

MRS MELDON: One moment, Henry. I want you to try and realize my point of view, the point of view of an ordinary woman without any pretensions. Think of Eddie as I think of him! ...

CORRIE: This isn't good for you.

MRS MELDON: Oh, yes, it is. I go back now to the very beginning, and I think of Tom and me, very young and foolish, I suppose, but very happy, too, Henry, and our queer pleasure and fright when we knew that Eddie was coming. And I think, too, of myself, sometimes at night, awake, with Tom lying asleep beside me; and how I thought about the little child

I was going to bear him, and how I loved it and loved him for being its father, and how sure I was that it would be a boy! I was frightened, too, sometimes, because I thought I might die and never know my son, who would grow up and have no knowledge of me. And then he was born, such a dear, little, clutching child, so terribly dependent on me. Tom was very pleased and proud, but never so pleased and proud as I was. We both watched him grow – you know how handsome he was!

CORRIE: Yes, he was a good-looking lad.

MRS MELDON: And we made plans for him. He was to be great and liked – people did like him; even you liked him, Henry, didn't you?

CORRIE: Yes, I ... I liked him. He was an attractive boy. But don't you think –

MRS MELDON: And then he was ill. You remember how we all thought that he would die, and Tom, poor Tom, who never could express himself very aptly, went about as if he were stunned. I can't tell you what I thought then, Henry. I just can't tell you, but oh! I prayed for him, Henry – prayed for him so that my whole mind was a prayer. Well, he got better, and seemed to grow stronger, and at school he did very well. I can see him now, the first time he played in a cricket match, very pleased with his blazer, and how excited he was when he came to tell me that he had made ten runs. Ten runs he made, my little son, in his first cricket match. All the other boys of his age were very respectful to him, and I was so glad when he let me walk about with him, just as if he hadn't had a triumph. And Tom was frightfully pleased, too, and gave him a sovereign! ... (*Her tears overcome her, and she raises her hands to her lips in a gesture of grief.*) My little boy! ...

CORRIE: This is distressing you, my dear. Don't talk about it any more.

MRS MELLON (*recovering herself*): He hadn't been at Oxford long when the War began, and then he went off and enlisted. We didn't know whether to be proud of him or to be angry with him, but chiefly we were proud. I loved him in his clumsy uniform and his great, rough boots, just as much as I loved him later on in his officer's uniform. And when he went off to France, I tried to be worthy of my son and not to cry. It was frightfully hard to smile, Henry, but I did smile. I felt that that was what Eddie would wish me to do, not to shame him before the other people, and so I smiled and made a little silly joke about the fear of the Germans when they heard of his arrival. But I was in terror, Henry, and all the time that he was away I was in terror. The sight of a telegraph messenger made my heart sink! ... And then he came home on his first leave, and my little son wasn't my little son any more, but a strangely grown man, young to look at, but full of extraordinary knowledge. I felt shy with him. He'd seen so much and knew so much. And then I think I felt prouder of him than ever before, because he was a man and I could depend upon him. We were very happy during that leave, Henry, so happy that I hardly had time to be miserable because it would so soon be over, and when he went back, although I cried a little when he wasn't looking, I didn't mind so much as I thought I should, because I persuaded myself to believe that he wouldn't be killed. When he had his second leave and was a captain, I was sure that he would come home to me, quite safe. Even Tom, who had always felt we should lose him, began to believe that he'd come home again. But he didn't. Immediately he got back to France, he had to go into the line, and eight days later he was killed – just obliterated, as you say, by men who had never seen him, who didn't even know that they'd killed him. And all my years of love and hope and desire and pain – gone! I'd nursed him and cared for him and taught him little lessons and been proud of him – and then in a moment my beautiful son was ... obliterated, Henry! (*There's a slight pause while she recovers herself.*) You see, don't you, Henry, that I can't take a broad view of that. I can only see my son's body mutilated and destroyed. That's all.

CORRIE: Well, of course, I quite see your point of view, Charlotte. It is hard. I admit that. But we have to keep our feelings under control. And after all, there's the consolation that Eddie did his duty to his country. I dare say he accounted for a good many Germans! ...

MRS MELDON: That doesn't comfort me, Henry. I can't get any pleasure out of the thought that some poor German woman is suffering just as I'm suffering. No, Henry, I feel that I should want to take sides with her against men like you!

CORRIE: Men like me!

MRS MELDON: Yes. People with broad views. Because you're such fools. Someone like me, not clever, creates a beautiful thing like my son, and you, with all your cleverness, can only destroy it. That's why I think you're a fool, Henry.

CORRIE (*nettled*): Well, of course, Charlotte, with your views, I can hardly expect you to appreciate me or my work, but I fancy that my countrymen, if they have any sense, will know how to value me. My bomb will make my name known to the most ignorant men in the country. People will talk about the Corrie bomb, just as they used to talk about the Mills bomb during the War. I shall have to ask for a large lump sum in payment of the invention, because a royalty wouldn't pay me at all. Mills got a royalty on each of his bombs, but then they were small and hundreds of thousands of them were used. My bombs will be big, and one of them will suffice for a city. Yes, I shall have to ask for a large lump sum. Now that they're spending several million pounds on a battleship that is generally believed to be useless, I'm entitled to ask for a very large sum for my bomb which will certainly decide the war. I wonder how much I ought to ask for? Charlotte, how much ought I to ask for? They won't give me what it's worth, that's absolutely certain. They might pay a quarter of a million. Charlotte, what would you ask for if you were me?

MRS MELDON: I should ask for my son.

CORRIE: Now, now, now, Charlotte, not again, please. Not again. We must think of the future, not of the past. I don't want to ask for too much, because I shan't get it, and I don't want to ask for too little, though I shall probably get that anyhow. What do you think, Charlotte? Do you think it would be better to let them name a price?

MRS MELDON: I don't know.

CORRIE: Well, you might take a little interest in the matter. It's very important to me. They ought really to give me a title, too. Supposing I say a couple of hundred thousand pounds and a peerage! …

MRS MELDON: Why not say thirty pieces of silver?

CORRIE (*thoroughly angry*): Really, Charlotte, you're insufferable! You're absolutely insufferable! I put up with a great deal from you because you're in distress, but there are limits to endurance, you know. You haven't congratulated *me*, even perfunctorily, and you've made yourself and me thoroughly miserable by this … this moaning over what can't be helped. You've even made Hannah miserable. My dear Charlotte, I'm talking to you now for your good. You really ought not to let your mind dwell on things in the way you do. It isn't good for you, and it's very unpleasant for me and for others who associate with you. Your boy was killed – so were other people's boys – but we can't spend the rest of our lives in lamentation. I have my work to do! …

MRS MELDON: Your bomb?

CORRIE: Yes.

MRS MELDON: Which will make the bodies of men and women and little children rot if it does not blow them to pieces.

CORRIE: The fortune of war, my dear Charlotte. After all, what does it matter to a man whether he is blown to pieces by a bomb or stabbed to death by a bayonet? As a matter of fact, the bomb is the more merciful of the two. It isn't any use being sentimental about these things. The purpose of war is killing, and the side which kills the most people in the shortest time is going to win the wars of the future. My bomb will enable those who possess it to conduct a war in a rapid and efficient fashion. No reasonable person can deny that I have performed a service to my country in inventing this bomb for its use, and even you, if you were not distracted by what you heard this morning and the fact that this is the anniversary of Eddie's death, would agree with them.

MRS MELDON: No one but you knows the secret of your invention, Henry?

CORRIE: No – not that I am aware of.

MRS MELDON: If you were to destroy your invention, never reveal its secrets, thousands of boys like Eddie might live without fear of being destroyed?

CORRIE: Oh, I don't know. It's a fantastic thought, that, but there's nothing in it. Other people will invent things even deadlier than my bomb.

MRS MELDON: But, Henry, if you were to suppress your invention!

CORRIE: Suppress it!

MRS MELDON: Yes, if you were to destroy your formulae, and people were to know what you'd done, perhaps you'd do a great deal to change people's hearts! …

CORRIE: My dear Charlotte, most sensible people would think I'd gone off my head. A few cranks and religious maniacs might praise me, but the average person would think I was a fool – besides being damned unpatriotic.

MRS MELDON: Henry, I beg you to destroy your invention.

CORRIE: You what?

MRS MELDON: I beg you to destroy it. Let that be your memorial to Eddie! …

CORRIE: My dear Charlotte, I begin to believe that grief has unhinged your mind. Destroy my invention! …

MRS MELDON: Your bomb will destroy life, Henry. I beg of you to destroy it! …

CORRIE: Rubbish, woman, rubbish.

MRS MELDON: Then I will destroy it for you! (*She goes to the table where the retorts are and hurls the table over so that the retorts are smashed.*)

CORRIE: What the hell are you doing?

MRS MELDON: I'm destroying your foul invention.

CORRIE (*laughing harshly*): That won't destroy it. I've got it all in my head. All that you've done, Charlotte, is to make a mess on my floor. Damned silly, I call it. (*He stoops down and begins to clear up the mess.*)

MRS MELDON (*standing behind him*): It's all in your head!

CORRIE: Of course it is. Anybody but a fool of a woman would have realized that. Making a confounded mess like this! ...

MRS MELDON: It's all in your head?

CORRIE: Yes, yes. Don't keep on repeating yourself, but come and help to clear up this mess you've made.

MRS MELDON: Henry, won't you do what I ask you?

CORRIE: Don't be a fool. (*Looking round.*) Give me that cloth over there so that I can mop up this stuff. (*He continues to collect the pieces of broken glass, etc., while she goes towards the table where the cloth is. When she reaches the table, she sees a long knife lying there, and half unconsciously she picks it up and looks at it.*)

CORRIE (*impatiently*): Hurry up. What on earth are you doing?

MRS MELDON: I'm looking at something – this knife!

CORRIE: Well, you can look at it afterwards. Fetch the cloth now. Here's Eddie's wreath under the table. You've made a mess of it, too!

MRS MELDON: Eddie's wreath! (*She comes towards him, the knife in her hand.*)

CORRIE: Yes.

MRS MELDON: If you were to give up your invention, Henry, I wouldn't mind about the wreath. Your offering would be better than mine.

CORRIE: Well, I shan't. Give up my invention for a lot of damned sentiment! Not likely!

MRS MELDON: It'll destroy life, Henry.

CORRIE: What's that got to do with it? Give me that cloth. (*He snaps it out of her hand, but does not see the knife in her other hand.*)

MRS MELDON: You won't destroy it, Henry?

CORRIE (*almost in a snarl*): NO!

MRS MELDON (*raising the knife above him*): Then I ...

(*With a queer moan of despair, she drives the knife into his back. He sways a moment, uttering a choking sound, and then, clutching at the air, he pitches forward on to his face. She stands above him, looking down on his body in a dazed way. She is crying hysterically, and suddenly she stoops and picks up the broken wreath. She holds it to her breast, and stares distractedly in front of her.*)

MRS MELDON: Eddie, dear, I had to, I had to, Eddie! ...

CURTAIN

A Silk Dress
(*Une Robe de soie*, 1933)

Henriette Charasson

Characters:
Albert, 48 years old
Germaine, 40–42 years old

A Study

Germaine is still beautiful and sexy. There may be a hint of grey in her hair. She is wearing a stylish negligée. Albert is going grey at the temples. He is in his dressing gown, working at a desk. A desk lamp is lit and the curtains to the window are closed.

GERMAINE (*gently opening the door and standing in the doorway*): Albert, I'd like to speak to you.

ALBERT (*working*): Mmmm ...

GERMAINE (*nervously taking a single step forward*): Am I disturbing you?

ALBERT (*all the while, continuing to write*): Clearly. You can see that I'm at my desk working. And if I'm working, then you're disturbing me. (*He continues writing for a moment without looking at her then he looks up.*) Can't it wait until the morning? (*Germaine hesitates.*) If it's money you want, just tell me what it's for and I shall give it to you, but for goodness sake, let me get on with my work!

GERMAINE: I don't need any money. (*Suddenly and decisively, like a mouse that roars, she closes the door and advances.*) Albert, our daughter is crying.

ALBERT (*his face suddenly hardening*): So what? Let her cry. (*All the while writing.*) She can't keep it up all night long.

GERMAINE: This is not some kind of game.

ALBERT (*putting down his pen in exasperation*): When I say 'no', then

I mean 'no'. I am not in the habit of going back on my word. (*Picking his pen back up.*) Is that understood?

GERMAINE (*shaking*): No.

ALBERT (*looking up in surprise*): No?

GERMAINE (*courageously*): No. (*Pause. With effort she continues courageously.*) No. As I said, I need to speak with you. (*He shows signs of anger.*) You're not going to shut me up this time, like you usually do, by frightening me.

ALBERT (*with derision*): Frighten you? Do you think I'm going to eat you up or something?

GERMAINE (*shaking*): This time it's a question of my child and I won't back down so easily.

ALBERT (*with derision*): Your child! She's also my child, I believe! I think I'm a good father. Tell me, if you think I'm such a terrible father!

GERMAINE: May I sit down? I'm shaking so much, I'm not sure I can stand up any longer.

(*She collapses into an armchair.*)

ALBERT (*getting up, going over to her and, with a hint of a smile, placing a hand on her shoulder*): Not even the strength of a chicken! And you want to be the equal of men! My poor dear!

(*He bends over and gives her a kiss on the forehead.*)

GERMAINE (*a little calmer*): You know full well that I've always been scared of you. You can be so bad-tempered, so violent.

(*Albert sits down on the arm of the chair.*)

ALBERT (*gently*): So, what now?

GERMAINE (*confidently*): Now, to the matter of our daughter ...

ALBERT (*standing up impatiently*): I've told you, I don't know how many times, I will never consent to this marriage. There's no point in going on about it. You know full well that when I say 'no', I mean 'no'. (*He goes back to work.*)

GERMAINE: And what makes you think it's all right to accept your decisions without any discussion? Especially when it's such a serious issue. With a marriage it's a whole life that's at stake. Why should it be up to you to make the decisions about your daughter's life, about whom she should fall in love with? (*All the while Albert is working and gives a snort of derision. Germaine is offended.*) That's right, answer me with rudeness! Being rude isn't an argument! Just because you try to shut someone up by being rude, doesn't stop them having an opinion!

ALBERT (*working at his desk*): You can think what you like, as long as you don't go on about it.

GERMAINE (*shaking*): Albert, you are mistaken … you are mistaken if you think things are going to carry on like this. You know, sometimes I can't bear it any longer.

ALBERT: Ah, so you can't bear it any longer? And what can't you bear any longer? A husband who provides you with a comfortable house, servants, clothes, money whenever you ask him for it …?

GERMAINE: There's more to life than money. And anyway, if you give me what I need, then I think I've already paid you back. Everybody says I'm beyond compare as a housewife.

ALBERT (*interrupting with sarcasm*): If you only listened to what people say. They just want to flatter you!

GERMAINE: You can't pretend that for the twenty years that we've been married I haven't known how to keep a good house – and all whilst spending less than everybody else! And haven't I always spared you any worries?

ALBERT: On the contrary, there's been no shortage of worries! When a man like me endlessly grafts away all day long and then carries on working nearly every evening after dinner, he has the perfect right ….

GERMAINE (*trembling*): Perhaps I would have preferred a man who grafts less and pays more attention to me. A little less comfort and … (*pensively*) a little more love.

ALBERT (*with irony*): Oh, yes, fine words indeed. That's all it ever is with you women – just words!

GERMAINE (*offended*): If you hold women in such contempt, then why do you bother with them at all? It's so easy for you to dismiss them: 'Women, eh?! Huh! Women!', but just imagine trying to get on without women in your life. You're a fine one! You wouldn't even know how to cook a steak, remove a stain from your waistcoat or sew on a button.

ALBERT: And that's the only reason we put up with your never-ending sentimentality.

GERMAINE: You can't really say that my 'never-ending sentimentality' has ever been a great burden to you. I don't think I've been one of those who bore their husbands with, 'Do you love me?' Ever since I gave birth to my daughter …

ALBERT (*cutting her short*): So, I'm not important to you any more? Well, thank you!

GERMAINE (*unsettled*): That's not what I meant. I meant to say that ever since I've been able to hold our child in my arms,that has given me comfort, in spite of everything else.

ALBERT (*raising his head suddenly*): Everything else?

GERMAINE (*very quickly*): Your coldness, your temper.

ALBERT (*bitterly*): You might say that you're one of those women who is more of a mother than a wife.

GERMAINE (*violently*): What do you know about that? Who knows what it would have been like if you had been different?

ALBERT (*angrily*): There we are, that's decided then! I'm not going to be allowed to work this evening!

GERMAINE (*courageously*): No, you won't be allowed to work, as long as our child is crying.

ALBERT: Still?

GERMAINE: Yes, still. And she'll carry on with it! God knows, I'm not one of those women who gives in to their children on everything. The power that I didn't have to stand up to you, I had when it mattered for Jeannine, when it was for her sake! And I have it again today for her, because it's a question of her happiness.

ALBERT (*with derision*): Her happiness?! Always these grand statements! Don't make me laugh. You women don't half exaggerate … as if a twenty-year-old child knows what's best for her! Marry in haste, repent at leisure!

GERMAINE: But …

ALBERT: Come now, do I have to prove it to you? (*with a patronizing tenderness*) My dear wife, wasn't it the case that before we got married, you gave your poor innocent heart to Eugène Grandier? And when your father would not allow you to become engaged to him because his father had gone bankrupt – in those days, such things counted for something – did you not agree to marry me instead? (*She makes a movement as if to reply, but he continues.*) Did that prevent you from loving me? Did that prevent you from being happy?

GERMAINE (*profoundly*): Do you think I was happy?

ALBERT (*cross*): I really don't know what's wrong with you!

GERMAINE (*upset*): No, you really don't, do you? You don't know at all! You're not aware of anything! You don't understand how your own little girl can be in love and how she can be loved by a decent young man. The heart is full of things that are corrupted by life's unpleasantnesses, the same old lies that wear us down. (*forgetting who she's speaking to*) To be in love for the first time, to give yourself completely in spite of everything, to prize the one you love, to trust, to believe in everything: in him, in life, to think of him as beautiful and good, for there to be nothing but laughter, hope and tenderness …

ALBERT (*angrily, in a low voice*): You're just making it up!

GERMAINE (*dreamily, lost in her memories*): You have no idea why it's this person and not that person, why it's this particular face, these particular eyes, that particular voice, that has this effect on you. That makes you go weak at the knees when he comes near, makes your heart ache so deliciously. It makes you crazy, dizzy, dazzled, happy … Even if the love is unrequited, it is nonetheless marvellous, to love and nothing else. To have this desire and to sacrifice oneself to it. You would die with a smile on your face. You want to cry out, 'Thank you, God', just for feeling completely fulfilled. And then, if you know that the love is returned, oh, that is just too good to be true. Yes, you think, that would be too good to be true, that will never happen, God would never allow such happiness … such a complete and fulfilled life … (*with a sob*) And, indeed … he does not allow it. Almost never, very rarely. He didn't allow it in my case. And then afterwards, once Father had ruined everything, I married you.

ALBERT (*raging*): Second-best then am I? Well, thank you very much! It's been an absolute pleasure!

GERMAINE (*confused*): You knew very well that I was in love with Eugène Grandier. I told you that when we got engaged.

ALBERT: Oh yes, you certainly did. But … not like that!

GERMAINE (*animated*): It was completely innocent! We didn't even exchange kisses – not even in jest. We held hands, that was all.

ALBERT (*raging*): I think that's quite enough! The Devil take me if I'd known you loved him like that …

GERMAINE (*interrupting him animatedly*): Did you ever ask me?

ALBERT (*continuing*): … that you held him in your heart like that.

GERMAINE (*a little fiercely*): At least I still have a heart.

ALBERT: Do you think I enjoy seeing you standing there trembling and speaking to me in that tone of voice about this young man …

GERMAINE (*smiling faintly*): A young man … he'll be forty-five now … and I've never seen him again.

ALBERT (*violently*)*: Maybe it would have been better if you had seen him. He's probably bald … and with a paunch! That's always disgusted you. (*Slapping his forehead.*) It's really too much, after twenty years of marriage, for a chap to have to listen to his wife talking like this about a scoundrel … before your engagement as well!

(**It's important that Albert has remained slim with a full head of hair.*)

GERMAINE (*with bitterness*): Is it my fault that you never managed to rid me of his memory? That you did nothing to make me forget? You thought you only had to appear, to call out ...

ALBERT (*acidly*): An honest woman ...

GERMAINE (*with a touching simplicity*): I am an honest woman, Albert. I am an honest woman. Not a single thought of betrayal has passed through my mind – I can't be reproached for that! But it's one thing to be in control of one's thoughts and another to be in control of one's heart.

ALBERT: I've heard it all now! Why don't you just say that you don't love me, that you've never loved me! Just say it!

GERMAINE (*tearfully*): Why should I say something that isn't true? I love you very much, Albert, I love you as the man to whom I promised my whole life before God, to whom I have borne children, with whom I have wept, when together (*her voice starts trembling*) we laid one of those children in a coffin ...

ALBERT (*quietly*): Shut up.

GERMAINE (*passionately*): I love you as my husband and everything that represents, all things considered, through all the troubles, the arguments, the joy, the grief, the successes and the failures. I love you very much, like a part of myself, like a part of my children. My life is tied to yours. You can make me tremble with your temper, frustrate me with your pig-headedness. I have cried on your account, Albert, without telling you, because tears only irritate you. You are my husband and I love you.

ALBERT (*reassured*): Very well then. What now?

GERMAINE (*gently*): It's just that I don't love you in the way I could have loved. I have not been happy in the way that I could have been happy. (*dreamily*) This flower of joy that was stolen from me, this blanket of love, this precious thing. (*reaching a quick crescendo*) This blossoming, this laughter, this joy, this passion, this belief, everything that I didn't have and that I could have had and that I wanted to have, well ... (*decisively*) that will not be denied my daughter. She is in love and she is loved. She has a chance to be happy and she will be happy. This marriage that you're against, Albert, that you object to without any reasons, it will happen. I want it to.

ALBERT (*at his desk, slapping his forehead*): And I say this marriage won't take place. I do not want it to. I think I'm the master of the house, am I not?

GERMAINE: No.

ALBERT (*stunned*): No?

GERMAINE: No. You are the master of your own life. You are not the master of your daughter's life. You do not have the right to deprive her of her happiness for no reason.

(*A pause.*)

ALBERT (*with difficulty*): I have my reasons.

GERMAINE (*coldly*): Oh?

ALBERT (*more forcefully*): Yes, I have my reasons.

GERMAINE (*ironic and cold*): And might one be permitted to know those reasons?

ALBERT (*disconcerted*): No.

GERMAINE (*with increasing irony*): Ah!

ALBERT: No. (*Pause.*) No. I can't tell you. It's a matter of honour.

GERMAINE (*shrugging her shoulders*): Oh, really?

ALBERT (*imitates*): What, don't you trust me?

GERMAINE (*strongly*): No. Not exactly. You see I can't trust you.

ALBERT: It's too much! What do you mean?

GERMAINE: Precisely because I know the reasons.

ALBERT (*disconcerted*): Oh?

GERMAINE: Yes. (*Long pause. Germaine, ironically.*) Well, aren't you going to ask me what they are?

ALBERT (*very embarrassed*): No.

GERMAINE (*ironic, quietly*): No?

ALBERT: No. (*Changing the subject.*) What womanly nonsense.

GERMAINE: You think so? Don't you really mean, manly nonsense, Albert, manly nonsense? (*Short pause.*) What. Haven't you got an answer?

(*He puts down his pen and rummages through his papers.*)

ALBERT (*finally*): I would like to work now, if you don't mind. I have work to do.

GERMAINE (*authoritatively*): Your work can wait. (*with intensity*) Albert, we have never before been as honest as this with each other. We have never before spoken like this as equals. You scared me so much. I simply went along with everything without saying a word. (*Pause.*) Do you know what I mean by 'everything'?

ALBERT (*turning away and pretending to work*): No.

GERMAINE (*upset*): I would never have spoken to you like this if it hadn't been a matter of Jeannine's happiness. I have felt alone with everything without a single word. Today is the very first time. You might have thought that I wasn't at all interested.

ALBERT (*bitter and pained*): If you kept quiet, perhaps it was because you didn't love me enough for it to matter much to you that I ... (*He stops suddenly.*)

GERMAINE (*sadly*): Spit it out then! 'That I cheated on you'. I know full well that you cheated on me and not just the once either.

ALBERT (*protesting*): Oh!

GERMAINE (*with authority*): And not just the once! Do you really think I didn't know? As if a woman with a modicum of intelligence would not know when her husband is thinking of another woman, of when he is with another woman!

ALBERT (*bitter*): If you had loved me, you would have been upset.

GERMAINE (*gently*): That's not my style. (*Almost in spite of herself.*) And how do you know that I didn't cry when I was alone? (*Short pause.*) All the tears I shed when you weren't there ... (*Pulling herself together.*) But perhaps you're right after all to say that perhaps I wouldn't have been able to put up with it, perhaps I would have cried in front of you, if I had loved you more, if you had been the man of my choice and not my father's.

ALBERT (*with anguish*): Germaine!

GERMAINE (*softly*): Do you understand why I don't want my daughter to suffer what I did and have her marriage of love denied her? Forgive me for saying it like this, Albert (*with tenderness*) my husband, but perhaps you would not have cheated on me, if I had loved you more, as well, and perhaps you would not have gone elsewhere in search of love, in search of the happiness I didn't give you? But (*with passion*) you never asked it of me! (*Silence. Germaine, slowly.*) We both made a sensible marriage (*smiling sadly*) a good, practical, sensible marriage, like a comfy old woollen jumper.

ALBERT (*animated*): It's worn well though.

GERMAINE (*smiling sadly*): Yes, except all the ladies prefer something out of silk, you know. It's a silk dress that I dream of for my daughter.

ALBERT: You're not still on about that? Even though you know, Germaine, *because* you know ... well, I don't understand it, I don't understand it any more.

GERMAINE (*politely*): What don't you understand? You don't understand that even though you had an affair with Madame Morin, I'm still happy that our daughter marries Edward Morin?

ALBERT (*getting up*): I'm in the right here, for God's sake! If you had a moral compass, like I do ...

GERMAINE (*with a melancholy smile*): Do you really think that, of the two of us, it's me who lacks a moral compass?

ALBERT (*embarrassed*): Let's not talk about the past. Let's not go back over the past. It's less a matter of the past than ...

GERMAINE (*forcefully*): Than what?

ALBERT (*picking up the thread again*): I behaved badly. I admit that. I gave in to temptation. But it's all in the past now! It was twelve years ago.

GERMAINE (*with a bitter irony*): Yes, there is a statute of limitation. Isn't that what you call it?

ALBERT: I made sure never to see Madame Morin again. With your brains you should realize that this affair is now long behind me. It's a long time since we've seen the Morins. Is it my fault that our children have got to know each other and fallen in love? What can you expect in a town like Paris? But, anyway, don't you realize how awful, how intolerable it would be if our children … and for you … if you loved me, if you hadn't become obsessed with this idea.

GERMAINE (*with melancholic irony*): You can't make me jealous about this any more.

ALBERT (*painfully*): Please … don't make fun of me.

GERMAINE (*vibrantly*): I can assure you, I'm not in a laughing mood. I simply know one thing: my daughter is suffering. And I have watched Edward, he's nothing like his mother, he's a good lad with a heart of gold. He is worthy of our child. When I think of our child's happiness, I don't think of you nor me … nor of the love that this woman stole from me for a time, nor of the tears I shed. You, me, her, you see we all step back into the wings. We step out of the limelight and leave it for the new generation. These young ones have each other. They are so much in love, they are devoted to each other. I will forgive everything, I will forget everything. I don't even know if there's anything to forgive any more. I don't even know any more if you weren't always the husband I needed. I am nothing more than a mother who loves … if you had loved like that, like a mother, you would understand!

(*The tears softly run down her cheeks and she places her face in her hands on the table.*)

ALBERT (*overcome, standing up and placing a hand on her shoulder*): My dear wife …

GERMAINE (*lifting her head*): I know that it will be awkward for you and for her … and for me. But the Morins no longer live in Paris. We wouldn't have to see them very much. And this discomfort, this shame, this remorse … won't you just put it all behind you? For the sake of your daughter's happiness …

ALBERT (*gently*): Germaine …

GERMAINE (*very quietly*): Her happiness … like I never had! (*They both have pained expressions.*) You agree? (*Albert's expression softens. Then Germaine, full of joy, her face lights up.*) Can I go and tell her?

ALBERT (*tenderly*): Yes, in a moment. Just stay a little. (*She sits down next to him. He seems bashful.*) Tell me, we've still had some good times together, haven't we? I wasn't always bad-tempered ... or unfaithful. (*Pause.*) And I do love you very much, you know, in spite of ... in spite of what you know. Tell me you don't really regret marrying me? (*with an almost comic jealousy*) Tell me that you don't still think about this young Eugène?

GERMAINE (*smiling in spite of herself, tenderly*): You're crazy!

ALBERT (*moved*): If only you knew, in spite of how I am ... all my faults, if only you knew that you are always in my heart. I know that I've never told you that often enough. I've never told myself often enough. I didn't dare to. I didn't have the time. Being a husband, though that *is* something, all the same, isn't it? (*She goes to stand up.*) Stay a little longer.

GERMAINE (*affectionately teasing him*): I thought you wanted to work?

ALBERT (*leaning towards her, very quietly*): I ... I love you so much, my darling.

CURTAIN

The Great Terror (*La Grande épouvante*, 1916)

André de Lorde and Henri Bauche

Characters:
Tâni
Frank Burton
Warden
Harris
Williams
Amann
Parker, detective
James, servant
Coroner
Policeman
Miss Evelyn Burton

ACT ONE

A cosy room in a London Colonial club. Dark panelling. On the walls hang Egyptian and Indian landscapes. Tables, coffee tables, leather armchairs, all expensively sober and comfortable. On one coffee table there is a glass and two bottles. Upstage centre is a large doorway, leading to a lit corridor on the walls of which can be seen a collection of tribal weapons. To the right of the doorway, at the back, there is a large window through which can be seen London by night. Downstage right there is a door, downstage left another door. On one of the tables are newspapers and books.

A man in evening dress, Major Warden, is standing in front of a window, his back to the audience. There is also James, a servant in livery.

WARDEN (*standing in front of the window*): What a night! Good God, such filthy weather!

JAMES: Oh, Sir, in London it's quite normal for this time of year.

WARDEN: Very true. (*Pause.*) What time is it?

JAMES: Nearly nine o'clock.

WARDEN: Thank you. Fetch me *The Times*!

JAMES: Of course, Sir.

(*He exits.*)

WARDEN (*alone, he goes over to the fireplace*): Brr! You can feel the cold just by looking at the fog.

JAMES (*entering*): Here's *The Times*, Major.

(*Warden, thanking him with a nod of the head, takes the newspaper and starts to read. Silence. Sound of the wind. In the distance, the noise of a bus passing can be heard. Then, the sound of a door closing. Harris enters by the door on the right. Warden does not move.*)

HARRIS: Ah, there you are, Warden ...

WARDEN: Pardon?

HARRIS: I thought you were sleeping. Burton hasn't arrived yet then?

WARDEN: No. Are you expecting him?

HARRIS: Yes. We're off to a musical evening with his sister.

WARDEN: Do you like that kind of thing?

HARRIS: It passes the time.

WARDEN: And, of course, Miss Evelyn is rather pretty, isn't she?

HARRIS: She is charming.

WARDEN: And rich too!

HARRIS: Well, that's perfectly possible ...

(*Silence.*)

WARDEN: I was out shooting yesterday. He was there too.

HARRIS: Who?

WARDEN: Burton.

HARRIS: Ah, sure. He often goes.

WARDEN: Yes, he's a first class marksman, distinctly first class!

HARRIS: Oh, yes, we're not short of good marksmen in the British Army.

WARDEN: Yes, but there's not another like him. When he was over in Egypt in the army ...

(*There is noise on the staircase at the back, off stage.*)

HARRIS: There we are, that must be him now, I heard him on the stairs.

(He goes to the door upstage and has a quick look.)

Yes, it's Burton!

(Evelyn Burton enters, followed by Frank Burton. Frank is in evening dress, Evelyn in a ballgown.)

FRANK: Good evening!
WARDEN: Good evening, Burton, it seems that you won't be joining us for poker this evening.
FRANK: No, I'm accompanying my sister to Lady Hampton's.
EVELYN: Yes, Frank's accompanying me this evening, playing the role of a good father! (*to Warden*) Good evening, Major, are you well?

(The Major bows and shakes Evelyn's hand.)

EVELYN (*to Harris*): Good evening, Mr. Harris.
HARRIS: Good evening, Miss Evelyn.
WARDEN (*to Frank*): A good idea, Burton, to bring Miss Evelyn here. A pretty female face lights the place up. (*to Evelyn*) But we're embarrassed to receive you like this ...
EVELYN: Why?
WARDEN: Why, it's like a public house! There's tobacco!
HARRIS (*picking up the thread*): And alcohol!
EVELYN (*smiling*): That does not bother me, as long as I don't have to drink it.
HARRIS: Oh, you have nothing to fear from me. I can't stand the stuff!
WARDEN: Unlike our friend Major Williams!
HARRIS (*smiling*): Oh, yes, him ...
FRANK: I thought he would be here ...
WARDEN: He'll be on his way.
HARRIS (*to Evelyn*): Whenever you would like to leave, I'm all yours.
FRANK: Oh, let's wait a little. I've arranged to meet someone.
WARDEN: Ah!
FRANK: Someone who you've certainly heard people talking about. Doctor Tâni.
HARRIS (*searching his memory*): Tâni?
WARDEN: I know that name!
FRANK: Of course. He's the Egyptian doctor who has settled here in London, in Kensington, for a few months now.
HARRIS: Ah! The famous doctor ...
EVELYN: That's him!
WARDEN: Yes, I remember now!
FRANK: There's been so much about him in the papers.
WARDEN: Isn't he the one who lives in that extraordinary house?

FRANK: Exactly. It's a house that belonged to another Egyptian before him. Part of it has been built underground. Inside it has been furnished and decorated like a house on the banks of the Nile. I've often been there. It's really very strange. There are all sorts of things there. Mummies, for example, and also this strange lighting that gives everything a most queer appearance.

HARRIS: And doesn't he also have his own tomb, nearby him in a vault in the house? I'm sure I read that somewhere. And it's always open, ready for him at any time.

FRANK: Yes, that's part of its uniqueness.

WARDEN: And its notoriety!

FRANK: He's had some strange animals sent over from Egypt. He makes up his remedies with their blood.

WARDEN (*smiling*): And fools buy them at inflated prices.

EVELYN (*also smiling*): Everyone has to make a living!

WARDEN: There are too many people these days who swear by these stupid ideas that are as old as the hills. Magic, sorcery, occultism …

HARRIS: Excuse me. Occultism is really very interesting!

WARDEN: Interesting? You think so?

HARRIS: Certainly!

WARDEN: That depends on your point of view. As far as I'm concerned, I don't very much care for all that. These other-worldly things. Believe me, they are best left well alone.

EVELYN: Yes, they are indeed a trifle unpleasant …

WARDEN: Yes, unpleasant … even unsettling.

HARRIS (*ironically*): Really?

WARDEN (*to Frank*): And what's he like this … doctor? He must be terrifying?

FRANK: Not at all …

EVELYN: You've seen that Mulatto chap in the small ads in the papers? That fellow with the completely white eyes, who claims to reveal the past and the future? He's just like that!

HARRIS (*to Evelyn*): Do you know him then?

EVELYN: We made the crossing back from Egypt together.

WARDEN (*to Frank, with some surprise*): Burton, are you a friend of this shady gentleman?

FRANK: He's not exactly a friend. But he was a great help with certain projects I undertook over there in ancient Egypt.

WARDEN: Ah, yes, your book on the Third Dynasty. And why is he coming here this evening?

FRANK (*slightly nervously*): I wanted to introduce you to him. He would like, if possible, to become a member of the club.

WARDEN (*coldly*): Ah!

FRANK: But why not?

WARDEN: I'm not sure that everybody would feel comfortable with that …

(*Enter Williams in a rush. His face is red and his manner is wild. He slams the door behind him. He is wearing a coat and hat.*)

WILLIAMS (*without seeing Evelyn, shouting*): James! Hey, James! Damned fool! (*Suddenly noticing Evelyn.*) Oh! I beg your pardon!

(*He removes his hat and stands still, embarrassed. Evelyn smiles, good humouredly.*)

FRANK (*presenting Williams to Evelyn*): Major Williams. (*to Williams*) My sister, Miss Evelyn Burton.

WILLIAMS: Charmed!

JAMES (*entering*): Sir …

WILLIAMS (*gruffly, handing him his hat*): Here you are, take this.

(*James takes the hat and helps Williams take off his coat.*)

JAMES: Shall I fetch the whisky?

(*Williams looks at Evelyn.*)

EVELYN: Oh, Major Williams, don't be concerned on my account.

WILLIAMS (*bowing his head*): Miss Burton.

HARRIS (*pointing to Warden's glass*): You can see that drink has already been taken here!

WILLIAMS (*to James*): Very well, then. Yes, off you go!

(*James takes the coat and hat and exits by the door at the back. He returns almost immediately and goes toward the door on stage left.*)

WARDEN: Tell me, James, will the President be returning this evening, as he said in his letter?

JAMES: Yes, Mr. Warden.

WARDEN: Good. Thank you.

(*James leaves by the door stage left.*)

FRANK (*to Williams*): You don't seem to be in a very good mood, Williams! What's wrong? Is there an ill wind blowing?

WILLIAMS: No, no, it's nothing. I don't know what's the matter with me today. I'm all on edge.

WARDEN: Everyone has bad days.

WILLIAMS: Every day is a bad day for me!

(*James enters with a bottle of whisky, a glass and a soda bottle.*)

HARRIS: Here comes something to cheer you up.

WILLIAMS: In any case, in this weather it can't do any harm, even if it's just to warm you up.

JAMES (*in hushed tones to Williams*): Shall I leave the bottle?

WILLIAMS: But of course, you fool!

(*James exits, after serving the whisky.*)

HARRIS (*to Evelyn*): The Major can't handle the weather in London. He misses Egypt too much!

WARDEN: His beloved Egypt!

WILLIAMS (*with a sigh*): Ah! Egypt! Alexandria, Cairo … oh happy youth!

FRANK: Come on, now. Don't get sentimental! You'll soon be going back there.

WILLIAMS: Me?

FRANK: At least that's what I heard.

WILLIAMS: I'm not sure …

HARRIS: But seeing as you miss it …

WILLIAMS: I miss the old days. There you are! But going back now, that's another thing. Any way it's the only place, you know, where they appreciate the beauty of life, the freedom to be your own master, to do whatever you want. But you can have a bit too much of that sometimes. Yes, there comes a time when you have to move on.

(*Silence.*)

FRANK: Williams, I'm expecting somebody … somebody you know.

WILLIAMS (*make a gesture of indifference*): I don't know anyone any more … apart from the members of this miserable club where you can lose whatever you like.

WARDEN: Always the life and soul of the party!

FRANK: But you do. He's an Egyptian. A man you knew in Egypt.

WILLIAMS (*looking at him suspiciously*): Me?

FRANK: Doctor Tâni.

WILLIAMS (*suddenly getting up*): Tâni … (*Long pause.*) What does he want coming here?

FRANK: Oh, you don't seem exactly thrilled at the prospect?

WILLIAMS (*repeating himself with increasing anger*): What does he want here?

FRANK (*awkwardly*): What? I don't suppose he means any harm ... At his request, I am going to introduce him to everyone this evening. He would like to become a member of the club.

WILLIAMS (*violently*): Him? Are you mad!?

WARDEN: Calm down, Williams, calm down!

HARRIS (*to Evelyn*): He's always losing his temper like this. (*to Williams, very softly, but with a hint of deep irritation*) Williams, you're being a bore!

WILLIAMS: But you don't know anything about this man.

FRANK: Oh, but we do!

WARDEN: We have it on good authority ...

WILLIAMS (*to Warden*): No! You don't know him.

WARDEN: He's eccentric, a bit of a quack, perhaps.

WILLIAMS: A quack? It's worse than that!

FRANK: Oh!

(*Williams gradually calms down, but his voice remains shaky.*)

WILLIAMS: I'm telling you ... I'm telling you. He's not a man you want anything to do with. There were things that happened over there ...

HARRIS: In Egypt?

WILLIAMS: Yes. It was said he had the evil eye.

FRANK: Oh! Really! The evil eye!

HARRIS: We don't believe in things like that in Europe!

WILLIAMS: He brings unhappiness with him. That's right, he brings unhappiness! Anybody who has had anything to do with him ...

FRANK (*interrupting*): That's ridiculous!

WARDEN: I didn't think you were the superstitious type!

WILLIAMS: I'm not superstitious! But there are some things you have to accept! There is something not right about this man! Even animals are afraid of him. Yes, it's true, dogs avoid him ...

FRANK: Oh really! This is infantile! (*He laughs.*)

WILLIAMS: Don't laugh, Burton!

FRANK: Oh, come, come!

WILLIAMS: No, Burton, no! You mustn't laugh at things like that. Very often animals have a deep sense of when anything is wrong, anything evil or malevolent. Besides I've heard things about him ...

HARRIS: Such as?

WILLIAMS: Terrible stories! He was always to be seen with a sinister individual who he used to refer to as his master, a certain Storah, a hypnotist, a thief ... and it all ended badly!

FRANK (*shrugging his shoulders*): Now, look here!

WILLIAMS: But it's true! In any case, I don't want to see him. No, I don't want to ... I'm leaving!

(*He finishes his drink and gets up.*)

HARRIS: You shouldn't do that!

WILLIAMS: Why not?

HARRIS: It'll look as if you're afraid of him!

WILLIAMS (*violently*): I'm afraid of no one! No one, do you hear!

WARDEN: We know that! There's no need to shout ...

HARRIS: It's precisely because you're not afraid that there's no need to behave like that.

WILLIAMS: You think so? Very well, I'll stay then!

JAMES (*entering by the door at the back, carrying a coat*): Doctor Tâni to see Mr. Burton.

(*Williams physically recoils. Warden watches him and smiles.*)

FRANK: Yes.

(*The men all rise and move apart. A moment of silence. Tâni appears in the doorway. He stays there, motionless.*)

FRANK (*approaching Tâni*): Please come in, Doctor.

(*Tâni slowly enters.*)

FRANK (*to Warden and Harris, then to Tâni*): Allow me to introduce you. Doctor Tâni, Major Warden, Mr. Harris. (*Handshakes. To Williams.*) I believe you know each other ...

WILLIAMS (*dryly*): Yes, yes, most certainly.

TÂNI (*with irony*): It's been a long time. I had the great pleasure of meeting the Major in Egypt. (*Turning to Evelyn.*) Miss Eveyln ...

EVELYN: Good evening, doctor, how do you do?

(*She offers him her hand. Ceremoniously Tâni kisses it.*)

TÂNI: I am most happy to see you again! It is the first time that we meet in Europe.

EVELYN: That is right. How time flies!

TÂNI: But the memory remains.

FRANK (*to Tâni*): I have explained to these gentlemen that you are a great scholar.

TÂNI: I have studied a great deal ...

HARRIS: Not only the history of Ancient Egypt, but of the other, more mysterious spheres of knowledge too. Is that not the case, doctor?

TÂNI: Well, these other, more mysterious spheres of knowledge … (*Pause.*) But let's not talk about that. You are officers, men of action, such things are of no interest to you.

HARRIS: But on the contrary! They interest me greatly! It seems that there are some extraordinary phenomena …

TÂNI: I'll say it again. It would be better left alone. Now is neither the time nor place. There's no need … not unless you wish to pass through the Doors of the Night!

(*During this latest exchange, Williams has shown signs of becoming agitated and has emptied his glass many times.*)

WILLIAMS (*smiling nervously*): Ah yes, the Doors of the Night? And what lies behind those I wonder?

TÂNI: There lies … there lies the Path of Mystery.

WILLIAMS (*still smiling*): Yes, it's as if I'm actually there! And where does it lead, this Path of Mystery?

TÂNI: For some people it is the path to enlightenment, for others it is the path to fear.

WARDEN: Oh! What a strange expression!

WILLIAMS: Very strange! Very strange indeed! And stupid! Ah!

(*He laughs nervously for a long time.*)

WARDEN (*with a glance towards Tâni, as if to apologize for Williams's bad behaviour, to Frank, in hushed tones*): Leave him. You know it's always the same when he's been drinking.

HARRIS (*to Tâni*): I also studied once upon a time – oh, very superficially – certain spiritualist phenomena. There are certainly some very troubling incidents. I have read Professor Sélim-Phràh's book on Modern Magic.

TÂNI: It is a serious, well-researched volume.

HARRIS (*to Tâni*): For example, is it true that, through pure will, pure will alone, it is possible to produce phenomena such as being able to move physical objects?

TÂNI: Yes.

WILLIAMS (*laughing*): Ha! Ha!

HARRIS (*to Williams*): There are certain things that are a mystery to us! There's no need to dismiss them as ridiculous, just because they are beyond our wit!

WARDEN: Very true, very true! In India, the Yoghis, the Bagaths, the Fakirs, can all perform astounding feats!

TÂNI: Terrifying ...

WARDEN: At such times it is as if they have power over the forces of nature, living beings and even inanimate objects. (*To Frank and Evelyn.*) Isn't that true?

FRANK: I have certainly seen some extraordinary things.

EVELYN: Oh! I've never seen anything like that myself and I don't want to either.

HARRIS: They say that they can make objects move just by looking at them and that they can make these wonderful plants grow in an instant, with strange flowers that miraculously blossom ...

WILLIAMS: A trick! Swindle!

FRANK (*appearing*): Come on now, Williams!

WILLIAMS: It's just a way of getting money out of you! The police would do better to round them all up! They're nothing but crooks!

TÂNI: Crooks, Major Williams? You really think so?

WILLIAMS: They are no more able to do these things than the next man.

TÂNI: You are mistaken!

WILLIAMS: Don't imagine for a minute that I'd let myself be taken in by these conjuring tricks.

(*A knock at the door stage left – James enters.*)

JAMES: Gentlemen, the President is here.

FRANK: Ah, good!

WARDEN: Dear old Adams!

FRANK (*to Tâni, apologetically*): The president of our club has just returned from a long trip.

WARDEN: We must go and welcome him.

FRANK: Well then, I'll leave you for a minute.

WARDEN: Would you excuse us?

TÂNI: Why, of course!

(*The men exit.*)

EVEYLN (*after a pause*): Now, don't you go taking any notice of Mr. Williams. Men like that, you know, who have lived out in hot countries are often a little vulgar and get carried away. But deep down they are good people.

TÂNI (*seriously*): It doesn't do to be so vulgar with somebody who inhabits the higher echelons of science! (*Pause.*) No! The body must not rule over the mind ... but it matters little. (*Pause.*) I haven't seen you since our voyage.

EVELYN: No, that's right.

TÂNI: I am pleased to find you as radiant now as you were back then, in my country, on the banks of the Nile, the great eternal river that I will never see again!

EVELYN: Never again? How can you know that?

TÂNI: There are things I just know …

EVELYN (*with irony*): So you can see into the future?

TÂNI: No, not at all. Nobody can see into the future. Sometimes, however, it is possible to catch glimpses of it. If you like, perhaps I could show you how …

EVELYN: Oh! No! I'd rather not know!

TÂNI: Why not?

EVELYN: I don't like that sort of thing. It frightens me …

TÂNI: You, frightened, Miss Evelyn? You who were so brave back then during that terrible storm that caught us off the coast of Sicily? I can just see you, calm and smiling, in your white dress …

EVELYN: It wasn't as dangerous as all that! Besides, you were not frightened either!

TÂNI: Nothing bad could have happened to me. I knew that my time hadn't come …

EVELYN: You knew?

TÂNI: My knowledge is not so great, alas, unlike that of my beloved Master, who is now freed of the shackles of this life … But my power, the power that I got from him, this power is, all the same, immense … Do you not believe me?

(*He looks at her for a while. Then shouts can be heard from the side room behind the door, as the club members are leaving.*)

VOICES:

– Ah! Just a splash of soda!
– Your good health, President!
– Ah. Ah! Dear old Adams …
– Drink up then!
– That's enough, Williams, watch out!

(*Tâni remains motionless still looking at Evelyn.*)

EVELYN: Why are you looking at me like that?

TÂNI: I love you … (*He takes her by the hand. She gently withdraws it.*) I love you.

EVELYN (*embarrassed*): Don't say that!

TÂNI: I have loved you for a long time. If only you knew …

EVELYN: No! Don't talk like that! I don't like it!

TÂNI: I speak as I must speak! Why have you never come to see my house?

EVELYN: Well ... I know there are things at your house that are odd, strange ... a little too strange for my tastes.

TÂNI: Well, come with your brother then! Why don't you come with your brother some time? You must come with him the next time ...

EVELYN: We shall see ...

TÂNI: He must come this week.

EVELYN: That's not very likely. Frank has to go away.

TÂNI: What do you mean, 'go away'?

EVELYN: Yes, he has to go to Scotland for a few days.

TÂNI (*after a pause*): And he's leaving soon?

EVELYN: Tomorrow or the day after.

TÂNI: Ah! So he'll be leaving you? (*Pause.*) Very well then, you shall come when Mr Burton returns. Oh, I shall not forget that you owe me a visit. You must ... you must come and see me! (*A long pause, during which he stares at her in a strange fashion.*) I shall very much look forward to that!

FRANK (*coming back with Warden*): Dear old Adams, his travels seem to have done him the world of good.

WARDEN: I've never seen a fellow in such fine form!

(*At this moment the voices of Williams and Harris can be heard off stage.*)

VOICE OF HARRIS (*to Williams*): Yes indeed! I shall tell him ...

VOICE OF WILLIAMS: After all, it does concern you!

WILLIAMS (*enters, a little unsteady on his feet*): Yes! I shall tell him that such shenanigans are all very well in the hot, exotic countries like India or Egypt, playing to a bunch of gullible savages – and it must be said, as a friend! (*to Tâni*) Isn't that right?

(*Tâni does not reply. Smiling, he watches Williams.*)

FRANK (*to Warden*): He's terrible when he's been drinking!

WILLIAMS (*starting up again*): I, as you know, have a generous spirit ... I do understand everything. But I don't like having one put over on me. I don't like being made a fool of.

WARDEN: The President's champagne has already done that!

WILLIAMS (*increasingly getting worked up*): But here, if you have the audacity to force such things on people ... it's not enough simply to pull the wool over their eyes ... you have to ... you have to prove it! Do you hear? You have to prove it!

HARRIS (*stepping in*): That's enough!

TÂNI (*coldly*): Leave him!

WILLIAMS (*picks up a glass and speaks to Warden, whilst holding it in his hand*): They can make objects move just by looking at them. Ha! Ha! Ha! (*to Tâni*) Perhaps our magician here can make something move a little without touching it, just because he wants it to!

TÂNI: No!

WILLIAMS: But come now! Take this table … this chair … this …

TÂNI: No!

WILLIAMS (*grinning*): There you are!

TÂNI (*forcefully*): No, I don't want to! It takes great willpower … such reserves of energy!

WILLIAMS (*grinning to the others*): There, you see! These people, you only have to call their bluff …

TÂNI (*decisively*): Very well then! So be it! Major Williams, this glass … this glass you are holding …

WILLIAMS: Eh? So what? This glass?

TÂNI: Just look at it!

(*Williams looks at it. Little by little, under Tâni's gaze, his hand loosens its grip on the glass and, suddenly, the glass falls to the floor and shatters.*)

EVELYN (*frightened*): Ah!

HARRIS: Extraordinary!

WARDEN AND FRANK: Yes …

HARRIS: How on earth, did you …?

TÂNI: By force of will!

(*Silence.*)

HARRIS (*to Tâni, smiling, in hushed tones*): The Major seems to be an excellent stooge for this kind of thing.

WARDEN (*in a low voice to Harris*): Harris! No more!

WILLIAMS (*having heard, becomes furious*): A stooge? Me?! A stooge! I won't have you saying that! I won't have it! I'm not a stooge for the tricks of this … of this … (*to Tâni*) As for you, I will not allow you to make a fool of me ever again with your stupid tricks. No, I won't allow it! And you, especially, everyone knows you for what you are!

WARDEN (*intervening, to Williams*): That is enough!

WILLIAMS (*to Tâni*): Oh yes, everyone knows you for what you are! There should be a law against people like you coming to a decent club, into the company of gentlemen …

FRANK: Williams!

WILLIAMS: You're just like the other one … yes, the one that you call your master! He came to a bad end, didn't he? He came to a bad end!

TÂNI: Now, I'm telling *you* to shut up!

WILLIAMS (*shouting*): He was hanged! Yes, he was hanged! Hanged as a thief. And also because he ...

TÂNI (*enraged*): Shut up!

WILLIAMS (*suddenly stammering, as Tâni stares at him*): Because he ...

TÂNI: Major Williams, it is dangerous to speak ill of the dead. Take care that they don't come back to take revenge ... And when one has a past of one's own ...

(*He stops and stares at him.*)

WILLIAMS: What do you mean?

TÂNI: Out there, in the East, you are your own master to do whatever you desire. Whatever you desire. But sometimes, one goes a little too far ...

WILLIAMS (*violently*): Oh!

TÂNI: And if people knew what Major Williams got up to when he was in Khartoum seven years ago ...

WILLIAMS: You're lying!

(*He lunges at him, frothing at the mouth. Williams is restrained. Tâni does not move. He stares at Williams, who gradually becomes quiet, and shaking, sinks down to the floor and curls up in a ball.*)

WILLIAMS (*to the others*): No, no, leave me alone! I'm not going to do anything! (*more quietly*) I ... I won't do anything!

(*He collapses into an armchair, stage left.*)

FRANK (*to Harris and Warden*): Gentlemen, if I had imagined that such an incident ...

(*Harris, Warden and Evelyn speak almost together.*)

HARRIS: Indeed, very regrettable ...

WARDEN: In a club such as ours ...

EVELYN: Frank, we're leaving!

WARDEN (*very embarrassed, abrupt and slightly formally to Harris and Frank*): Gentlemen ... (*Pause.*) I am the eldest member here ... I ask you to hear me out ... this scene ... well, it must never happen again! Never. (*Pause. To Tâni.*) I would ask you to forget the whole thing!

TÂNI: Forget? Me? Certainly not! The soul of my master has been insulted! Who will now stop my master avenging himself?

(He bows quickly to Warden and Harris and returns to the door at the back. To Frank.) Burton, I hope I will see you again?

(He makes a vague gesture as if to take Evelyn's hand and bring it to his lips. Evelyn turns away slightly, without affection. He leaves. A very long pause.)

WARDEN *(approaching Williams with furrowed brows)*: As for you, Williams …

WILLIAMS: For the love of God, Warden, leave me alone! You too, Burton, just leave me … Oh! *(He slowly gets up.)* I don't know what I have … *(Pause. He looks at everyone with astonishment, then fearfully, distraught.)* Excuse me! *(He goes to move, then stops.)* Oh, that man! That man!

(He leaves slowly by the door at the back.)

FRANK: Gentlemen, I don't know what to say …

WARDEN: Is there any truth in what that man said?

HARRIS: Yes, what about his accusation against Major Williams?

FRANK: Anything is possible, given his passion for alcohol!

WARDEN: Yes … but if there is something else …

HARRIS: It has to be brought into the open!

WARDEN: I can't believe it. And besides, this Egyptian is a perfectly disagreeable sort.

FRANK: Once again, I do apologize!

(A noise is heard as if something is being torn.)

EVELYN *(with a shudder)*: Oh!

(Pause. Everyone looks around nervously.)

HARRIS: Listen!

(Then, suddenly, a terrible noise and a loud cry, followed by groaning.)

EVELYN: Oh, my God!

FRANK: What on earth can that be?

HARRIS *(runs to the door at the back)*: Wait! I shall have a look …

(He disappears.)

EVELYN: Oh, I'm frightened …

(The sound of voices, shouts, orders being given, footsteps, doors opening and closing.)

HARRIS *(appearing in the doorway, frightened, not entering)*: Come, quick! Warden! Burton! There's been a terrible accident! Major Williams ... on the stairs ... he must have slipped!

(*Warden runs out with Harris.*)

EVELYN (*grabbing hold of Frank*): Frank! Frank!
FRANK: Now, calm down!
EVELYN: It's that man who brought bad luck! He's taken his revenge!
FRANK: Revenge? What do you mean? Don't be silly!
EVELYN: I tell you, it's him!
FRANK: Not you too, believing in these ...? The Major was drunk. He couldn't have seen where he was putting his feet, and then ...
HARRIS (*reappearing*): He is dead.
EVELYN (*with a loud cry*): Dead!

(*Voices are heard.*)

VOICES:
– Put him down here!
– No ...
– If I tell you ...
– Has anyone gone to fetch a doctor?
– You know perfectly well it's no use ...
– It should have been prevented.
– No, nobody could have prevented it.

HARRIS (*to Evelyn*): Miss Evelyn, don't stay here! It's a terrible sight ...
EVELYN: Oh! Frank!
HARRIS: Come on now, please! Come on!

(*Just then Warden enters followed by men carrying Major Williams, dead. His face is crushed, a terrible sight.*)

EVELYN (*hiding in the arms of her brother*): What if it's true, though?!
FRANK: What?
EVELYN: His power! It would be terrible!
FRANK (*looking at Williams's corpse*): Terrible!

CURTAIN

ACT TWO

A low vaulted room in the Egyptian style with columns of hieroglyphics painted on the wall. At the back is a large door with two strong bolts. Downstage left is a small low door. On the right along the length of the wall is a stone staircase which leads up to another door near to the back wall. On the right hand wall near to this door above the staircase is a small barred window. Alongside the staircase is a sarcophagus. Another sarcophagus stands to the left of the door at the back. Between the door at the back and the left hand wall hangs a large, dark curtain.

Tables, chairs and a sofa.

A man with a terrible face, covered in scars and with the look of a mad man, is sitting facing the audience, his eyes staring and his fists clenching the side of his head.

A long pause.

The curtain moves slightly. Then the sound of barking can be heard, followed by the rattling of chains being strained. The man, who is sitting not far from the curtain, gives a start. He recoils as if seized by repugnance and terror.

AMANN (*watching the curtain*): Oh! There is no end to this groaning! (*A muffled cry from behind the curtains.*) Be quiet! Be quiet! Oh! Please, be quiet! (*The sound of wings beating against the bars of the cage, followed by a long almost human, groaning.*) I must … I must rest! (*Another cry.*) No … No! I can't take any more, I can't take any more!

(*Amann puts his hand to his head as if the noise is causing him painful blows to the head. Silence. Then, behind the door on the left, can be heard footsteps descending. The door opens. Tâni appears, shrouded in a large black cloak. He closes the door then stands absolutely still. He looks at the man without speaking. The man slowly turns his head towards Tâni.*)

AMAAN: It's the beast … the beast. She's been howling all night long. You must have been able to hear it up there on the street.

TÂNI: This place is so cut off it doesn't matter.

AMANN: Oh, Master! Why … why have you brought this terrible thing over from Egypt?

TÂNI (*smiling*): Does she frighten you?

AMANN: She very nearly tore my hand off …

TÂNI: Does it hurt much?

AMANN: Yes, it hurts.

TÂNI: That's a good thing. Suffering is a necessity … my master said, 'Suffering is the crucible of life'. (*From beneath his cape he pulls out a black package and places it on the table.*) There we are! It's becoming increasingly difficult to get hold of … there's a new gravedigger down at the Chinese cemetery in Whitechapel. The fool wouldn't listen to reason.

AMANN (*pointing to the curtain*): It's for her …

TÂNI: It's the only thing she can eat. She has to have flesh that has been long dead. You shall feed her. And afterwards you must draw some blood from her for the mixture …

AMANN: Yes, Master.

(*He goes over to the table to pick up the packet.*)

TÂNI: Tomorrow you must go over to the other cemetery yourself.

AMANN (*terrified*): No! Please, no!

TÂNI (*very calm*): You will go back to the other cemetery, just as you did before. And behind the wall of the church you'll knock at the old woman's door who will take you to the foundlings' workhouse.

AMANN: No … no … never! I won't do it again!

TÂNI: You will do it.

AMANN: No, No! The last time when I was very nearly caught I had a dream afterwards, a terrible dream! I was in prison … the rope … the hangman … the black hood placed over the head! No … no, I don't want to!

TÂNI (*slowly*): You won't go?

(*He stares at him for a long time.*)

AMANN: Don't look at me like that! Don't look at me like that!

(*Amann struggles against Tâni's control. His fists are clenched, he has rolling eyes, his head is tipped back. He grinds his teeth. He is about to throw himself at Tâni. Suddenly he stops, as if gripped by an iron hand. Amann grips the back of his neck with his hands, then his throat, then his forehead. Silence. His arms fall. He looks at Tâni. Then suddenly he sits up straight and cries out, completely transformed.*)

Yes! Yes! I shall go! I shall go and do whatever you wish.

Like I did before, just like before! Just like over there in Egypt with the Master ... Storah!

TÂNI: Silence!

AMANN (*exhausted*): I shall go! I shall go to the cemetery! And if there are no corpses then I'll take the living and turn them into corpses! Ah! Corpses ... corpses!

(*He falls to the ground roaring and foaming at the mouth. Then he is quite still, stiff as in a cataleptic fit.*)

TÂNI (*looking at him in silence*): Another fit! This happens every time now.

(*He gives Amann's body a gentle kick. The muffled sound of a doorbell is heard in the distance. Silence. The doorbell rings again. Tâni climbs the stairs to the right and leaves by the door at the top. He disappears. Silence again. Then Tâni's voice is heard, saying*):

Is that you Burton? At this time? Come in!

(*Frank Burton enters. He is in evening dress and a long black coat. Tâni offers him a seat.*)

FRANK: No, thank you. I won't be staying. I have to be at the club by eleven o'clock.

(*He notices Amann stretched out on the floor. He recoils.*)

TÂNI: Oh! It's nothing to worry about. He is susceptible to these fits ...

(*Tâni gestures towards Amann who automatically gets up. He remains standing, stock still, like an erect corpse. Tâni awakens him from his trance by waving his hands in front of his eyes. Amann looks around in confusion. Tâni mutters a few words in a strange guttural language. Then he says*):

TÂNI: I'm delighted to see you, my dear Burton. But I thought you were away on your travels.

FRANK: No, I was forced to remain here for ... (*He stops.*)

TÂNI: For?

FRANK: Major Williams's funeral.

TÂNI: Ah yes, the Major's funeral.

FRANK: Yes.

(*Pause.*)

TÂNI: You see, Burton, in ancient Egypt the dead were embalmed so that the corpse could not decompose at all. Alcohol was unknown then, it's one of the wonders of modern times. The Major's body won't decompose at all because all the alcohol he's drunk will perfectly preserve him. Ha, Ha!

(*He grins.*)

FRANK: I'd ask you not to speak about one of my friends in that manner. He may well have had his faults, but he was a friend all the same … and an Englishman!

TÂNI: Don't get worked up …

FRANK (*continuing*): And a friend who died in a rather strange manner.

(*He stops.*)

TÂNI: Strange? I was told that he fell down the stairs. Such things happen …

FRANK: Yes, such things happen, but in this case there are particular circumstances …

TÂNI: What do you mean?

FRANK: You were present at the time …

TÂNI: So, what of it?

FRANK: That ridiculous discussion! And your threats …

TÂNI (*grinning*): Threats? Surely you don't think there is a connection between this accident and my being there?

FRANK: Me? No! But if I ever thought you had anything to do with this accident … (*quickly*) I'd smash your face in!

TÂNI (*amused*): Oh! Really?

FRANK: Yes, because you'd be a despicable and dangerous creature that would have to be dealt with!

TÂNI: Dealt with? And who says that even when I'm dead I won't need to be feared anymore?

FRANK: Oh, I know … I'm used to these kinds of threats. You're always bandying them about. Well, it doesn't bother me. You don't scare me!

TÂNI: Fighting spirit, eh?

FRANK (*drily*): Let's leave it at that! I came here to tell you … … regarding this business with the Major … and I say again that I don't believe what they're saying … but there are coincidences – yes, I'll call them coincidences – albeit unfortunate ones …

TÂNI: Unfortunate ones?

FRANK (*continuing*): It would be best if we severed all relations.

TÂNI: Oh!

FRANK: And I came to ask you to return to me the papyrus scrolls that I entrusted to you.

TÂNI (*going to a desk and taking out some papyrus scrolls*): You mean these? (*Silence*.) Burton, are you standing by what you just said?

FRANK: Yes … I shan't come here again and I would ask that you no longer visit me …

TÂNI: Look, Burton, you can't be serious. This is me, who has such affection for you … and for your sister!

FRANK: My sister has nothing to do with it!

TÂNI: Burton, what have you got against me? You're quite mistaken! Your sister …

FRANK: What?

TÂNI: Ever since I first saw her over there in sun-scorched Egypt, so pretty, so graceful, so youthful, so beautiful, pure eyes … Listen to me, Burton, I'm a rich man … you know that … I am rich … very rich. And I've had to work so hard. Yes, I've had to work so hard just to get here. But I wanted to be here more than anything else. I have ambition and a love of science … The thirst for knowledge. But there is something else that is stronger than all of my knowledge and ambition … it's …

(*He stops*.)

FRANK: It's what?

TÂNI: Burton … your sister … Miss Evelyn … I love her! If you have no objection I would like to take her for my wife …

FRANK: Her? Evelyn? You're mad! How does a man like you set your sights on a young girl like her? Where are you from? Who are you? What did you do back there in Egypt? And what else were you up to? And how did you manage it? Besides, there are rumours …

TÂNI: Lies …

FRANK: Who knows? After all, as far as we're concerned you're racially inferior!

TÂNI (*reddening with anger*): Burton!

FRANK (*brutal*): Yes, racially inferior! Can you really see it working – a mulatto wanting to marry a young English girl?

TÂNI: Burton!

FRANK: And of all things, Evelyn! My dear Evelyn, the purest, most dignified, the best! Really! I can see that you won't admit that there's a gulf that separates you.

TÂNI (*with intense fury*): Nevertheless … if I wanted …

FRANK: That's enough!

TÂNI: If I wanted … if I wanted.. ! Now listen to me, Burton, regardless of what you wish, regardless of everything, even regardless of what she wants, she will come to me. And if I want it ... if I want it, she will love me!

FRANK: I pity you!

TÂNI: She will be mine! Mine! Now and for ever more!

FRANK: I won't even dignify that with a response!

(*He goes to leave.*)

TÂNI: Be careful, Burton!

FRANK: Are you threatening me?

TÂNI: Be careful!

FRANK: You don't scare me!

(*He starts to climb the staircase up towards the door at the top.*)

TÂNI (*stopping him*): No, not that way!

FRANK: What!

TÂNI: Not that way! Leave through this door!

(*He points to the door at the back, moves over to it and opens it. Tâni closes the door again after Frank. He immediately strikes a gong. Amann enters through the door on the left. Tâni signals to him without speaking. Amann opens the door at the back and leaves. Silence. Slowly, Tâni climbs the staircase as far as the small door at the top. He opens it. Evelyn is behind it. She is wrapped in a large coat. Tâni goes back down the staircase and stands in the centre of the room. Evelyn remains motionless behind the open door.*)

TÂNI (*calling her*): Evelyn!

(*She slowly comes down the staircase and stands at the foot of the stairs. Tâni goes towards her. She holds out her hand, he takes it and gently leads her to the sofa and makes her sit down. She removes her coat. Then he sits next to her. He takes her hand again, holding it tightly in his own. Evelyn looks at him with a pale and sad smile on her face.*)

TÂNI: Evelyn! Here you are, next to me, at my home, alone with me! I've longed for this moment ... Evelyn ... (*He takes her in his arms.*) Oh! How soft your young body is ... (*He holds her tightly against him.*) And your eyes ... such beautiful big eyes, so gentle, so pure, so deep ...

(*His face is pressed up against hers and he makes to kiss her on the lips. She does not resist but continues to smile, motionless. A short silence. Tâni looks passionately into her eyes.*)

TÂNI: How beautiful you are my dear Evelyn! (*He impulsively embraces her. Suddenly he gets up and retreats a few steps.*) No, no, not her! Not her, the others, maybe, all the others, but with Evelyn it's not just her body that I desire, but her soul, her love. Evelyn it's not your unresponsive flesh that I want, but I want your living body to be mine!

(*He approaches Evelyn who remains motionless. He grabs hold of her wrist in his left hand.*)

You came here on a day and at a time of your own choosing, of completely your own accord.
You came in, took off your coat and sat down on the sofa. You will not remember my orders, my orders that you are obliged to obey, my orders that have brought you here. You will remember nothing of that, do you hear, nothing!

(*He quickly waves his right hand in front of her face and says.*)

Awake!

(*Evelyn slowly brings her hands up to her forehead. Tâni's voice suddenly switches to a friendly conversational tone.*)

Ah, Miss Evelyn, I am delighted that you wanted to come and visit me!

EVELYN: But ... yes ... I came.

(*She appears confused, struggling for words. Tâni is leaning slightly towards her. Just then Amann enters through the door at the back. At a sign from Tâni he goes to bolt the door at the back and also at the top of the stairs. He exits by the door on the left, passing in front of Evelyn who shudders at the sight of him. The door on the left makes a noise as it closes and in response a long moaning is heard behind the curtain to the side of the door. Evelyn gives a start.*)

EVELYN (*trembling*): What was that?

TÂNI: Nothing at all! There's no need to be frightened any more! Come here! I'm going to show you what fear is. You're going to be face to face with fear ...

(*Amann re-enters through the door on the left. He carries a glass bowl full of blood. He goes behind the curtain. A roaring and wailing is heard. Evelyn shudders in fear but regains control of herself.*)

TÂNI: (*gently pulling back a corner of the curtain behind which *can be seen the bars of a cage*): Behind this curtain you will find all the terror in the world and all the horror of the shadows. (*He draws the curtains again.*) That is something you cannot see, because you would die of fright. But you can listen!

(*The sound of flapping wings and terrible cries can be heard. Evelyn remains quite still, trembling slightly. Tâni, taking her by the arm, leads her to the sarcophagus to the left of the door at the back.*)

TÂNI: When I asked you to come her the first time – do you remember? I told you that I would initiate you into the mysteries of our art. And now you have come! So ... I present to you the most sublime of things! The sarcophagus!

EVELYN: No, leave me alone! I don't want to! No!

TÂNI: This is my beloved master ... he of mysterious powers and the master of all masters on this earth ... (*Pause.*) As Major Williams used to say ... and he too is dead now ... they hanged him! Yes, hanged him! Because in the eyes of the world he was a criminal ... but he knew things that nobody else did. (*Pause*) I had his body dug up and I kept it with me ... here ... because he is everything to me, the very essence of my power comes from him. Death does not destroy us, those who have been initiated. The Master will be born again, not into a new body, but into his own body, his own body ... the repository of his great mind ... Watch!

(*Whilst he has been speaking, he has lit a lamp and opened the sarcophagus. On the body there are signs of strangulation – Evelyn flinches. Tâni forces her to approach the corpse. Pause.*)

TÂNI: At night time, yes, at night time it seems to me that my master is alive again ... that this corpse comes alive and that he gives me orders, orders that I have to obey! Yes, sometimes he appears in the darkness ... when I'm alone with him, with my own thoughts, with his own thoughts ...

(*A long pause, then he repeats*): With his own thoughts ...

(*Quickly he turns off the light. Another pause. Suddenly Evelyn cries out in fear.*)

TÂNI: What's the matter?

EVELYN: His hand ... his hand ... it grabbed hold of me ... It held on to me ...

(*Tâni switches the lamp back on.*)

TÂNI (*with irony*): Are you saying that the hand of this corpse grabbed hold of you?

EVELYN: Yes ... Yes ... Oh!

TÂNI: You silly thing! Do you really believe that a dead person can move ... that their hand can grab hold of the hand of a living person like that? For a start, just look ... it's a long way from you ...

EVELYN: He came ... he came to me ... in the darkness ... he grabbed hold of me ...

TÂNI (*smiling*): Ah yes, it is true that there are strange things on this earth! (*After a pause, he speaks quietly and intensely.*) Yes, one day, his hand will move and write something from a mind that has come alive again. But not yet ... look, the hand is dead, just as the whole body is dead. Quite dead!

(*He undoes the bandages that cover the upper body of the corpse and without doubt it is certainly a corpse ... terrifying! Whilst he does this, Evelyn retreats to the door at the back.*)

TÂNI (*continuing*): Come here ... come and look ... he is quite dead ...

EVELYN: Yes ... he is dead.

TÂNI (*watching her for a while*): So you see it's true. Well, then! Am I not more knowledgeable, more powerful, more impressive, more noble than the others, more handsome in these grand surroundings. Can you not love me, Evelyn, as I love you? Can you not long for my love, my embrace, as I long for yours? But you've already come to me, because here you are, at my house, in my arms, nearly ... Evelyn, Evelyn, my love ...

(*At first Evelyn is taken by surprise, not understanding what is happening, then she is overcome with horror and disgust, terrified and screams. She stretches out her arms and steps away from Tâni. Suddenly he launches himself at her and grabs hold of her, picks her up in his arms and carries her to the sofa. There is a silent struggle, teeth are clenched. Evelyn defends herself with all her might. But Tâni gets the better of her. He tears her dress so that her breasts are all but exposed. He lays her down on the sofa. She screams and struggles.*)

EVELYN: Save me! Save me! Help!

TÂNI: You are mine ... mine for ever and ever!

(The violent struggle continues. Evelyn is dishevelled and ravaged and starts to succumb. Tâni soars with desire and delights in a final effort. The young woman manages to raise herself and push Tâni away who totters back a few paces. When he goes to attack her again, the skylight window shatters and a hand holding a revolver appears through it. A shot is fired. Tâni collapses in a heap at Evelyn's feet, repeating these words):

TÂNI: You're mine, d'you hear me?! Mine!

CURTAIN

ACT THREE

Same scene as Act Two. The stage is lit only by a small electric torch which has been placed on a table. Things are barely visible.

A man is sitting motionless on a chair stage left. A long pause. Suddenly the door to the left opens. Somebody enters. The man in the chair suddenly stands up and screams in terror.

HARRIS *(closing the door behind him)*: Well then! Mr Parker, it's me, Harris. Weren't you expecting me?

PARKER *(a little out of breath)*: Yes, yes. I knew you were coming, but …

HARRIS: Yes, I'm a little early. It was agreed, wasn't it,that they would come tonight with the coroner?

PARKER: Yes. It's time this was over and done with!

HARRIS: I understand. This watching over the unknown …

PARKER: I'd rather be guarding the enemy any day of the week!

HARRIS: That's what they say.

PARKER: That's what I say and that's what I think! *(Suddenly getting up.)* Can't you see how I've aged since I've been in this damned house!

HARRIS: Come on now, calm down! *(Pause. The sound of wind blowing around the outside of the house in a sinister fashion.)* It's a terrible business, to be sure.

PARKER: Oh, if only you knew how it's affected me being here. The things I've heard, the things I've seen … well I've seen some terrible things in my time as a detective, but nothing like this before!

HARRIS: There are times, when you're alone in the darkness, when you imagine things …

PARKER: No, no, I've not imagined anything. I've been of sound mind. Something came, a creature, I don't know what … it walked … or rather it glided gently along … a bit like a beam of light passing through water. But this was nothing to do with light. On the contrary, this was something darker, something of the night … more intense … like a night fog that quickly filled one of the corners of this room.

HARRIS: A figment of your imagination! In your state of anxiety …

PARKER (*continuing*): And it made a noise … a faint, muffled noise, very close to me, yet at the same time like a distant wailing, passing through the walls. There, behind that door. (*He points to the door at the back that leads to the cellar.*) There is a staircase down to the cellar. It was there that it came from. It came from the crypt vaults beneath the house, you know?

HARRIS (*after a pause*): And tell me … this thing … did it come every night?

PARKER: The first few times, I don't know. Around that time I was overcome by sleep. But it must have come because I dreamed that it was leaning over me … Well, afterwards, I fought against falling asleep, I resisted … and I saw it …

HARRIS: How often?

PARKER: Two nights in a row. Then it didn't come any more.

HARRIS: But once you'd seen it and knew what it was, you could have tackled it.

PARKER: No, I couldn't … I couldn't … I didn't dare …

HARRIS: Oh, come on! A brave fellow like you?

PARKER: Cowards may be used to fear … but when fear seizes you and you're not used to it, it's terrifying. You can fight it with all your might, but you are in its grip, dominated by it, crushed by it and it is as if terror itself, rather than blood, is coursing through your veins.

HARRIS (*after a pause*): Then why are you sitting in the dark? A little light would not have been amiss. This is enough to fill your imagination with dark thoughts … how do you turn the electricity on?

PARKER: It's useless. It doesn't work.

HARRIS: Doesn't work?

PARKER: No, not since the fellow died.

HARRIS: Oh, why ever not?

PARKER: I don't know.

HARRIS: Well, that is odd. (*Pause.*) Have you a lamp at all?

PARKER: Yes.

HARRIS: Well, why don't you light it?
PARKER: Yes, now we can light it so they can find their way in.

(*Parker goes to light the lamp. A pale light fills the stage. The scene is as it was at the moment of Tâni's death, except that the corpse that was in the open sarcophagus has disappeared and the curtain at the rear has been drawn, revealing a wide recess, on the wall of which are fixed iron chains and there is also a large cage with iron bars. The sofa on which Tâni was killed is no longer centre stage but to the right.*)

HARRIS: Ah! There we are – that's better.

(*Voices are heard off stage.*)

PARKER: Here they are!

(*The Coroner, Frank and a uniformed Policeman enter through the door on the left.*)

HARRIS: Ah! There you are!
FRANK (*shaking his hand*): My dear chap ...
THE CORONER (*to Parker*): Anything to report?
PARKER: No, sir.
THE CORONER (*to the policeman*): Would you turn up the lamp please. I need to write. (*The Policeman turns up the lamp. The Coroner sits at a table.*) Now, gentlemen, let's get on and do what we have to do without wasting any time. (*to Frank*) Mr. Burton, as a condition of the court setting you free – which it does on the grounds that you behaved according to what you had to do in order to protect your sister – you promised that you would place yourself fully at my service ...
FRANK: Of course, Sir.
THE CORONER (*continuing*): ... in the interests of justice in this strange and difficult enquiry into this Tâni fellow. It is without doubt that this man – regardless of what he may have done in Egypt – has, since his arrival in England, committed terrible deeds which contravene the law, with his accomplice ... (*to the detective*) Come and stand next to us please, Mr Parker. (*continuing*) ... the man who resided with him, by the name of Amann, whom you arrested.
PARKER: Yes, sir. Immediately after the death of his master, he first of all disappeared without trace. But I arrested him a few days later wandering around the house.
THE CORONER: Well, now this chap is in a lunatic asylum. Since he was arrested all he has said is 'Now he is more terrifying than

ever! Now he is more terrifying than ever!' Evidently he is alluding to the death of his master.

FRANK: Yes, evidently …

THE CORONER (*continuing in hushed tones*): Since his death, however, some strange things have presented themselves. First of all we discovered here behind this curtain (*he points to the curtain*) something quite terrifying, a kind of vampire, but much bigger … a monstrous creature that looked as if it was made of the bodies of several different animals … moreover, shortly after it was taken away, the creature died and immediately began to decay. Then, inside the sarcophagus was a mummy, or rather a corpse, that disappeared the day after our search without our knowing who took it away or for what purpose. Then, Mr Parker assures us – and it is impossible to believe that he is the victim of hallucinations – somebody came in here during the night, which indicates either an accomplice or a ghost! But I don't think any of us believe in ghosts, do we?
If we dismiss the latter theory, it remains for us to try to solve one of the most curious mysteries ever to come to the attention of the police. Which is why, if you'll indulge me, we are going to precisely reconstruct the scene of the drama one more time. Mr. Burton, remind us of the circumstances. Meanwhile, Mr. Parker and you, Green, put everything here back as it was on the night in question.

(*Parker and the policeman place the sofa centre stage as it was when Tâni was shot. To Frank*):

I will ask that you are precise and leave nothing out, as unfortunately, since this terrible business, your sister has not been able to help us at all.

HARRIS (*to Frank*): How is she, by the way?

FRANK: The same as ever. Since we took her away from the house unconscious she hasn't left her bed and she still hasn't spoken a single word.

HARRIS: My poor chap, I'm so sorry … really I am … If there's anything I can do …

THE CORONER: Mr. Burton, we are waiting.

FRANK: Ah, yes, of course … I was unaware that my sister had come here. Nothing could have led me to believe that my sister would have come to this man's house! Whenever she spoke of him, since the accident on the staircase, it was never without fear and loathing. The man's power must have been quite something!

THE CORONER: Yes, she came here whilst in an hypnotic trance.

FRANK: Hypnotic, perhaps! Or demonic. There are things that I never used to believe in, but now I'm not so sure. Not sure at all! (*He wipes his forehead with his hand and looks around the room anxiously.*) Well, I came here to retrieve the papyruses that I entrusted to this Tâni ... we had worked together ... you see, he was a scholar ... a true scholar! He also knew about certain other supernatural things. So I asked for the papyruses back and he returned them immediately. And then I told him ... I told him what was on my mind ... that our friendship was over! And that's when he started talking about my sister. He told me he loved her – that should have opened my eyes, or at least made me a bit suspicious, but at that time not a bit of it! Instead I was just consumed by anger and I couldn't think of anything except throwing my contempt in his face and I left. Once I was outside, I was thrown into confusion and I headed off to the club where I met my friends ... you, Harris.

HARRIS: Yes, that's right.

FRANK: Then suddenly I was shaken out of it. I waited a little while and then retraced my steps. I felt I had to go back to this house. I don't know why. I suppose now that it must have been some kind of telepathy. You know how close my sister and I are. It's as if there is a thread that attaches us to each other and pulls us together in moments of danger. Yes Harris, I believe in these things now. (*Pause.*) So I came back here. All the doors were locked. I went all around the outside of the house and I stopped beneath this skylight. Then, just at that moment I heard a piercing scream. I managed to clamber along the wall as far as the skylight ... I was armed ... I saw him ... and I killed him! ...

(*At that moment the sound of gusts of wind can be heard, like wailing all around the house. The lamp flickers all of a sudden and then comes on again. Long pause.*)

PARKER (*worried*): It's time!

THE CORONER: What?

PARKER: This was the time, when the thing came the other night ...

THE CORONER: What are you saying?

PARKER: I don't know! Perhaps ... (*The sound of the wind gets stronger. A door is heard closing.*) Listen!

THE CORONER: Yes! Now, Parker, you go over there! Green, come here! Everyone else come with me ... turn off your torches. (*They turn off their torches and all go towards, the curtain.*) That's good. Now turn off the lamp. (*The lamp is turned off.*) Not a sound now! Nobody move!

(*A long pause in the complete darkness. The door on the right opens slowly. A figure enters through the door and slowly makes its way to the centre of the stage. A hoarse, throaty breathing is heard. The figure stops in front of the sofa, long pause, interrupted only by the sound of the wind and the breathing of this thing. Suddenly, the men rush out from where they are and cover the stage with the beams of their torches.*)

FRANK (*with a loud cry*): Evelyn!

(*Indeed it is Evelyn, dressed in black, as pale as death, with mad eyes.*)

FRANK (*continuing*): Evelyn!

THE CORONER (*quietly*): But you told us that Miss Burton was unwell, that she hadn't left her bed since ...

FRANK: But what does this mean?

HARRIS (*to Frank*): She seems to have frozen!

THE CORONER: She doesn't appear to hear a thing!

FRANK (*in a trembling voice, whilst Parker and the Policeman relight the lamp on the table*): Evelyn! Oh, Evelyn! Why have you come back here? Why? And what are these black clothes? Why are you dressed in mourning? What's the matter with you? Say something! Speak to me! (*Evelyn does not respond.*) Please, speak to me! (*Evelyn remains quite still and mute. Holding his head in his hands, Frank speaks to the others.*) Oh, my God, what's going on? She doesn't recognize me any more. The poor thing has lost her mind!

(*Long pause.*)

EVELYN (*in a sombre, low voice that is barely recognizable*): He's calling me ... I'm coming ... I have to go ... the power is too strong ... the voice is too strong ... Oh! He wants me to go to his tomb, over there, it is his command, it is his command ...

(*She straightens up and moves towards the door.*)

FRANK (*running after her*): Evelyn! Evelyn! Where are you going?

EVELYN: I am going to join him ...

FRANK (*holding her by the arm*): But you are mad ...

EVELYN: I must! I must!

FRANK: But that's insane! (*He takes her in his arms and restrains her.*) There, there, Evelyn! My dear sister! It's me, Frank! Listen to me!

EVELYN: Frank … yes … I know who you are … but I really have to go to him … because, he's calling me, you see.

FRANK: Evelyn! Get a grip on yourself!

EVELYN: He's calling me to his tomb!

FRANK (*still holding her in his arms*): No, he's not. No, he's not. Nobody's calling you. Nobody!

EVELYN: He wants me in his arms … in his arms. He wants me to lie down next to him, in his coffin. The dead are calling the dead …

FRANK: But you … you are alive!

EVELYN: Oh, keep hold of me … keep me alive …

FRANK: I've got hold of you and I'm strong. I'll protect you from him.

EVELYN: Yes, yes … protect me … stop me from leaving … Oh! Don't let me go! Otherwise I'll never come back! Frank! Frank! Be strong … you must be stronger than him. You mustn't let him take me away or I'll be lost! Keep hold of me! Don't let me go!

FRANK (*struggling in vain*): But I can't! (*To the others who are watching all this, petrified.*) Help! Help me!

(*The Policeman and Parker go to help Frank. Harris follows them. The Coroner remains standing nearby.*)

EVELYN: Oh, your hands … your arms aren't strong enough! Ropes, chains … yes, chains … please, please! … he's dragging me away … into his fleshless arms … (*in desperation*) Tie me up … I beg of you … tie me up!

FRANK: We have to do what she says! The ropes … the chains … quickly!

HARRIS (*whilst Evelyn continues to incessantly struggle and moan*): She's having an appalling fit!

THE CORONER: Do as she says! Tie her up!

FRANK: The chains … get the chains … there … behind the curtain …

THE CORONER: Yes ….

(*Harris goes to fetch the chains. The men chain Evelyn up, whilst she continues to moan and scream.*)

EVELYN: Oh! Hold on! Hold on tightly! With all your might! Oh! You must keep me alive with these iron chains! These chains of steel! So that he doesn't take my soul … so that he doesn't take me away into the dark night, into the shadows, to the gates of darkness.

(*There is a large gust of wind. The lamp goes out. Complete darkness. A kind of long moaning is heard around the house. Silence, then the sound of footsteps. The door at the back slowly opens as if it is being pushed by an invisible hand. Through the door can be seen a faint, mysterious light coming from who knows where. Then there is the sound of footsteps slowly coming down the staircase. Suddenly the sound of chains falling to the ground and Evelyn emits a terrible scream, a scream of complete terror. The light suddenly disappears.*)

FRANK (*rushing around*): Evelyn!

HARRIS: What is it?

THE CORONER: Oh, my God!

FRANK: Light! Some light!

HARRIS (*to Parker*): The lamp! Light the lamp!

(*The Policeman relights the lamp. Evelyn is lying on the sofa dead. The chains are lying next to her, undone.*)

PARKER: The chains are undone!

(*He lifts the body by the head. Evelyn's face is terrifying: it is the face of a corpse in full decomposition. They all look at her in horror.*)

FRANK: She's not moving!

THE CORONER (*to Frank*): She's dead!

PARKER (*to Harris*): Dead ... yes ... and decomposing as if she's already been dead a very long time!

FRANK (*covering his eyes with his hands, insane with horror*): That's not her! That's not her, this horrible thing! No! No! I won't look at her! Take her away! Take her away ...!

CURTAIN

THIRD PROGRAMME:

The Wax Museum
The Lovers
The Man Who Met the Devil
The Man Who Killed Death

Preface

The third programme in this volume consists of four plays that were performed at the Théâtre du Grand-Guignol in Paris, although the final play, *L'Homme qui a tué la mort* (*The Man Who Killed Death*), was also performed in an English translation as part of a revival of the London Grand Guignol in 1928, the same year it premiered at the rue Chaptal. The other two horrors, *Figures de cire* (*The Wax Museum*) and *L'Homme qui a vu le diable* (*The Man Who Met the Devil*), both emerge from the latter years of the *Belle Époque*, 1910 and 1911 respectively. All three of the horror plays here are linked by their central use of different iconic horror imagery from popular culture: the inanimate (or perhaps all too animate) doll or waxwork; the crumbling Gothic pile harbouring a long-held family secret; and the reanimated severed head.

In contrast, the comedy presented here, *Les Amants* (*The Lovers*), is superficially a gentler piece, although with a profound resonance and not without sexual tension and ruthless satire of contemporary relationships and morality. First produced in 1901, it is an example of an early Grand-Guignol comedy, but was not the first Mirbeau play to be produced there. *Vieux ménages* (*The Old Couple*) premiered at the Théâtre d'Application in 1894 but was revived extremely comfortably at the Grand-Guignol in October 1900.

The Wax Museum tells the story of a young man who is literally frightened to death whilst trying to spend a night, as a 'dare', alone in the museum of waxworks.[1] As with other Grand-Guignol dramas, such as *The Man Who Met the Devil* and *Le Baiser de sang* (*The Kiss of Blood*), it plays upon traditional Gothic and supernatural iconography, in this case the iconography of the doll that comes to life and commits horrific violence, as can be found in Mary Shelley, E.T.A. Hoffmann and others. In cinema it first appears in German Expressionist Paul Leni's 1924 silent portmanteau

1 Interestingly, in the first published edition of the play, readers are invited to contact Paul Ratineau, described as the artistic director (*régisseur general*) of the Grand-Guignol, for further details of the play's staging. It signifies the importance of the actor and stage designer Ratineau to the whole enterprise at this time.

or anthology-form film *Das Wachsfigurenkabinett* (*Waxworks*). Leni later emigrated to America, where he made the 1927 version of John Willard's comedy horror *The Cat and the Canary* for Universal Pictures – more famously remade in 1939 with Bob Hope. However, consistent with Grand-Guignol practice, the true horror is not a supernatural one, but one firmly rooted in the reality of the urban jungle. The threat to Pierre is not of waxworks that might come to life, but of prowlers and thieves who might murder him for his wallet. The greater significance lies in two aspects of the play that are core to the Grand-Guignol aesthetic, namely class and the dynamic between artifice and reality.

There are three distinct social classes represented in the play. First, there is the honest, grafting working-class, as represented by Bourrache, the owner of the fairground wax museum, the unnamed waiter and cashier in the Montmartrean café, and even the two police officers. Second, there is the Parisian underclass of prostitutes and vagabonds. Third, there is the dissolute aristocracy, as represented by Pierre de Lionne and his cronies. It is the first two groups that are treated most sympathetically and represented as victims, brutalized by a capitalist society. Whilst there may be tension between these two groups, their behaviour is shown to be entirely determined by their economic need. The prostitutes and thieves risk imprisonment (and worse) on account of their poverty; Bourrache is on the edge of bankruptcy; the café workers chase out the prostitutes for fear they will scare their wealthy customers away. As Bourrache says, 'Everyone has to make a living somehow.' Such representations are true to the Grand-Guignol's early roots in Zola-esque radical naturalism.

It is the young aristocrats who come off worst, portrayed as pompous, self-indulgent, irresponsible snobs. Pierre's descent into a jabbering wreck inside the wax museum is as much pathetic as it is horrifying, and the real horror is not so much Pierre's untimely death from natural causes but the fact that the innocent and nameless prostitute might be wrongly led to the guillotine for his murder.

It is quite fitting for a genre that evolved from a combination of melodrama and naturalism that the interplay between reality and artifice should be a recurring theme in the Grand-Guignol. Indeed, the very playfulness of horror at the rue Chaptal was dependent on both the realist execution of the special effects and moments of horror and the 'contract' between actor and audience that recognized the pretence and illusion of the spectacle. Likewise, the wax museum itself represents this very interplay: the waxworks are valued both for their realism (seen, for example, in the irony of the policeman mistaking Pierre's body for a waxwork with the declaration, 'That's amazing! You'd think it was real') and for the fact that they are models. It is this same tension that is Pierre's ultimate downfall, terrified as he is of both real-life prowlers and the creepy mannequins in the museum. Furthermore, it is a tension that is foregrounded early on in the play when, in a moment of self-referential irony, it transpires that the young swells are on their way home after a night at the Grand-Guignol. So it is for the audience at the theatre watching the play; they find themselves sitting in a real theatre, watching an artifice that refers to the very same theatre as a piece of fiction. The extensive use of the darkness in Act Two is a further example of the use of interplay between the imagined and the real, the physical and the psychological, and the playful and the serious that lies at the heart of so much Grand-Guignol horror.

A further reference may be made here to the well-known European folktale 'The Boy Who Knew No Fear', in which a young boy, like Pierre, claims to have never been frightened and volunteers to stay overnight in a haunted house in the hope of experiencing fear. The difference is that, in the folktale, the boy remains unperturbed by whatever the devils and ghosts that haunt the house may throw at him. In *The Wax Museum* there are no ghosts, but it is the overwrought Pierre who is scared to death by the imagined fear of a real threat, not unlike the murderous lovers Thérèse and Laurent in Zola's *Thérèse Raquin* (1867), who are haunted by hallucinations of the dead Camille.

Octave Mirbeau (1848–1917) was a contemporary of Zola and just as controversial, politically speaking. He was a journalist whose politics evolved from his being a Bonapartist, a monarchist and a republican prior to becoming an anarchist. Mirbeau, who deliberately made himself provocative and controversial, remains one of the most fascinating and eloquent voices from late nineteenth-century and *Belle Époque* France. Leo Tolstoy believed Mirbeau to be 'France's greatest contemporary writer' and the preeminent example of French culture's 'secular genius' (Lemarié and Michel, 2011, 1181).

Mirbeau consistently presented – in his journalism, fiction and plays – an acerbic critique of what he perceived as the widespread hypocrisy and corruption in French society. Mirbeau is most famous in our own time for his novels, above all for *Le Jardin des supplices* (*Torture Garden*, 1899) and *Le Journal d'une femme de chambre* (*The Diary of a Chambermaid*, 1900). Neither novel has lost its power to shock and disturb.

Le Journal d'une femme de chambre is an unsettling masterpiece of erotic fiction and a devastating critique of bourgeois France. As the title suggests, the novel is presented as a servant's diary which contains a catalogue of numerous sadistic and fetishistic employers, although, significantly, the eponymous narrator is not a naïve victim but a woman fully capable of exploiting the situation as much as being exploited. The novel presents a damning portrait of *fin de siècle* France and its hypocrisy and moral bankruptcy. It is testimony to its power as a novel that *Le Journal d'une femme de chambre* has had the privilege of being adapted to the screen by directors as celebrated – and dissimilar – as Jean Renoir (1946) and Luis Buñuel (1964).

In the context of the Théâtre du Grand-Guignol, *Le Jardin des supplices* is an especially significant work. In this novel, Mirbeau presents wealthy, decadent Europeans sojourning in the Far East. These pleasure-seekers have a voracious appetite for sadism, not least in the torture garden of the title, where they watch, in sexual delirium, the prolonged torture and execution of Chinese criminals. Mirbeau's brilliant coup is to have the narrative fed to us through the voice of one of the European travellers: a man whose moral uprightness is gradually worn away until he is as depraved and cruel as the other voyagers, not least the debauched young English widow, Clara. The novel remains a shocking and inexorable 'journey', not dissimilar in its narrative, structure and theme of anti-imperialism to a contemporaneous work of English fiction: Joseph Conrad's *Heart of Darkness* (1899). However, Mirbeau's unremitting focus on sexual depravity and 'horror' makes '*Torture Garden* the sadistic and sexualized *Heart of Darkness* of the *fin de siècle*' (Hand, 2011, 3).

Le Jardin des supplices was, of course, adapted for the Grand-Guignol in 1922 (five years after Mirbeau's death) in a stage adaptation written by Pierre Chaine and André de Lorde (see Hand and Wilson, 2002, 195–230). Although the dramatization essentially transforms Mirbeau's decadent novel into an espionage thriller, the play does put atrocity centre-stage, with a prostitute skinned alive and Clara getting her eyeballs burned out with red-hot needles (significantly, no 'just' retribution is delivered on the sadistic Englishwoman at the end of the novel).

Not only were Mirbeau's novels adapted for the stage by other writers: he wrote some original plays for the Grand-Guignol himself. Given the themes in his fiction, one might expect him to have produced works of explicit sadism and graphic violence for the rue Chaptal. In fact, Mirbeau's one-act plays for the Grand-Guignol seem remarkably restrained, at least at first glance. The comedy genre was as important to the Grand-Guignol as horror, and Mirbeau's plays for the Grand-Guignol are all masterful examples of Grand-Guignol comedy. After all, Mirbeau was a gifted comic writer, even if his fame abides in works of the erotic–grotesque. His two most successful full-length plays, *Les Affaires sont les affaires* (*Business is Business*, 1903) and *Le Foyer* (*Charity*, 1908) are works of satire in the Molière tradition, notable for their wit and humour as much as their eviscerating critique of the hypocrisy and corruption of contemporary France and its bourgeoisie.

The Lovers opens meta-theatrically with a Host character who, we are told, 'could be the director of the theatre' (not dissimilar to the Stage Manager in Thornton Wilder's *Our Town* (1938)), who talks to the audience about the location and what they are about to witness. The play presents the rendezvous of two lovers and is a battle of the sexes. The Man is passionate and anticipatory, the Woman is cool and upset. The play presents their mounting argument, which grows in accusation and aggression. But at its climax all is resolved, their passion is on fire and the curtain politely descends. It is a well-written pastiche of the discourse of love, but, being Mirbeau, it shows that love and sex teeter on the brink of destruction: provocatively, Mirbeau demonstrates that the point at which aggression and the repellent are at a climax is the zenith of arousal and the prelude to sexual union.

Far removed from the bourgeois domesticity of Mirbeau's comedy is the heavily Gothic setting of Gaston Leroux's *The Man Who Met the Devil*. Gothic literature is generally agreed to originate with the publication of Horace Walpole's *The Castle of Otranto* in 1764, yet the influence that the Gothic imagination has exerted on literature, theatre, film, fashion and popular culture more generally throughout the nineteenth and twentieth centuries, and even into the twenty-first, is difficult to overestimate. Victorian melodramas and ghost stories, Hammer horror films, dark brooding Nordic Noir crime fiction and twenty-first-century teenage vampire films all borrow liberally from the imagery and motifs of the Gothic form.

The Grand-Guignol itself was also no stranger to the Gothic. This was partly the result of the theatre's early connections to the 'blood and thunder' melodramas that played along the 'Boulevard du Crime' in nineteenth-century Montmartre and is also evident in the Grand-Guignol's writers' exploitation of the *faits divers* in the popular press of the time – lurid descriptions of true-life crimes. With this in mind, many of the concerns of the Gothic (such as the transitions between and transgressions across the boundaries of dark/light and sanity/madness) can be found throughout the Grand-Guignol repertoire, although *The Man Who Met the Devil* is more unashamedly an homage to the Grand-Guignol's Gothic roots.

When the play was first premiered at the rue Chaptal in December 1911 Leroux was already established as a journalist and writer of crime fiction, having introduced the French reading public to the detective Joseph Rouletabille in *Le Mystère de la chambre jaune* (*The Mystery of the Yellow Room*) in 1907; 1911 was also the year in which what is arguably Leroux's most successful work, *Le Fantôme de l'Opéra* (*The Phantom of the Opera*), appeared in book format, having first been published in serial form the previous year. Whilst Leroux's efforts were more usually steered towards prose fiction, rather than drama, he had enjoyed some success with *Le Lys* (*The Lilly*) in 1909; however, *The Man Who Met the Devil* – an adaptation of his 1908 short story 'L'Homme qui a vu le diable' – was his first and only contribution to the Théâtre du Grand-Guignol.

Gaston Louis Alfred Leroux was born in 1868 in Paris and was educated in Normandy, where his grandparents owned a shipping company. His father was also a wealthy public contractor, so the young Leroux enjoyed a privileged childhood. In 1889 Leroux's father died, leaving the young law graduate a sizeable inheritance, which he immediately set about squandering over a period of six months on the kind of lifestyle that any young man in Paris, with unexpected money in his pocket, might be tempted to lead.

By 1890 Leroux was broke, and he turned to journalism for a living, becoming the court reporter and theatre critic for *L'Echo de Paris*, a rather suitable on-the-job training for a budding Grand-Guignol playwright. In this capacity he covered the notorious Dreyfus Affair of 1894. He later became the international correspondent for *Le Matin*, covering the 1905 Revolution in Russia. From 1907, however, Leroux focused on his career as a novelist, remaining prolific until his death in 1927.

The Man Who Met the Devil is, at first glance, a fine example of a Gothic melodrama. Its setting in a grand old house (the archetypal 'Gothic pile'), located somewhere in the Alpine border region of France, Italy and Switzerland, is typical of the Gothic form; the majesty and awe of the mountainous landscape encapsulates Edmund Burke's notion of the 'sublime' as outlined in his *Philosophical Enquiry into the Origin of our Ideas of the Sublime and Beautiful* of 1757, which had a strong influence on Gothic writers. We can also see typically Gothic motifs and imagery in the tensions between rationality and superstition; the real and the imaginary/fantastical; sanity and madness. In addition, there is the motif of the weather – the wild and uncontrollable forces of nature (the storm), reflecting not only the grandeur of the landscape but also the psychological turmoil of the aged owner of the mansion and anticipating the descent into madness of the character of Allan. The plot structure itself, concerning a group of young travellers having an accident and taking refuge from a storm in an isolated mansion owned by a wealthy eccentric cared for by old faithful servants, is one that has been repurposed time and again in the Gothic tradition, especially in film. There is also an underlying sexual tension, especially revolving around the character of Claireli and her relationship with the men in her party, although it is Allan's confusion that is one of the key drivers of the narrative. As David Blair says, 'Gothic also dabbles in male – not merely female – sexual anxieties' (2002, XII).

Where the play departs from the Gothic tradition, however, is in its treatment of the supernatural. Here it pins its colours more definitely to the Grand-Guignol mast. The horrors of the Grand-Guignol were real-life horrors, in accordance with the genre's primary roots in naturalism, and the supernatural horrors, common enough in much Gothic writing and melodrama, be they ghosts, vampires or monsters, were generally banished from the stage at the rue Chaptal.[2] Where they do appear there is usually a rational explanation: a trick of the mind or a devious plan to drive a

[2] An interesting footnote, however, is that the actor Réné Chimier (1902–1997), who succeeded Paulais as Maxa's stage partner in the 1930s and attracted the moniker of *le roi de l'épouvante* ('The King of Fear'), was a keen spiritualist. After leaving the Grand-Guignol at the end of the Second World War and after the return of Eva Berkson, the English owner, to the rue Chaptal, Chimier became the founding General Secretary of the *Centre spiritualiste de France* (Pierron, 2002, 138).

victim to madness, as in Jean Aragny and Francis Neilson's *The Kiss of Blood*. The monsters at the Grand-Guignol were strictly of the order of 'la bête humaine' – those created by society itself. At best there is a certain ambiguity towards the supernatural, such as that enveloped in the mantle of the Orientalism of *The Great Terror*. In *The Man Who Met the Devil*, whilst certain 'supernatural' events are not always explained in rational terms (arguably leaving a hint of ambiguity), there is a clear push towards a psychological explanation for the events that take place. The appearance of the 'Devil' to Allan in the mirror, for example, is never manifestly explained in rational terms, yet the fact that the Figure is described as resembling Allan 'like a brother' and 'making identical yet opposite movements' suggests that he is merely seeing his own reflection and what we are witnessing is the effect of suggestion (the old man's story and Claireli's criticism of him for not killing her husband) on the unstable and susceptible mind of a vulnerable individual. At least the play could be read as such. The Grand-Guignol's interest in psychology and the disturbing effect of suggestion on the vulnerable mind can be seen in early plays such as André de Lorde and Charles Foleÿ's *Au téléphone* and *The Wax Museum*, although it was not until the inter-war period that the psychological drama began to feature more predominantly in the theatre's programming.

The Man Who Killed Death is a good example of such a psychological play and also draws upon classic horror iconography. Its author, René Berton (1872–1934), was a doctor before moving to Paris in 1908 to become a full-time writer, where he worked as a journalist, poet, theatre critic and playwright. His lyrical dramatization of the Orestes legend – *Oreste* (1923) – was particularly acclaimed when staged at the Comédie-Française. He was also perfectly suited to the Grand-Guignol, being able to draw on his medical knowledge for ethically concerned horror dramas such as *L'Euthanasie, ou le Devoir de tuer* (*Euthanasia or The Duty to Kill*, 1923), while his playful sense of irony and farce continues to shine in sex comedies such as *Après coup ou Tics* (*Tics ... or Doing the Deed*, 1908). In *The Man Who Killed Death* Berton returns to medical science, but in a more ambitious play which explores the themes of unethical scientific experimentation and the judicial system and boasts a lurid and technologically inventive dénouement. Although *The Man Who Killed Death* was performed only during the season beginning 9 January 1928 and not revived, it is an emblematic classic of the Grand-Guignol repertoire thanks in particular to the striking poster design from the time of its premiere, which shows the Grand-Guignol at its most gruesome, technophobic extreme.

The Man Who Killed Death belongs to a Grand-Guignol subgenre of guillotine plays which includes works such as André de Lorde and Jean Barnac's *Au Petit jour* (*At Daybreak*, 1921), Charles Hellem and Pol d'Estoc's *Vers l'au-delà* (*To the Beyond*, 1922) and Eugène Héros and

Léon Abric's comedy *La Veuve* (*Chop-Chop, or The Guillotine*, 1906). The guillotine is a cultural icon in France, being a symbol of the Revolution and, by implication, the Republic and democracy itself. Indeed, executions were still sometimes held in public in France until 1937 and the death penalty was not finally abolished until 1981 (Pierron, 1995, 875). The cultural and political status of the guillotine is reflected in the scandal that surrounded *Au Petit jour* in 1921, which gave rise to one of very few instances of censorship of the Parisian Grand-Guignol.[3] The fact that the play ends with the beheading of a condemned murderer on the guillotine caused outrage (Antona-Traversi, 1933, 72), and the theatre owner, Camille Choisy, and the authors, de Lorde and Barnac, were ordered by the police to ensure that the curtain fell before the convict mounted the scaffold. The controversy of *Au Petit jour* was not the presence of a guillotine itself or the fact that it was a gruesome stage effect (this was the Theatre of Horror, after all), but rather that showing a functioning guillotine was regarded as an insult towards a national icon and symbol of French justice. Although *The Man Who Killed Death* is concerned with ethical issues of justice and capital punishment, the guillotine is offstage (although very much audible from construction to deployment) and, after the execution takes place, the dramatic focus shifts to the (pseudo)scientific theme of resuscitation.

Berton is a writer of considerable skill and *The Man Who Killed Death* is a finely structured and scripted work full of choice roles for actors: whether it is the wardens and their bosses, or the three key roles of Morales, Gauvain and Fargus, there is the potential for dynamic and even ironically humorous characterization. Berton takes us through the details of the preparation for a guillotine execution from the perspective of the prison wardens, keeping the audience in suspense while it is being factually informed before we encounter the condemned murderer, Morales. The fact that Morales insists on his innocence creates a tension of ambiguity which is a powerful juxtaposition to the high-flying but naïve and conceited lawyer Gauvain. Once this is established, the audience meets Fargus, the eponymous death-defeating man of the title. Whether we find in Fargus and his assistant Marec a complex satire of unethical and uncaring science or an all-out precursor to the Dr Frankenstein and Igor of countless horror movies, their driven, ruthless vision takes the audience on an inexorable journey into horror where science is out of control. However, although it

---

[3] According to Pierron, 'From the very start, the Grand-Guignol was under the watchful gaze of the police' (2011, 16), although attempts at censorship appear to have been ineffective, as any performance that was halted began again after midnight, once the police had gone home (2011, 16). Furthermore, Pierron suggests that it was this relationship with the authorities that encouraged Méténier to name his theatre after the Guignol, the satirical Lyonnais puppet-show, which had likewise been subject to police interference. Nearly a century later, Méténier believed his theatre was a Guignol on a larger scale (2011, 16–17).

is a journey into horror with a shocking finale, Berton takes the audience there through well-crafted moral debates appertaining to the legal system, and through persuasive examples of (pseudo)science.

The great horror set-piece of the play is the reanimated head in the dénouement. Before this, the audience hears the guillotine outside the window, the descriptive dialogue permitting the audience to 'see' the execution in a manner not unlike the way in which the 'real-time' description of a trepanning in the opening scene of Jean Aragny and Francis Neilson's *Le Baiser de sang* (*The Kiss of Blood*, 1929) allows the full horror of the operation to be realized, whilst the actual procedure is obscured by the body of the surgeon. When the freshly severed head is attached to Fargus's invention, Berton explains in his stage directions that a false head is replaced with the actor concealed beneath the scientist's table. The successful animation of Morales' head appalls all the witnesses (with the exception of the delighted Fargus) and drives Gauvain insane, his final declaration a grotesque echo of his summing up in court.

The decapitated head has always had a powerful significance across all cultures. It occurs in Biblical texts, with the beheading of John the Baptist or the account of Judith seducing then decapitating the conquering general Holofernes (dramatized by, among others, Howard Barker in *Judith: A Parting from the Body* (1992)). In Classical mythology it is associated with Perseus's slaying of Medusa, the monstrous female who retains her power to petrify (literally) even after decapitation: an apt metaphor for the mortifying power of the emblem of the severed head. This cultural phenomenon has fascinated critics such as Julia Kristeva, whose *The Severed Head: Capital Visions* (2011) examines the philosophical and cultural significance of decapitation, especially in works of art.

Historically, the power of decapitation has been exploited by those who have wanted to demonstrate, most unequivocally, the destruction of their enemies. The act of beheading is an iconic image in specific histories, whether in the form of the axe-man dispatching Henry VIII's two most unfortunate wives or the use of the guillotine in the White Terror that followed the French Revolution. Appallingly, the mortifying power of decapitation is still exploited in contemporary times, as evidenced by the graphic decapitation videos which have been issued by groups as diverse as Al-Qaeda, Islamic State and the drug cartels in Mexico. They may be widely different in ideological or geographical terms, but all have used beheading footage to demonstrate their ruthless determination to annihilate their enemies and 'petrify' their opponents.

Core to Berton's play is, of course, the fact that the head is resuscitated. The debate as to whether consciousness is sustained for any period of time in a severed head has been recurrent. It is claimed by some that severing the spinal cord and blood supply causes instantaneous death and that any movement is merely muscular spasms; the contrary argument is that documented examples of facial and ocular motion are evidence of continuing consciousness, even if for only a brief period. It is claimed, for instance, that Anne Boleyn's lips continued to move in prayer for a few seconds after her execution (1536). Similarly, one of the legends of the French Revolution is that Charlotte Corday (assassin of Marat) grimaced in indignation at the crowd when her face was slapped after decapitation on the guillotine in 1793. There is no doubt that Berton is, as well as exploiting a particularly macabre popular legend and debating point, basing his play on the real-life activities of a number of French scientists who experimented on guillotine victims. For example, in an interview in *Le Matin* (3 March 1907), Dr Dassy de Lignères claims that in 1880 he restored blood circulation to the guillotined head of the child killer Louis Ménesclou by using a living dog, during which, for two seconds, Ménesclou's eyes blinked and the mouth spoke silently. Less implausible is the experiment of Dr Gabriel Beaurieux, who obtained permission to attend the guillotining of Henri Languille in 1905, tested the head for signs of consciousness and concluded from lip and eye movements (for a period of approximately thirty seconds) that it showed such signs. If Dassy de Lignères and Beaurieux's investigations claimed that consciousness continues or can be brought back, the son and father doctors E. and G. Descaisne reached another conclusion. In 1879 they tested the guillotined head of murderer Théotime Prunier by pricking it with needles, holding a candle to its eye and inserting ammonia into its nostrils, before concluding that it was lifeless (Dash, 2011).

In more recent times, the scientific debates around head resuscitation and transplantation have captured attention and provoked controversy in equal measure. In 1970 the American surgeon Robert White conducted the first successful head transplant of a monkey, which survived for nine days before the host body rejected it (Thomson, 2015, 10). Developments in immunology, neurology and transplant surgery have meant that the possibilities are once again being explored: medical researchers in China have successfully transplanted mice heads, while, in 2015, the Italian neurological surgeon Sergio Canavero launched an international project to attempt the first transplant of a human head (Thomson, 2015, 10).

The Grand-Guignol was a theatre of possible horrors that often exploited the world of *faits divers* and the popular press, and there is no doubt that some of its audience would have been aware of contempraneous experiments and scientific conjecture; as a consequence, *The Man Who Killed Death* was an example of drama not so far from the truth.

In other performance contexts, the powerful, abject symbolism of decapitation has been exploited in television dramas such as *Game of Thrones* (2011 onwards) and *Rome* (2005–2007). When it comes to the appearance of life after beheading, one example can be found in *Aguirre, Wrath of God* (Werner Herzog, 1972), in which a decapitated conquistador utters his final word as his head lies on the ground. Another memorable animated head is featured in the television series *American Horror Story: Coven* (2013–14). Marie Delphine LaLaurie (Kathy Bates) is a New Orleans socialite from the 1830s who drinks an elixir of eternal life and is buried alive. Disinterred into the contemporary world, this unreformed racist from the era of slavery is decapitated by her nemesis, the voodoo queen Marie Laveau (Angela Bassett), and her still-living head is forced to watch the complete television series *Roots* (1977). The postmodernist excesses and playfulness of *American Horror Story* are frequently characterized by hideous horror and humour and LaLaurie's head is reminiscent of examples of camp and kitsch popular horror such as the grimly hilarious *Re-Animator* (Stuart Gordon, 1985). In this cult movie – loosely based on H.P. Lovecraft's short story 'Herbert West – Reanimator' (1922) – a precocious Frankensteinian genius, Dr Herbert West (Jeffrey Combes), murders his rival Dr Hill (David Gale) and brings Hill's head (and separated body) back to life. The scientific rivalry continues unabated, and when Hill threatens to tell the world about the science of reanimation, West declaims: 'You'll never get credit for *my* discovery … Who's going to believe a talking head? Get a job in a sideshow!'

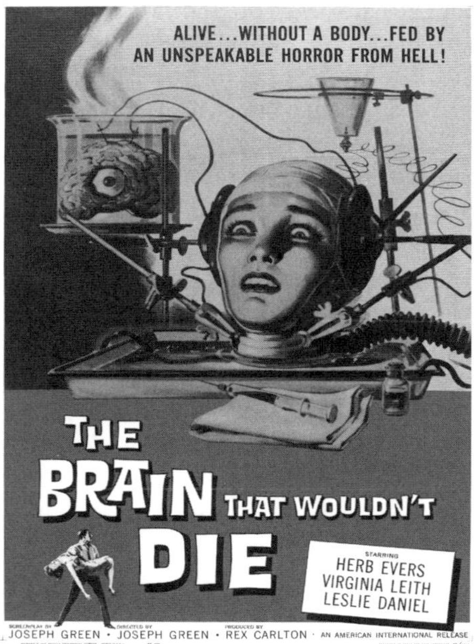

10 Film poster for *The Brain That Wouldn't Die* (Joseph Green, 1962)

Produced a generation before *Re-Animator*, *The Brain That Wouldn't Die* (Joseph Green, 1962) is a science fiction B-movie that has since become a camp classic, not least because it featured on *Mystery Science Theater 3000* in 1991. In *The Brain That Wouldn't Die* a scientist, Dr Cortner (Jason Evers), saves the head of his fiancée Jan (Virginia Leith) when she is decapitated in a car accident and successfully brings it back to consciousness in his elaborate Grand-Guignolesque invention. The first 'act' of the film maps closely to *The Man Who Killed Death*, with more than a touch of André de Lorde and Alfred Binet's *L'Horrible Expérience* (*The Horrific Experiment*, 1909), in which a young woman dies and her father and fiancé (both doctors) attempt to revive her with dreadful consequences. After this, the film develops the plot, with the mad scientist seeking to find a woman whose body would be an appropriate match for his girlfriend's still beautiful head.

The iconography of the poster for *The Brain That Wouldn't Die* is unmistakably reminiscent of the 1928 poster for *The Man Who Killed Death*, although the influence was almost certainly more directly the comic-book story 'The Trophy' in *Tales from the Crypt* 25 (August 1951) (see Hand and Wilson, 2012).

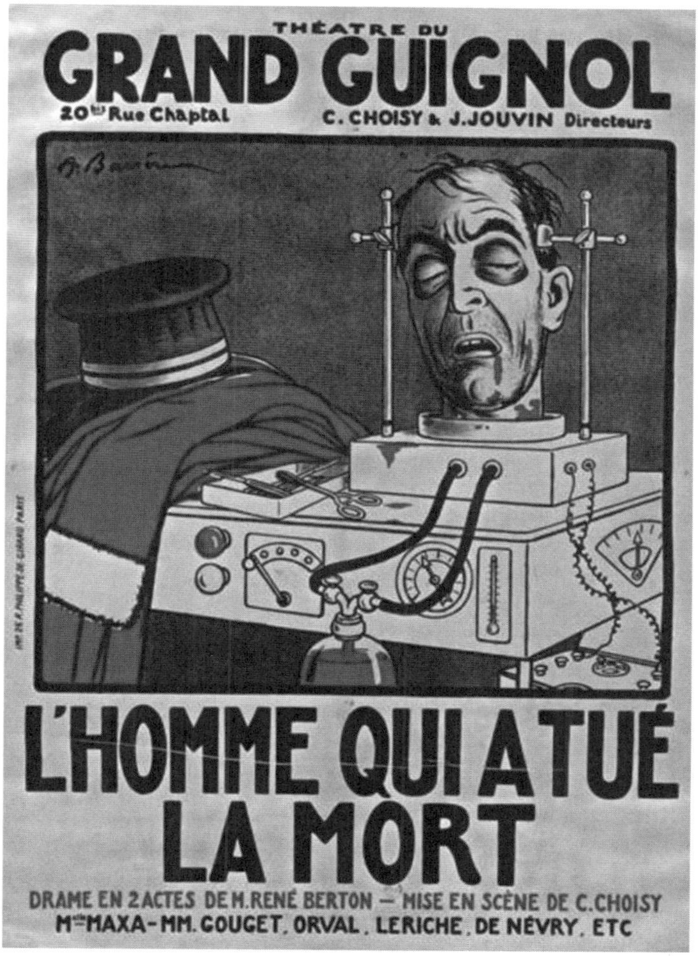

11 Poster for the premiere of René Berton's *L'Homme qui a tué la mort* at the Théâtre du Grand Guignol in 1928

The Wax Museum (*Figures de Cire*, 1910)

André de Lorde and Georges Montignac

Characters:
Bourrache
Cashier
Waiter
Woman
Pierre
Divonne
Jacques
First Cop
Second Cop
Voices of two prowlers

ACT ONE

A very small café in Montmartre. On the right, a panel door leads out onto the street. Outside a gas lamp casts a dim red light.

Mid-stage left is the counter. Upstage there are tables and chairs. Upstage right, next to the door, is a ceramic stove.

Downstage right, on the other side of the door, is a table and bench. As the curtain rises, the cashier is reading her newspaper at the counter. A waiter is sleeping on a chair downstage left, a newspaper lying at his feet. Outside can be heard the sound of gusts of wind, lashing the rain against the windows. The door suddenly opens and Bourrache enters, muffled up and shivering. He is wearing a fancy suit and a hunting waistcoat. His hair is turning grey and he has the appearance of a fairground showman. His entrance wakes up the Waiter.

BOURRACHE: Oh God! The newspapers always get the better of us! No sooner has somebody beaten up some poor fool or smothered some rich old woman, they stick up photographs of the victim and the murderer for you with the kind of detail that's almost impossible to reproduce in wax. If it's a thrill they want, the public buys a newspaper for one sou. They won't pay ten to come into our place any more.

CASHIER: You're right there!

WAITER (*who meanwhile has been serving Bourrache with a drink*): A drop of Cognac, M. Bourrache?

BOURRACHE: With pleasure! (*continuing*) And then there are these theatre swine. I don't know where they get their stories from, but there are writers who will tear your heart apart in less than five minutes. I tell you, I've nothing left to fight with. So, I'm going to sell up and retire to the country.

(*The Waiter, having served Bourrache his glass of cognac, has returned to the counter where he is drying glasses and sorting out the saucers.*)

CASHIER (*smiling*): You may say that, M. Bourrache, but you love your work too much!

WAITER (*playing along*): That's for sure!

CASHIER: Next year you'll be back here again at the Montmartre Fair.

BOURRACHE (*remaining seated*): Not if the weather is anything like this. There are too many storms in Paris. It's wearing out my canvasses.

WAITER (*having finished his work, has sat down on a chair, stage left*): Have you seen the paper? The crime in the rue Fromentin!

BOURRACHE (*banging on the table*): Another crime! In the name of God! The weather! The newspapers! The theatres! It's all a conspiracy against the showmen! There's nothing to do but pack up and bugger off!

(*At this moment shouting can be heard outside, along with whistles and the frenzied shrieks of women being chased during a vice-squad raid. The door suddenly opens and one of them enters, bare-headed, out of breath and trembling, and comes down mid-stage after closing the door behind her.*)

WOMAN (*putting her hand on her heart*): Oh, I'm so scared!

WAITER (*getting up*): What do you want?

WOMAN (*very upset*): Oh, monsieur, please, just give me a minute …

CASHIER: And what a way to make an entrance!

WAITER (*moving towards her*): What's going on?

WOMAN: I beg your pardon, it's …

WAITER (*harshly*): Well, what is it?

WOMAN (*pleading*): It's a raid. Do you mind if I stay for just a moment?

(*The Waiter goes to open the door and gestures for the woman to leave.*)

WAITER: Sling your hook, slut!

WOMAN: But, monsieur, the cops are out there. They'll catch me.

BOURRACHE (*taking pity*): Leave the poor woman be!

WAITER (*taking the woman by the arm*): I don't give a damn! Now, clear off!

CASHIER (*very dignified*): This is a decent café, it is, M. Bourrache. We don't let in unaccompanied women …

WOMAN (*to the cashier, tears in her voice*): For pity's sake, Madame … I beg you … just until the cops have gone past … if they, catch me, I won't get off. It'll be Saint-Lago prison!

WAITER (*leading her by force towards the door*): How about I help you make a speedy escape from here?!

WOMAN (*gripping on to him*): Monsieur, please!

WAITER (*pushing her outside violently*): Or I'll call the cops myself! (*He closes the door behind her.*) Upon my word, what vermin!

BOURRACHE: The poor bitch! Everyone has to make a living somehow.

CASHIER (*dignified*): There are houses for that kind of thing!

BOURRACHE: I'm saying nothing. But even so, the poor thing …

WAITER: Give them an inch and they'll take a mile!

CASHIER: And then there are all these stories about the police.

BOURRACHE: The police would do better if they arrested the murderers rather than rounding up women. Well, there you are – murderers are more dangerous.

(*The door opens as Bourrache speaks these words. Pierre enters, followed by Divonne and Jacques. All three in evening dress and in high spirits. The Waiter goes to greet them, very obsequiously.*)

PIERRE (*standing aside for Divonne*): Well, yes, let's go in here.

WAITER (*standing to attention*): Gentlemen, Madam.

DIVONNE (*entering*): In here? Do you really think so?
PIERRE (*following her*): Why not?
JACQUES (*entering last*): This will be fine.

(*These comments are spoken almost at the same time.*)

DIVONNE (*looking around*): This'll suit me fine.

(*The sound of the rain outside can be heard.*)

PIERRE: We should wait until this downpour passes.
JACQUES: What a dump it is round here! Not a cab anywhere …
DIVONNE (*having taken off her coat and giving it to Pierre, she goes and sits at a table at the back, she is very well dressed with plenty of jewellery*): The waiter will find us one.
WAITER (*wiping the table at which Divonne has sat down*): Of course, Madame, and what would the gentleman like to drink?
DIVONNE: Just a moment. (*to the others*) What would you like?
PIERRE (*places Divonne's coat on a chair and sits with his back to the counter. Jacques sits on the bench to the right of Divonne*): I don't know. (*to Jacques*) What do you think?
WAITER: A drop of champagne?
PIERRE: Yes …
DIVONNE (*animated*): No! We've had enough to drink this evening!
PIERRE (*protesting*): Oh!
DIVONNE (*to the waiter*): Well, say something!
WAITER: Well, what can I get the lady and gentlemen?
PIERRE: Give me a cherry in an eau-de-vie, if you have one.
CASHIER (*interrupting, having checked a jar on the counter*): Yes, there are some left.
DIVONNE: Now, there's an idea! I'll have one too.
JACQUES: Well … (*thinking for a moment*) Me too.
WAITER (*announcing in a thunderous voice*): Three cherries in eau-de-vie! Three!

(*He goes to get them from the counter.*)

JACQUES: Tell me, waiter, are they good?
WAITER: What?
JACQUES: Your cherries?
CASHIER (*indignant*): They are a speciality of the house.
PIERRE (*smiling*): Well, perhaps I shouldn't have one then.
DIVONNE (*giving Pierre a kiss*): My darling little Pierre, you are silly!
JACQUES: We're not going to hang around here for long, are we? Aren't we going to go home to bed?

DIVONNE: You great softy! (*To the Waiter who is tipping the cherries into the glasses.*) Waiter, a jug of water for the gentleman!

JACQUES: What I said wasn't that stupid. It's late. What the hell are we doing here?

(*The Waiter brings over the cherries.*)

DIVONNE: We're waiting for the rain to stop.

PIERRE: Waiter, go and hail a motorized taxi.

WAITER: But, monsieur, a motorized taxi at this hour?

PIERRE: Well, just an ordinary cab, then.

DIVONNE: Look, whatever you can find. (*Hanging the towel around his neck, the Waiter quickly goes out. To Jacques.*) You're always moaning about something! I for one have rather enjoyed this evening. I've never seen a police raid before. It's great.

PIERRE: Does it give you a thrill?

DIVONNE: A thrill! Are you crazy?

JACQUES: It gives me the shivers.

PIERRE (*smiling*): Are you afraid you'll get carted off to Saint-Lazare?

JACQUES: No, but this stampede of hunted animals in the middle of the night, it unsettles me.

DIVONNE (*all the while eating her cherries*): Yes, those poor girls. It's a terrible job all the same!

JACQUES: It's upsetting in a different way to what we just saw at the Grand-Guignol.

PIERRE: That wasn't that bad either.

DIVONNE: Believe you me, that *System of Doctor Goudron*, it didn't half give me a fright! I wouldn't have dared go home alone.

PIERRE (*smiling*): Really?

DIVONNE: I'm not kidding … those plays really scare me.

PIERRE: Then why do you go and see them?

DIVONNE: Because I like it!

JACQUES: I don't get it!

DIVONNE: It's difficult to explain. It's a strange feeling. It gets you right in here. (*She draws a cross on her stomach.*) It churns you up inside. It's both one thing and the other. It is quite distasteful, but at the same time … thrilling!

JACQUES: Ah well, it's quite different with me. I don't like getting frightened.

PIERRE: Frightened? But does fear really exist?

JACQUES: But, of course!

DIVONNE (*to Pierre*): Are you stupid? Of course it exists.

PIERRE (*affirmatively*): If you are rational, if you are balanced, you are never frightened.

JACQUES: It's not a question of reason, old boy. It's a feeling. When you are frightened, you are frightened of everything and nothing, without a reason. A case in point is vertigo. Tell me, have you never been frightened?

PIERRE: Never!

DIVONNE: Oh! You liar!

PIERRE: It's the gospel truth, but no matter how hard I try, I simply can't remember a time …

JACQUES: You mean you've never once experienced one of those stupid, idiotic moments of fear that makes no sense?

PIERRE: No! And I bet nothing will ever happen to me either.

(*Bourrache, who has been listening to the discussion whilst silently smoking his pipe, interrupts good-humouredly.*)

BOURRACHE: And perhaps you will be wrong.

DIVONNE (*to Pierre*): Who is this fellow?

PIERRE (*to Bourrache*): What do you want?

BOURRACHE (*getting up and approaching them, greets them very politely*): Excuse me, gentlemen, madame, I got carried away. When I hear somebody saying that fear is just rubbish, I can't help laughing.

PIERRE (*taking up the challenge*): What do you want, my dear chap? It may not be your opinion, but it is mine. When faced with danger I have never once lost my nerve or my clarity of mind.

DIVONNE (*feeding him a cherry with her fingers*): Really? You are amazing! Have one of my cherries!

BOURRACHE (*getting up*): Very well, monsieur. Look at me, I have strong arms and legs. Do I look like a wilting leek? Well there has been one time in my life, when I was up against the devil himself.

DIVONNE (*leaning her elbows on the table, interested*): Really? How was that?

BOURRACHE: First I need to tell you that I am the owner of a waxworks museum.

DIVONNE: A waxworks museum?

BOURRACHE: Yes, madame.

PIERRE (*also interested*): Ah!

JACQUES: A waxworks museum? At the fair?

DIVONNE (*impatient*): Yes, that's right. A waxworks museum. Now, let the gentleman speak.

PIERRE (*to Divonne*): Be quiet, then.

BOURRACHE (*continuing*): Yes, just over there, it's very close, almost opposite. I tell you I know all about horror. That's what I sell. The severed head of the Murderer Gamahut or the acid attack on the Neuve. They don't bother me at all. When I dust them it does nothing to me … it was a night very much like tonight …

(*The rain can be heard outside getting heavier.*)

JACQUES: What a night out there! (*to his friends*) I say, the waiter is taking his time getting that cab.

DIVONNE (*furious*): Ah! Shut your mouth! Let the gentleman tell his story. (*to Bourrache*) Well?

BOURRACHE: Well, at ten o'clock,I was doing my rounds, checking for prowlers, who sometimes sneak in under the canvas to shelter for the night …

DIVONNE (*smiling*): A well-chosen spot altogether!

BOURRACHE (*continuing*): The canvas was a little loose and then a gust of wind blew out my lantern. When I found myself all alone in the darkness surrounded by my motionless gentlemen, I started to get the shivers and these damned beads of sweat started to form on my forehead. I thought my ticker was going to pack up and that I was going to pass out. (*He puts his hand on his heart.*) Well, I just scampered out of there as fast as I could.

PIERRE (*smiling*): A strapping fellow like yourself! You do surprise me!

BOURRACHE: Well, monsieur, it got me thinking. It's quite natural. You can be brave when you know what the danger is, when it's there before your eyes, right in front of you. If I see some ruffians coming towards me, then I tell myself, 'Look out, old boy, be on your guard.' They sent me off to war against the Prussians. 'That's fine', I said, 'I'm ready for that.' I knew the danger, I expected it, I wanted it. I was mad for it! Whereas in the darkness, in the silence, amongst figures who don't move, there are shadows, things you can't understand and can suddenly grab you by the buttocks and give you a fright, believe me, no matter how intelligent you might be.

(*He goes back to his table and empties his glass of cognac.*)

PIERRE: Your fear is quite ridiculous, my dear chap. One cannot be frightened by something that doesn't actually exist … by the dark or by silence …

BOURRACHE: You can think you've heard more things in complete silence than in the midst of a howling mob. And as for the dark, well that's the stuff of nightmares!

PIERRE: You have a vivid imagination, my friend!

BOURRACHE: No, monsieur, I am just a simple man and you are probably just the same, if you don't mind me saying so.

JACQUES (*to Pierre*): Well, old boy, there's a way of proving to us that you're not so impressionable and the gathering here can provide it now: spend the night in his waxworks museum.

PIERRE: Certainly! I'll spend the night there (*indicating Divonne*), as happily as in her bed.

DIVONNE: Well, thank you very much!

PIERRE (*giving Divonne a kiss*): It's just a figure of speech, my darling. (*to Jacques*) Would you like to have a little wager?

JACQUES: How much?

PIERRE: Whatever you like.

DIVONNE (*working to stop them*): Now, look here!

PIERRE: Leave us alone!

JACQUES: Fifty guineas?

PIERRE: Fifty guineas. Agreed.

DIVONNE: Fifty guineas! But you're drunk!

PIERRE: Leave us alone, I tell you. (*to Jacques*) Only I'll be charged with stealing your money.

JACQUES: I wager you fifty guineas that you won't spend the night in his gaff.

PIERRE (*smiling*): Oh my word!

JACQUES: Do you accept the bet?

PIERRE: Of course!

JACQUES: It's a deal!

PIERRE: It's a deal!

(*They shake hands on it.*)

DIVONNE (*to Pierre*): But, my darling this wager is idiotic! You're not going to walk out on me like this, are you?

PIERRE: Jacques will take you home and tomorrow first thing I'll bring you the fifty guineas he'll be handing over to me when he comes to set me free. (*He gets up.*)

DIVONNE (*smiling*): Well, in that case, that's absolutely fine!

PIERRE (*to Bourrache*): So then, did you hear all that?

BOURRACHE: Yes, monsieur.

PIERRE: Will you let me have use of your museum?

BOURRACHE (*hesitating*): It's just that everything is so fragile there, monsieur …

JACQUES (*to Bourrache*): There'll be a guinea in it for you.

PIERRE (*getting up*): Perfect.

BOURRACHE (*delighted*): A guinea! Well, that's a different matter then. At that price, if monsieur would like to spend every night sleeping there, you can make yourself at home.

PIERRE: No, thank you, I wouldn't want to take advantage of your hospitality.

DIVONNE (*who has got up and put on her coat, helped by Jacques, speaks to Pierre*) Now, my little darling, are you quite sure there's no danger?

PIERRE (*smiling and pointing to Bourrache*): As long as these gentlemen aren't cannibals.

BOURRACHE (*taking his coat from the hat stand*): If monsieur will just take care not to break anything.

PIERRE (*smiling*): Don't worry. I have no intention of grappling with murderers like Gamahut or Pranzini.

WAITER (*coming in*): Your cab is here.

BOURRACHE (*putting on his overcoat*): If the gentlemen would like to follow me, I will take you to my museum.

JACQUES (*to Pierre*): I'm going to come with you.

PIERRE: As you wish. Waiter, what do I owe you?

DIVONNE (*pointing to Bourrache*): Perhaps monsieur would like a drink with us?

BOURRACHE: Thank you, madame, but apart from absinthe, I don't touch alcohol.

WAITER (*having added up the bill in his head, to Pierre*): That is three francs, monsieur.

PIERRE (*pointing to Bourrache*): And whatever the gentlemen had?

WAITER: That's another six sous.

PIERRE (*handing over a five franc note*): There you are. Keep the change. (*to Bourrache*) I hope you have some amusing exhibits in your museum.

BOURRACHE: Calm down, please, monsieur. I have three well-groomed assassins, the story of a convict, the explosion at Vincennes, an exact reproduction of the Morgue, an exhibition of various Chinese torture techniques …

DIVONNE (*smiling*): How lovely!

BOURRACHE (*half whispering*): I also have a collection of …

PIERRE: Yes, yes, very good, that's quite enough.

BOURRACHE: If madame and the gentlemen would like to follow me, I will show them to you.

(*He opens the door. The wind and the rain get stronger outside.*)

JACQUES (*looking outside*): Brrr!
PIERRE: Ok, ok, we'll follow you.
DIVONNE (*exiting*): What a night!

(*They all leave. The Waiter follows them, obsequiously saying farewell, and closes the door behind them. The noise of the car can be heard leaving.*)

WAITER (*to the cashier, as he comes back in*): Shall we close up?
CASHIER: I think so. Nobody else will come in tonight.
WAITER: Certainly not.
CASHIER: Certainly not clients like that! (*Shrugging her shoulders.*) They had three cherries!
WAITER: And that wager of fifty guineas.
CASHIER (*with another shrug of the shoulders*): Oh well, there you go. Would you pass me the rest of the cherries, Alfred?

(*She points to the glasses that are still half full, where Divonne, Jacques and Pierre have been drinking. The Waiter passes one to her and takes the other for himself.*)

WAITER: Your health, Madame Martin!
CASHIER: And yours too, Alfred!

(*They clink glasses and drink, whilst the curtain falls and there is another burst of wind and rain.*)

ACT TWO

The scenery represents the interior of a fairground waxworks museum. It is a large marquee with a wooden staircase with several steps upstage. At the top of the staircase there is a lockable door. Different groups of waxworks are laid out creating shadowy corners. Stage right, another part of the museum is hidden by a curtain that moves on an iron rail.

As the curtain rises the stage is empty and in complete darkness. In the distance can be heard bursts of wind and rain occasionally interspersed with rumbles of thunder. After a while there is the noise of a key being turned and the door at the back opens. Then Bourrache appears, holding a lantern. The lantern only illuminates the upper body of the waxworks figures. Pierre, Jacques and Divonne remain behind him.

It is not difficult to show a waxworks museum with several boards or mannequins that can be painted or dressed. The darkness affords the objects an air of mystery, as they are barely visible and there is little point in seeking out authentic props. The garrotting chair can be represented by a wooden chair with a plank, painted red, which extends beyond the back of the chair by half a metre, fixed to the back of it. Likewise the guillotine can be represented by two large rods and a piece of wood with a hole in the middle. The severed limbs can be represented by plaster mouldings that have been painted, etc.

BOURRACHE (*leading the way*): This way. (*The visitors enter. Bourrache descends the staircase. Now his lantern illuminates just the bottom half of the wax figures.*) Now, look out and tread carefully.

DIVONNE (*following them*): You could break your neck in here.

PIERRE: Your lantern isn't lit.

JACQUES (*smiling*): Not only is she deaf, but she's blind as well.

PIERRE: For sure.

DIVONNE (*to Pierre and Jacques*): And you've drunk so much champagne that you can't see very well either.

BOURRACHE (*to Pierre, who is close to a mannequin*): Careful monsieur. You're going to bang into the head of the murderer Tropmann. It's not fixed securely.

PIERRE (*smiling*): You mean to his shoulders?

BOURRACHE: Of course. But in the dark I would not be happy if the gentleman knocked it over. It's a head that cost me 45 francs. (*He illuminates a horrific head.*)

PIERRE (*pulling a face as he looks at it*): A bargain!

BOURRACHE (*slowly swinging his lantern around him*): There we are. Have a look!

PIERRE (*looking around*): It's not so bad ...

BOURRACHE (*going to the back with his lantern to the figures behind the curtain that can't be seen*): On this side we have a series of infanticides, along with the abortion at la Glacière, the little corpse of the Rue aux Herbes. And moving on, we have the charred remains from la Villette, the acid victims of Passy ...

DIVONNE (*affected*): Brrr!

BOURRACHE (*continuing with his commentary*): At the back you can see a replica of the crematorium oven. A little to the left is the guillotine that did service for a long time in the colonies. There's an exhibition of torture by the Inquisition. (*to Pierre*) You'll have to be careful not to prick yourself on the throat cutter of Vincennes. She has a knife in her hand.

(*As he is speaking, with his lantern he lights a candle fixed to the wall with an iron bar. The candle faintly illuminates the museum.*)

PIERRE: Don't worry, I won't be trying to seduce her.

JACQUES (*pointing to some kind of table*): And these heads here?

BOURRACHE (*with his lantern, he illuminates some heads, lined up next to each other on a table covered in a red cloth*): Those, monsieur, are the heads of famous guillotine victims.

JACQUES (*pointing to the right*): And behind this curtain?

BOURRACHE (*going to the right*): Those, monsieur, are the museum's most beautiful exhibits. There is a re-enactment of the crime in the rue Monge. The best is yet to come. (*He half-opens the curtain.*) If you would like to see. It's very realistic!

JACQUES (*recoiling*): No, thank you.

(*Bourrache closes the curtain again.*)

PIERRE (*smiling*): Yellow belly! (*to Bourrache*) Tell me, are you quite sure that the rain can't get in?

BOURRACHE: Not at all. I already checked the canvas this morning. There's perhaps a small vent – just enough to let a gentle breeze pass through, to keep things fresh ...

JACQUES (*to Pierre, smiling*): This'll suit you down to the ground.

DIVONNE (*looking around, she suddenly cries out*): Oh, what on earth is that?

PIERRE AND JACQUES (*running towards her*): What's the matter?

DIVONNE (*pointing to something in a chair*): There! Look!

BOURRACHE (*lighting up a severed arm and hand and starting to laugh*): Don't be frightened madame. It's nothing. Just a woman who has been cut up into pieces. I haven't yet had the time to put her on display. (*He picks up the limbs and takes them out of the way.*)

DIVONNE: Oh, the horror! (*to Pierre*) Ah, my darling, I don't want to see any more. I'm off!

PIERRE: Don't be silly. (*to Bourrache*) Tell me, old boy, is there somewhere I can sit down?

BOURRACHE (*indicating left*): On this side there is a chair that is an exact reproduction of the one they use in America to electrocute criminals.

PIERRE: Charming!

DIVONNE: And there's no danger?

BOURRACHE: None at all. It's not wired up.

PIERRE (*throwing an ironic glance around him*): I'm not so sure! I suspect something!

BOURRACHE (*indicating to the right*): And here we have a contraption that comes from Spain. It's for the garrotting torture. You take the condemned man, sit him down, tighten the screw, and bingo! It's neat and tidy. Now, if monsieur wants to have a little lie down, over here is the guillotine.

PIERRE (*laughing*): Yes, yes, very good. I can see that.

BOURRACHE: I've had good money from people like you before, who will always pay for an extra thrill by going to beddy-byes beneath the guillotine. But they always want to take it home with them.

PIERRE (*laughing*): We'll try that another time, eh, Divonne?

DIVONNE: Oh no, that's not my thing at all! I've had enough of this place. It gives me the creeps.

JACQUES (*to Pierre*): Very well, shall we leave you to it?

PIERRE (*to Divonne, kissing her*): Goodbye, my darling.

DIVONNE (*kissing Pierre*): Goodbye, my little darling, be good and don't cheat on me.

PIERRE (*smiling*): I'm sure I will – with the Throatcutter of Vincennes.

JACQUES: Until the morning then, old boy.

PIERRE: Don't forget your fifty guineas.

JACQUES (*looking around him*): I must have been drunk to take on this bet. There's nothing very much to be frightened of in a waxworks museum after all. Even I'd happily spend a night here.

PIERRE: Even so, old boy, it's too late for that.

DIVONNE (*climbing the staircase*): Ah yes, it's too late! (*to Pierre*) Goodnight, my darling.

BOURRACHE (*to Pierre*): I'm going to lock you in, because of the prowlers.

PIERRE: Very well, do it then.

BOURRACHE: I'll come and let you out at daybreak.

PIERRE (*accompanying him to the back*): That's it then. Good night and ... thank you.

(*They all leave and Pierre is alone on the stage in darkness. Jacques and Divonne can be heard laughing as they go away, whilst Bourrache locks the door. Then everything is quiet. A long silence. Then, outside in the night, stronger gusts of wind and rain.*)

PIERRE (*slowly goes back down the staircase onto the stage, his hands out in front of him, feeling around like a blind man*): Ah! Let's see if I can find my way around my bedroom. (*He knocks into a wax figure.*) Ah! There's one of my night-time companions. Good evening, old boy! (*He touches it.*) Is it a victim? Is it a murderer? I can't tell. (*He walks and bumps into a chair.*). Ah! It's the garrotting chair. (*He sits down and repeats Bourrache's words.*) You take the condemned man, sit him down, tighten the screw, and bingo! It's neat and tidy! (*He laughs. The rain can be heard running down the side of the canvas.*) Oh, it's pouring down! (*Pause.*) I've got such a headache. That's no surprise after all that we've drunk. It must be at least half past three, four o'clock. Time will pass quickly. (*The wind blows dismally. He turns up the collar of his coat.*) Brrr! It's not exactly warm. He calls that a gentle breeze! More like a biting wind. At least it'll sober me up. (*The wind blows.*) No, I can't stay here. There's such a draft. I'm freezing. (*He gets up and moves. At the same time a clock strikes in the distance.*) Damn, it's only three o'clock! Well, I can always have a smoke. That'll pass the time. (*He takes a cigarette, lights a match and looks around.*) The darkness is a strange thing! At first, it's as if you are completely blindfolded. Then, little by little it lifts, it dissipates, you can make out vague silhouettes. (*He goes back upstage.*) Over there I can make out two bars. Yes, two large bars, you might say. It's a gymnasium! (*Seeing better.*) But no, it's the guillotine, the famous guillotine that did service … Here's the basket … the blade … it's impressive all the same! (*He throws away the match, which casts a light on the ground.*) Earlier it was all very amusing, but now in the darkness, it makes you … (*Suddenly there is the sound of footsteps and voices behind the canvas. The voices get nearer and the following dialogue can be heard, in hushed tones.*)

FIRST VOICE: We just have to get in under the canvas.

PIERRE (*shuddering*): Eh?

SECOND VOICE: Have you seen what's inside?

FIRST VOICE: A waxworks museum.

PIERRE (*listening*): What on earth do they want?

SECOND VOICE: Oh well, nothing in there we can cook then?

FIRST VOICE: Maybe …

SECOND VOICE: There won't be. Let's go to Corvi's place. We can heat something up …

(*The footsteps and voices disappear into the distance.*)

PIERRE (*with a sigh of relief*): Ah! It was just prowlers. (*Thinking aloud.*) All the same, these voices, all of a sudden out of the darkness, when you're not expecting it. (*He shivers slightly.*) This darkness gets to you after a while. (*The wind blows.*) Oh, that wind! It makes the canvas slap! And I still have to spend many hours here. I'm already beginning to find the time dragging. (*Suddenly jumping at a whistling sound.*) What was that? (*Once again the whistle of a train passing in the distance is heard.*) I'm so stupid! It's a train whistle. It's strange that at night the smallest sounds acquire an extraordinary intensity. I can just make out the ticking of my watch! (*Feeling the pocket of his waistcoat.*) But no, I haven't got it with me. Well it's the beating of my heart. (*Putting his hand on his heart.*) My heart is beating fiercely. Nevertheless, I don't feel anything. It's ridiculous! (*Looking slowly around.*) Man is rational. There is something indefinable, mysterious, unnerving, that you can feel in this blackness amongst all these immobile forms that can't be seen, but can be sensed. It's like being in the morgue with all the corpses standing up. Ah! I can't stay here like this all night. (*He walks to the back.*) Now where's my chair, the famous garrotting chair? Ah! There it is. (*He bumps into the chair on which are the severed limbs of the butchered woman. He feels for the chair.*) No, I don't think this is it. (*Trying to orientate himself.*) We came in this way … yes, the door is definitely on this side … at the right … no, I don't know any more, I'm lost. If there was a fire and I wanted to save myself, I wouldn't be able to find the door. (*Giving a start all of a sudden.*) Eh? I heard a noise! (*Thinking.*) The wind must have knocked something over. (*He listens.*) But no … I heard something else. (*Calling out.*) Who's there? (*Pause.*) Perhaps it's outside. (*Calling more loudly.*) Who's there? (*Pause.*) Perhaps it's a rat. (*To himself reassuringly.*) Come on, old boy, don't get yourself into a state because there are rats in the place. (*Suddenly he stops in his tracks and looks ahead of him.*) What's that shadow there? I could have sworn it moved! It did! (*He starts to move forward.*) Ah! In the name of God! (*He stops.*) But no, there's nobody there. I'm alone here, quite alone. (*Pause.*) Well, there's nothing for it, but to go and see, it's as simple as that. (*He goes back upstage, his hand touching one of the heads on the table.*) What's that? (*He feels it, then feels the one next to it.*) Ah! They are the heads, the severed heads ... the famous victims of the guillotine. (*Quickly pulling his hand away.*) They feel cold to the touch ... it's horrible. (*Suddenly looks ahead of him, terrified.*) There. I'm sure the curtain moved. (*Trying to pull himself together.*) Come on! What's got into me? Am I scared? Scared of what? Scared of silence? Of the dark? Of all these mannequins ... Of these wax figures? Ah, that's stupid. (*He laughs nervously as he slowly moves forward.*) What can possibly be behind this curtain? (*He pulls back the curtain and looks, the faint glowing candlelight shines onto the wall at the side.*) It's the Crime at the rue Monge. A man who cut the throat of a woman ... (*Suddenly afraid, he turns around.*) Ah! This time, something did move! (*He moves forward and bumps into the garrotte, crying out in fear.*) Ah! (*Touching the chair.*) Ah, it's nothing ... (*Continuing to walk to the left.*) It's not possible. There's nobody there, I have to go and see, just to be sure. (*He moves to the left, stops in front of a group of mannequins and touches them.*) There, it's a mannequin. This one too. And this. (*Suddenly, reaching out his hand towards a group of wax figures, he cries out and recoils in fear and turns his head.*)

Ah! What was that I just touched? There by my hand it feels like ... (*He daren't look at it.*) Oh, but I'm going crazy ... I'm imagining things. (*Slowly he turns his head to look. Then he notices a shadow that is slowly moving. He cries out in fear and retreats upstage.*)

Oh, it's moving! It's moving! (*The shape moves towards him.*) The wax statue is moving! (*He cries out loudly and collapses into a chair in the middle of the other wax figures.*)

WOMAN (*from the first act, who has been hiding amongst the group of wax figures and, discovered by Pierre, has stood up and walked towards him*): For pity's sake, Monsieur, don't cry out, don't be frightened. I'm all alone, you have nothing to be scared of! (*She feels her way to Pierre's side.*) I slipped in under the canvas to escape the cops. There's been a crackdown this evening and those fellows are out to get me, because I wouldn't sleep with Brunaud, their boss. I'm not welcome in the cafes, so I came here. I didn't think anyone would find me. I never make any noise and you're the only person to come in here. But I've done nothing wrong. Don't turn me in to the cops. (*Thinking that Pierre has said something.*) Eh? (*Realizing he hasn't said anything, after a pause, she carries on talking.*) I'll be nice to you, if you like. I won't charge you anything. Would you like that? (*Flirtatiously, as she moves towards the group where Pierre is.*) You don't have to be a dirty old man to come to places like this, do you, my darling. (*She smiles, then suddenly, she stops.*) But where are you? (*She moves forward.*) I can't see you any more amongst all the other gentlemen. (*Pause. Suddenly afraid.*) Monsieur, speak to me! Where are you? (*Suddenly stepping back.*) Don't frighten me. I have a weak heart. I'll pass out. (*Suddenly, her eyes fall upon Pierre who is motionless.*) Ah! There you are. I can see you. Why aren't you speaking to me? That's not very nice! (*She goes over to him.*) Come on, speak to me! You're frightening me! (*She shakes Pierre, who suddenly slides off his chair and falls in a heap on the ground.*) Ah! What an idiot I am! It's a mannequin! Damn! I've gone and knocked it over. (*She gives him a kick.*) You bastard! You didn't half give me a fright! (*She bends down*) I'd better check that it's not damaged. (*She touches it, then cries out in fear.*) Ah! No! It's him! It's that man! And he's not moving. (*Bending over him.*) Monsieur! Monsieur! What's the matter? Monsieur! Monsieur! Perhaps he's dead. Oh! My God! What am I to do? And I'm all alone. Alone with a corpse! Ah! (*Crying.*) Help me! Help! (*Then she retreats to the other end of the tent, her teeth chattering and hiding her head in in her hands.*) I'm scared! I'm scared!

(*Suddenly there is the sound of voices on the other side of the canvas.*)

FIRST VOICE: Didn't you hear anything?

SECOND VOICE: In here?

FIRST VOICE: Yes. I tell you there's somebody in there.

WOMAN (*looking up and listening*): The cops! …

FIRST COP: Let's have a look. Let's go in under the canvas.

SECOND COP: Wait while I unhook the lantern.

WOMAN: If they find me here with him (*pointing to the body*), they'll think that …

FIRST COP (*suddenly appearing at the back, a lantern in his hand. Holding it in front of him, he sees the woman*): What the hell are you doing here?

WOMAN (*pleadingly*): Oh, officer …

SECOND COP (*coming in, to his colleague*): I told you there was somebody here.

WOMAN: Officer, I can explain everything ....

FIRST COP (*brutally*): Explain what?

WOMAN (*looking around*): Well, you see, there was a bust this evening wasn't there? Well, I slipped in under the canvas to escape the vice squad ... Brunaud's out to get me, because I won't sleep with him ...

FIRST COP (*interrupting her*): Yes, all right, all right. Who were you talking to just now?

WOMAN (*lying*): Er ... nobody.

SECOND COP: Ah! You bitch! You were with some feller you picked up at the fair and dragged in here!

WOMAN (*vigorously protesting*): But no, officer!

FIRST COP (*holding up his lantern to her and looking into her eyes*): Are you alone?

WOMAN (*staring at him*): Of course.

SECOND COP: So, who was it who shouted out?

FIRST COP: Come on, answer!

WOMAN (*after a short pause*): Er ... it was me ...

SECOND COP: And why?

WOMAN (*without too much difficulty*): Because ... very well ... when I realized I was all alone here ... in the darkness ... amongst all these gentlemen ... it gave me a real fright ... that can happen can't it? And it just made me cry out. There you are! (*She forces a smile.*)

FIRST COP (*to his colleague*): Very well, take her away!

SECOND COP: As you've nowhere to go to, we've got a nice cosy cell waiting.

WOMAN (*struggling*): Surely you're not going to nick me?

SECOND COP: Give me a reason not to! (*He takes her by the arm.*)

WOMAN: But, officer ...

SECOND COP (*leading her away*): Now, don't be difficult ...

FIRST COP (*lighting the way, to the second cop*): Ah! Look over there!

SECOND COP (*dragging the woman away, stops*): What?

FIRST COP: It's a funny thing, all the same, this waxworks museum.

SECOND COP (*looking around*): I've never seen anything like it. All these mannequins are a fine thing!

FIRST COP (*casting the light around and looking at Pierre's body*): And this one over here, stretched out on the floor. Look at this one!

(*The woman turns away, frightened, her whole body shaking.*)

SECOND COP (*going nearer*): That's amazing! You'd think it was real.

FIRST COP (*to the woman*): Come on then, let's go. Off with you!

WOMAN (*protesting*): But I won't go! I've done nothing! Leave me alone! (*The cops lead her away by force. She struggles.*)

SECOND COP: Ah, the slut!

FIRST COP: Put the handcuffs on her!

WOMAN (*crying as they drag her away*): Leave me alone, I say, leave me alone. You're hurting me! You dirty bastards! Leave me alone! Please! Listen ... I'll be nice to you ... leave me alone!

(*One of the cops lifts the canvas and the other pushes the woman through. Then they disappear.*)

And the curtain slowly falls to the sound of the woman's cries and the threats of the cops. And a distant clock slowly strikes four o'clock.

CURTAIN

The Lovers
(*Les Amants*, 1901)

Octave Mirbeau

Characters:
Host
Man
Woman

A moonlit park. To the right, a stone bench beneath a tree with overhanging branches. The stage is empty. The Host, who could be the director of the theatre, enters stage left. He is dressed very formally in black with white gloves. He moves with elegant little steps as far as the proscenium and bows to the audience.

HOST: Ladies and Gentlemen ... You see before you the quiet corner of a park one summer evening. It is a pleasant evening, tranquil, the air is thick with sweet scent ... Against the sky the foliage is bathed in moonlight and looks like black lace against purple silk. Between the shadows, between vague and strange silhouettes, you can see in the gloom, veiled by a silvery mist, the glimmer of water ... A pond? A lake? Who knows. You decide. But look at the setting – so misty, so divine! Love is everywhere. It is in the clearing and in the undergrowth ... It moves all around ... invisible. It stirs the branches of the trees, very, very, gently ... Delicious.

(*He indicates the bench. With emotion.*)

And here is a bench. An old bench. Not too overgrown. Not too mossy. A very old stone bench. Large and smooth like an altar ... An altar where you could offer the holy sacrament of *love*.

(*Declaims.*)

If benches be the seat of love ... Make yourself comfortable.

(*Pause.*)

Ladies and gentlemen, whenever a curtain rises and you see a bench beneath a tree next to a fountain or anything else for that matter, you just know that it can only be a love scene. I don't even need to tell you that any minute now, in this exhilarating night – oh, the melancholy of a heart in love! – a young man, according to custom, will sit on this bench beside a young woman. Once there, both of them will take turns in murmuring and moaning, weeping and sobbing, singing and extolling the virtues of things eternal ...

(*Looks across the park.*)

What did I say? I can hear the leaves rustling ... and I can see two shadows slowly coming through the branches ... There they are ... Oh, how sad they look!

(*The Man and the Woman enter slowly. They both look sad. The Woman is wearing lace and the Man is in a dinner jacket. As they appear, the Host salutes the audience, discreetly steps back and exits.*)

MAN: Ah! The bench ... That beloved bench ... (*He moves towards it, putting his arm around the Woman's waist. Tenderly.*) That old and beloved stone bench ... So often a witness to our rapture .... And our ecstasy ...

WOMAN (*aside*): Not the bench again ...

MAN: You seem tired ... Would you like us to sit down for a while?

WOMAN (*distractedly*): If you want.

MAN: Come along, then .... Give me your hand.

WOMAN (*aside*): Always the same bench!

MAN: You are so beautiful! You are particularly beautiful tonight, my dear ... And what a beautiful evening too. (*They sit down on the bench. The Woman, on the right, rather tensely; the Man leans towards her, takes both her hands and stares into her eyes. A lengthy silence.*) What a *delectable* evening ...

WOMAN (*still distracted and vague*): Delectable.

MAN: Isn't it just!

WOMAN: Yes.

MAN (*poetically*): Ah! What sweet mystery can compare with love? Every night, we come here ... The same things surround us every night ... the same starlight, the same dreamy moonlight ... and yet every night I seem to discover pleasures that are new ... and stronger .... And ... more ... more mysterious than before ... more unknown ... and so sweet ... so sweet! (*A bird squawks in fright and flies out of the tree above them. The Man stops talking abruptly. He is terrified and drops the Woman's hand, staring at where the bird flew from. Then he takes her hands again even more passionately.*) And so sweet. (*Silence.*) So very sweet! Wouldn't you say so?

WOMAN: What?

MAN: So very sweet.

WOMAN: Who?

MAN (*rather disconcerted*): But ... I don't know ... the starlight .... The dreamy moonlight ... the birds in the trees ... (*suddenly enthusiastic*) And our passion ... Our wild passion!

WOMAN: Ah yes ... sorry ... so very sweet. (*She sighs.*)

MAN (*after a short silence, very upset*): Why do you have to say it like that?

WOMAN: How do you want me to say it?

MAN: I don't recognize your voice any more ... I don't recognize *you* any more. You've completely changed. (*Pause.*) My darling. (*Silence.*) My treasure. (*Silence. Insistent.*) Darling treasure of my heart's desire. (*Silence. He reaches over and grasps her tightly. She recoils slightly.*) Why don't you say something? What are you thinking about?

WOMAN: Nothing.

MAN: Nothing? Are you angry or something?

WOMAN: Angry?

MAN: Yes.

WOMAN: Why should I be angry? Do you *want* me to be angry?

MAN (*tenderly*): Of course not ... I was just wondering ... I was only asking ... I beg you to tell me ... *Are* you angry?

WOMAN: Do I have any reason to be angry?

MAN (*very sad*): But you weren't saying anything. I was telling you ... telling you some things ...

WOMAN (*rather bitter*): 'So very sweet'.

MAN: Yes ... Well ... I was talking and you said nothing.

WOMAN: I'm not angry anyway.

MAN: Are you sad?

WOMAN: No. of course not. Should I be sad? (*She sighs.*)

MAN (*lively*): There's something ... there's something you're not telling me!

WOMAN: No, honestly, there's nothing –

MAN: I am not mistaken! My heart knows it! And my heart is never wrong! What is it?

WOMAN: Nothing.

MAN (*passionately*): Tell me! Tell me! What is it?

WOMAN (*irritated, she stands up and walks stage left*): Nothing ... Nothing, I tell you! (*She bursts into tears.*) Nothing.

MAN (*hurrying over to her*): You're crying! Oh, you're crying!

WOMAN: No, I'm not – I am not crying!

MAN: Yes, you are!

WOMAN: Let go of me!

MAN: I can hear you crying – why are you crying?

WOMAN: I'm just a bit emotional, that's all ... Maybe it's the night ... (*bitter*) Maybe it's the starlight .... The dreamy moonlight ... and our passion! Nothing, you see ... I'm not crying. (*She sobs.*) This is ridiculous! I don't want ... I don't want to cry ...

MAN (*searching for words*): My darling ... my beloved ... my sweetheart ... You are my sweetheart, aren't you? And I ... I ... I'm yours ... (*Woman shakes her head sadly.*) Yes, I am! We belong to one another! Of course we do!

WOMAN (*shaking her head and wailing*): Yes, we 'belong' to one another ... Nothing more than that!

MAN: Listen to me. I don't want you to cry. There's really no need. You mustn't cry. You don't have the right to cry. When you cry ... it drives me mad ... I simply can't bear to see it ... Look – just answer me. Have mercy on me ... Have some pity ... Answer me (*Looks at his hand.*) Oh look! A teardrop has fallen on my hand, a precious tear from your beloved eyes ... on my hand!

WOMAN: No, I tell you, no!

MAN: Yes, yes!

WOMAN: A drop of dew, that's all ...

MAN: Yes! A drop of dew from your eyes ... from your beautiful eyes ... on my hand. (*Kisses his own hand.*) Dearest ... dearest little teardrop ... on my hand (*Pause.*) Have I hurt you?

WOMAN: Do you think you have hurt me?

MAN: I obviously have ... but I don't know how ... I didn't mean to, I swear ...!

WOMAN: No, no.

MAN: Well ... has someone hurt you? (*heroically*) Ah! If anyone ever tried to hurt you! (*very agitated*) Them, for example! (*He gestures threateningly at some distant figures.*)

WOMAN: Calm down ... Stop it now ... What good would that do ... You don't understand ... It's not your fault ... You're a man and I'm a woman.

MAN (*tenderly and cynically at one and the same time*): Oh, come off it! If you weren't a woman, I'd –

WOMAN (*pushing him back*): Don't be so vulgar!

MAN (*clasping his hands together*): Oh!

WOMAN: It's very clear you'd never understand. Only a woman could understand. Only a woman would understand how I suffer. (*She takes a few steps.*)

MAN: Oh – you're suffering!

WOMAN: No, not quite …

MAN: I know it – I knew you were suffering …

WOMAN: Let go – I'm tired of you – take me back to the house.

MAN: Please – I beg you! Tell me all about your suffering … Your beloved suffering … Aren't I your … your … aren't I? (*quietly*) Your dearest friend? Not just your lover – not just the friend of your lips, your eyes … your hair … and every passionate and secret inch of your flesh –

WOMAN: Oh – that – obviously.

MAN: Aren't I also the friend of your thoughts … your heart … your soul? (*passionately*) Aren't I still deep inside your soul? Oh – how horrible! I beg you!

WOMAN: No – let go. Take me home. Nothing will change what I said. I was wrong to show you my feelings. I'd better be alone in my suffering.

MAN: Alone in your suffering? Ah – no! I will not allow it! Never! Never! I want to share your sorrow! I want all my share of your sorrow!

WOMAN: Don't keep asking … I won't do it … it's honestly better if I …

MAN (*exalted*): I want to share your sorrow! I want it, do you hear me? I want it all! All your sorrow! All your beloved sorrow! All of it, do you understand? To suffer *alone*? It's monstrous to hear you say such a thing … Ah! No! A thousand times no! (*caressingly*) I want you to be happy!

WOMAN: Ah! How could I possibly be happy since …

MAN: Since what?

WOMAN: Since you don't love me any more.

MAN: God in Heaven! Don't love you any more!?

WOMAN: Without a shadow of doubt.

MAN: Why on earth do you say such a thing?

WOMAN: I say it because you don't love me any more.

MAN: But … that's insane … it's … it's … totally crazy … It's madness … total madness … madness, I tell you … I don't love you any more? Why that's *blasphemous*! It's … it's … insane! (*Reacting to a movement of Woman.*) Completely!

I stand by what I said – it's madness ... You're out of your senses ... Where on earth did you get that crazy idea ... that I ... I ... I don't love you any more?

WOMAN: All at once I saw the whole picture.

MAN: The whole picture ... the whole picture ... But that's not enough ... You're being too vague ... Be precise ... You must be more precise ...

WOMAN: You're not like you used to be.

MAN: What?

WOMAN: I think you're bored with me.

MAN: What? *What*?

WOMAN: You've started smoking again.

MAN: But I never stopped, sweetheart. Just think about it – you know it's true. I've never stopped smoking now, have I?

WOMAN: Not like you smoke now ... before ... you'd never dare smoke ... *afterwards* ...

MAN: Let me – ah – let me ...

WOMAN: And now ... you're letting yourself go.

MAN (*stupefied*): What? What do you mean?

WOMAN: You take no pride in how you look any more. You neglect your appearance.

MAN: What? What?

WOMAN: Things like that do not escape the attention of a delicate lady ... a lady who loves –

MAN: Oh! I didn't expect that! That's really quite insulting, you know! Letting myself go? Everything else you've said, I can handle – maybe – but I draw the line at that. Let myself go. (*bitter and annoyed*) So, you think I'm dirty, do you?

WOMAN: Did anyone say that?

MAN: No – but you find me disgusting, do you?

WOMAN: Here we go – you and your exaggerations!

MAN: Come on now, in what way have I changed? This whole thing is extremely humiliating, believe me. Yes – I feel humiliated. Humiliated more than anything else. Very ... very humiliated ... (*affected dignity*) For my honour ... In the name of our love ... I demand an explanation ... I demand it. Because I am, after all, extremely humiliated.

WOMAN: I can't be more precise ...

MAN: That's easy to say ... good grief!

WOMAN: There is ... Something a little shady ... Something not quite palatable ... which seems to grow the more it remains unexplained.

MAN: Something 'shady'? Me – a man of my standing, my

reputation so well deserved, a man like me – 'shady' … It's inconceivable … It is absolutely humiliating. (*Silence.*)

WOMAN: I notice you don't deny it.

MAN: What? I don't deny it? You really are quite bizarre this evening … Yes, I deny it. I deny it with every fibre of my being!

WOMAN: No! This is why I sense that you don't love me any more. Before, you would've gone into a rage.

MAN: But I am in a rage … I am in a rage!

WOMAN: Not like before.

MAN: This is too much.

WOMAN: Nothing matters to you any more. Take this afternoon. I thought I was going to die.

MAN (*profoundly stunned*): Die? This afternoon? Come off it, I never saw you so happy … So charming … So joyful … So loving … Remember … in the drawing room … Remember the drawing room … The curtains closed … The divan … My caresses … Forgotten …! Your kisses … Meaningless!

WOMAN: What are you saying?

MAN: I'm reminding you that I held you in my arms … And when my hand strayed underneath your lace … Ah! How beautiful you were … swooning yet willing! I said –

WOMAN: Shut up! How vulgar you are!

MAN: And you thought you'd die? Die of happiness maybe!

WOMAN: Oh, you conceited oaf!

MAN: Well, what *did* you think you'd die of this afternoon?

WOMAN: You need to ask?

MAN: Yes … I'm asking … (*energetically*) I need to know.

WOMAN: You know only too well.

MAN: I swear –

WOMAN: Don't swear. It's not nice to swear.

MAN: I swear … I've tried to remember … I've racked my brains … What happened this afternoon?

WOMAN: Let's say nothing happened, shall we? I mean, what's the point of talking about it. You never see anything. You never feel anything. It's best that I hide my feelings from you. What do my feelings matter to you anyway?

MAN: Now … now … now … Let's not get in a muddle over this … It's not a question of your feelings … this afternoon … It's more a question of –

WOMAN: You see, you don't want to talk about it –

MAN: To tell you the truth, my darling, I haven't understood a word you've said … You are behaving very strangely this evening.

WOMAN: Strangely? That's right. I am strange. Ah! That's just what I need now – to be insulted!

MAN: Come on, now ... I didn't insult you ... I just said that you were acting a little strange this evening.

WOMAN: And you? What about you? Does it matter to you that every single minute you hurt my most delicate, intimate feelings.

MAN: I hurt your –

WOMAN: And you love me? Oh, for a man with courage! They often say that only a man with true heroism could love a woman as young, rich, beautiful and sought after as –

MAN: It's not a question of that.

WOMAN: And you think you have done all you need to for her, a woman who sacrificed everything for you, when you said ... between two puffs of a cigar ... that you loved her!

MAN: That's not fair, let me –

WOMAN: You love me? But are you ever interested in my happiness?

MAN: Of course ...

WOMAN: Had you only for more than a split second given your entire life to me ... a woman who has given everything to you – not just my life but my reputation ... my tranquillity ... my honour ... (*With a sudden romantic gesture.*) Yes! My honour!

MAN: But darling –

WOMAN (*interrupting*): Had you only avoided me, like a decent gentleman would have ... A gentleman who understands the modesty of a lady ... and respects a good family ... the terrible difficulties in being in a situation like mine. You? Never. I merely flatter your vanity ... your arrogance ... and, of course, you've used me like a trophy!

MAN: Oh! That's simply too much! Totally irrational – just like all women!

WOMAN: But you have used me like a trophy ... Can you honestly say that you haven't used me like a trophy?

MAN: Let me say something – let me speak, will you.

WOMAN: Restaurants ... summer fetes and garden parties ... boxes in the theatre ... Who knows where else? And your friends ... all those friends you dragged round to my house ... and who know every intimate detail of our personal life ... (*Man protests.*) Well, what do you have to say to that?

MAN: Be fair! Just think about it – my friends ... the restaurants ... the theatre ... they were all *your* idea! Sweetheart – you wanted all these things ... You insisted!

WOMAN: Me?

MAN: Yes ... you ... In the name of love, of course, all for love.

WOMAN: Well, at least one thing's clear. You have absolutely no sense of decency.

MAN: Just think about it ... just give it a moment's thought. How many times have I had to tell you to curb your bold behaviour?

WOMAN: 'Bold behaviour'. That's a pretty choice of words –

MAN: Your *charmingly* bold behaviour ... How many times have I tried to stop you being too impulsive ... how many times have I warned you against being foolish.

WOMAN: This is horrible!

MAN: I have never *stopped* you ... Try to understand, my dear, dear darling; on the contrary ... I was overwhelmed by you ... I was intoxicated! I said to myself 'What a noble spirit! What a free spirit! She loves me in spite of it all – in spite of gossip, prejudice, stupidity.' You were *sublime* ...

WOMAN: Really? Now that *is* impressive ... Your ignorance is beyond belief ... So you think that I had a desperate need to scream to the world: 'This is the man I love! Look at him – he is my lover!'? It's only natural, isn't it? (*angry*) So that's how much you estimate me, is it? What do you take me for? I'm just a trollop, am I?

MAN: Think about what you've said, just think about everything you've said. Where's your proof?

WOMAN: My God! It's perfectly clear ... I was just a slut to you ... one of those miserable creatures ... You never tried to spare me the presence of such women ... Now I understand why ...! Ah! I see it all ... How wicked! How despicable! (*Hides her face in her hands and sobs.*) Oh, the shame!

MAN (*lost*): Ah – now you're crying again ... My God! My God! I'm lost for words – I don't know what to say.

WOMAN: Did I deserve to be treated so cruelly? Did I? You are so *cruel*.

MAN: Listen (*He takes her arms and gently leads her to the bench and sits her down.*) Listen to me ... I beg you. (*He very cautiously kisses her.*)

WOMAN: No ... no ... I don't want you to ... never again ... You don't deserve it ... It's disgusting!

MAN: Don't cry. It *tortures* me to hear you crying.

WOMAN: Oh? What are you going to do about it? What can you possibly do?

MAN: Well ... yes ... I have wronged you ... my adorable love ... and I didn't even realize it ... you've been terribly wronged ... Yes, I admit it. But that's over now ... I'm deeply, deeply sorry! I beg you, please forgive me.

WOMAN (*through her tears*): I wish I'd never been born! I wish I was dead!

MAN: Don't talk like that ... please ... *Dead*? You really don't have the right to –

WOMAN: Yes! It's true! It'd be better if I were dead! Oh, now ... all my hopes are dashed ... forever ... don't you see? I am nothing to you ... Your true love? No, just an object ... just a bit of fun, that's all ... I am nothing to you ... my soul means nothing to you.

MAN: Your soul?

WOMAN: Yes, my soul ... my poor, wretched soul ... What is it to you?

MAN: Ah, your soul! Don't blaspheme, I beg you! Your soul means everything to me!

WOMAN (*gentle and weak*): Nothing ... nothing ... nothing at all ...

MAN (*strong voice*): Everything ... It means everything to me ... Your soul is my life ... my reason for being ... my joy – it means everything to me.

WOMAN: You forget, my dear, that I am a woman.

MAN: No! I think of nothing else ...

WOMAN: A woman ... You must understand that a woman can be like a child sometimes ... no more than a baby ...

MAN (*rocking her*): A tiny little baby ...

WOMAN: A tiny little baby ... a sensitive, vulnerable, weak little baby ...

MAN: Oh, my baby, my baby, my darling baby ...!

WOMAN: She needs to be cosseted, cuddled ... you have to sing sweetly to her soul ... and love her ...

MAN: I will cosset you ... I will cuddle you ... I will sing sweetly to your soul ... Oh yes ... I will sing to you so gently ... Oh yes ... I will sing to you so gently –

WOMAN: Often?

MAN: All the time! All the time!

WOMAN: And then ... Do you think I'm being silly?

MAN: No, of course not! How could you –

WOMAN: Do you think I'm stupid?

MAN: *You*?

WOMAN: Yes, yes, you do – you think I'm stupid, don't you?

MAN: Look ... (*He gives her a long kiss.*) My dear ... my darling ... stupid ... You? You are my sunshine ... my soul ... my everything ... my dear, dear everything ... (*cheerfully*) My little, ickle-wickle everything ...

WOMAN: Because ... if you *did* think I was stupid –

MAN: You are my heartbeat! My life force! You are all that I see! I am always with you – I am always inside you ... Without you ... I'd be nothing ... nothing ... nothing at all ... When we're apart I am lost ... I'm in despair ... like a traveller lost in a forest at night ... like a dog lost in the crowd ... Like ... like ...

WOMAN: More ... tell me more ... It's so wonderful ...

MAN: Never a day goes by ... never a minute ... never a second ... when I don't think of you ... Every day, every evening, every night ... in my dreams ... in my thoughts ... in everything I do ... Never a minute, do you see, never a minute when your heart, your soul ...

WOMAN: More ... more ...

MAN: Your heart ... your soul ... your eyes ... your hands ... your dear hands ... your dear eyes ...

WOMAN: Do you mean it? Swear!

MAN: Yes, yes, I swear! Your lips ... give me your lips ...

WOMAN (*almost swooning*): Oh, darling ... darling ... Never hurt me again ... never hurt your little baby again ...

MAN: Ssh ... I swear ... Never again ... your soul ... your mouth ... your –

(*Silence and passionate kisses.*)

THE END

The Man Who Met the Devil (*L'Homme qui a vu le diable*, 1911)

Gaston Leroux

Characters:
The Man (a handsome man of 80)
Allan (35 years old with a simple elegance and dressed in hunting gear)
The Figure (who resembles Allan like a brother)
Mathis and Mathieu (both thick-set and stocky with a heavy and coarse bearing, mountaineers from the Swiss side of the Jura and dressed in hunting gear)
Guillaume (servant of The Man, about 30 years old)
Claireli (young wife of Mathis, not at all countrified and with a determined and sneaky manner. In hunting gear)
Old Mother Appenzel (almost as old as The Man but is, nevertheless, still working as his servant)

ACT ONE

The two acts take place in the same setting. A gentleman's old dining room with large ceiling beams. An immense hearth is at the back. To the left there is a door with a view over the mountain. Next to the door, further to the left and at a higher level is a window with closed shutters. To the right, on the lower level, a small staircase leads up to the door of the man's living quarters. At the back, to the right of the fireplace, another door leads to the other rooms. To the left, at the back, is a partition, a peculiar-looking door, decorated with a large painted cross. A square table, a large armchair facing the fire. Chairs and stools. To the right, against the wall, is a dresser. It is old, simple furniture, a little gloomy, but nothing that stands out apart from the door with the cross. When the curtain rises on the first act, it is evening. Everything is locked up because the weather outside is atrocious and the wind is battering the old building right to its very foundations. The room is lit only by the fire in the hearth.

Old Mother Appenzel, then Allan, Mathis, Mathieu, Claireli.

At the start of the scene, as the curtain rises, knocking can be heard on the door, along with voices, above the sound of the storm.

APPENZEL (*looking suspiciously at the door*): Who's that knocking at this hour? (*She carefully approaches the door.*) Who's there?

VOICE FROM OUTSIDE: Open the door! Quickly, open up!

VOICE OF MATHIEU: Someone has been injured!

APPENZEL: Injured?

(*She unbolts the door and opens it. Mathieu and Claireli burst in. Allan, supporting Mathis, follows. The new arrivals are rigged out in hunting gear, rifles slung over their shoulders. Mathis is completely white, as if he has been rolling around in the snow. He is the only one without a gun.*)

CLAIRELI: Well, old woman, not a moment too soon!

MATHIEU (*carrying his own gun over his shoulder and Mathis's gun in his hand*): Were you going to leave us to die out there?

APPENZEL (*looks at the door and then at Mathis*): What on earth has happened to you?

MATHIS (*limping a little*): Fear, more than anything else – thankfully!

ALLAN: He took a wrong step and fell over into the snow.

MATHIEU: In the snow? Down a precipice more like! Poor old chap! I had to go all the way back down for him!

CLAIRELI (*taking off her rifle*): Oh, it's nice in here.

ALLAN (*to Mathis*): Come and sit down here by the roaring fire. (*Mathis sits down and Allan divests himself of his gun and game-bag which he places in the corner, upstage right, next to the wooden staircase. As he does this, he addresses Mathis.*) Hey, calm down, for goodness sake, you're trembling again.

MATHIS: Ah! I had such a scare.

MATHIEU (*putting his guns and game-bags down next to Allan's*): You know, I really think that if it hadn't been for …

MATHIS: That's right, if it hadn't been … and make no mistake … if Allan hadn't been right there to grab hold of my hand … when I think …

ALLAN: Well, don't think. Just get yourself dry.

(*Pause.*)

MATHIS: Well, Claireli, you're being very quiet! You were very nearly a widow, you know.

CLAIRELI (*darkly*): That's right, Allan, you saved my husband's life.

ALLAN: Just leave me in peace.

MATHIS (*half-jokingly to Claireli*): Perhaps you're having second thoughts?

CLAIRELI: I can see you're feeling better, Mathis! Joking away, as usual!

MATHIS (*looking at the others*): Yes, now I'm in the mood for a good laugh. Ah, my old friend!

APPENZEL: I bet it happened on the side of the Grande Marnière! It's a treacherous spot. Leduc met his death there only last year ...

MATHIEU: Are we by the Grand Marnière? I thought we'd gone past that ...

APPENZEL: Ah, there you are, you must have got lost up in the mountains.

MATHIEU: Hardly surprising really, what with the fog this afternoon and then the storm after that.

CLAIRELI: Yes, and fortunately we saw your lights burning ...

APPENZEL: Well, you must be very tired, my dear. Go and have a lie down and I'll get something to warm you up. (*She moves towards a chair.*)

ALLAN (*getting up and going to Claireli*): That's right, Claireli, we're forgetting all about you ...

CLAIRELI: Thank you, Allan, but look after my husband.

(*Allan looks at Claireli without answering.*)

MATHIEU: What filthy weather! Who'd have thought it? It just goes to show that the mountain is never predictable! (*He pats Mathis on the back, who is sitting in front of the fire, deep in thought.*) Well then, old chap, are you feeling any better? How's your leg?

MATHIS (*getting up and testing the mobility of his leg*): Everything's fine. My pride's a bit bruised, that's all.

(*Meanwhile Appenzel has taken the soup bowls from the sideboard and put them on the table.*)

MATHIEU: Can we spend the night here? Where are we exactly?

APPENZEL (*immediately retreating to the foot of the stairs as if unnerved by the question*): You're with good people, sir, people who won't see you starve or freeze to death. I'll let the master know ... (*She climbs the stairs.*)

ALLAN: Very good, my dear lady, very good! And come back quickly with some good soup. I, for one, am famished!

MATHIS (*turning round and surveying the scene, speaks suddenly, hesitantly and slightly nervously, eyes fixed on the door with the cross*): Look! ... Look!

ALLAN: What is it?

CLAIRELI (*looking at Mathis, to Allan*): What's got into him?

MATHIS (*takes a few steps towards the door with the cross and then stops, increasingly afraid*): It's the door with the cross!

MATHIEU (*quickly turning round*): The door with the cross!

MATHIS (*stepping back*): We're at *his* house!

MATHIEU (*taking a step towards the door with the cross, forcefully*): But yes … that's right! I wouldn't have thought it possible … but I thought we'd left the Grande Marnière far behind …

ALLAN: But whose house is this then?

MATHIS (*becoming increasingly worked up*): The Man Who Met the Devil!

ALLAN: The what?

CLAIRELI (*shrugging her shoulders*): It's just a fairy tale … local superstition …

MATHIS: There can only be one door like this in the whole of the mountains … (*To Appenzel who has stopped on the staircase.*) What's this door here?

APPENZEL: Nothing!

MATHIEU: Why is there a large cross on it?

APPENZEL: No reason!

MATHIS: Where does it lead, this door?

APPENZEL: Nowhere!

(*She exits.*)

ALLAN (*turning towards the door with the cross and going to touch it*): So what's the story about this door?

MATHIEU (*suddenly grabbing hold of Allan by the arm*): Don't touch that door!

MATHIS (*by the window*): You're right, we must touch nothing. Nothing! We have to leave!

CLAIRELI (*defiantly*): Leave?!

ALLAN: Leave?!

MATHIEU: Yes. This is a terrible place. Leduc must have come here and knocked on the door in the middle of a storm just like this, and they found him the next day at the bottom of the Grand Marnière.

ALLAN: Don't be ridiculous. If Leduc had spent the night here, he wouldn't be dead now.

MATHIS: What do you know about it? I'd rather be out there on the edge of the precipice than stay in this house.

ALLAN: Why?

MATHIEU: Because it is *his* house!

MATHIS: For no other reason.

ALLAN (*goes to Claireli*): They're both mad!

CLAIRELI (*deep in her armchair, warming her feet*): They should be locked up! You'll see, they'll both end up in the asylum with their old wives' tales!

MATHIS: It's not a joke! It's true, it's all true!

MATHIEU: There's proof!

ALLAN: What proof?

MATHIS: He might tell you himself if you stay here! But, believe me …

(*He indicates that he is leaving, fetches his gun and then returns to the table.*)

ALLAN: No! Seriously? You want to leave? Listen to the wind, it's battering the whole of the Jura to its core …

CLAIRELI: That's enough! We're spending the night here! (*to Mathis*) Now, if you'd rather pick your way along the path down to La Chaux-de-Fonds, then goodnight!

ALLAN: This is madness! You can't just let them go …

MATHIS: All right! All right! If that's what you want! On your own head be it! As long as Claireli has her way!

(*He puts down his gun. Mathieu does the same.*)

MATHIEU: We're making a mistake, you'll see, we're making a terrible mistake.

(*Old Mother Appenzel appears at the top of the staircase.*)

APPENZEL: The master sends you his compliments … Now before dinner I will show you to your rooms. (*She opens the door at the back.*) Ah! Keep away from that door! If he sees you there, he'll be very angry.

ALLAN: What's the story about the door then?

APPENZEL: That's nobody else's business.

(*She leaves, followed by Mathieu and Allan. Mathieu takes his gun with him.*)

MATHIS (*goes to follow the others, taking his gun before climbing the stairs*): You know that you're making a mistake in making us stay here?

CLAIRELI: Why?

MATHIS (*showing her the door with the cross*): Do you think it's natural to have this door with the cross on it?

CLAIRELI (*nervously*): Really, Mathis, there are times when I think you are so stupid!

MATHIS: Yes, I've also noticed there are times like that!

CLAIRELI: You drive me to the end of my tether with your insistence on contradicting everybody. You make it impossible for even your best friends. Allan won't come to see us so often ...!

MATHIS (*sombrely*): Allan is an old pal of mine, a childhood friend, a real friend, and earlier he really did save my life. But he did what anybody else would have done in his place. Well, if he doesn't come to see us any more ... (*Pause.*) I'll get over it.

CLAIRELI: What?!

MATHIS: Yes, I've noticed that when he's around, those are the times you find me stupid ...

(*He exits.*)

MATHIEU (*in the wings*): Mathis, come on! What are you doing?

(*Claireli watches Mathis with hatred as he leaves. She collapses with desperation into the armchair and stares into the fire.*)

ALLAN (*appearing in the doorway through which Mathis left*): So, are you not going to have a look at your bedroom?

MATHIS (*in the wings*): Yes, of course ... of course.

CLAIRELI: You know that he suspects something?

ALLAN: Yes, his friend keeps watching us!

CLAIRELI: Allan! ... Alan! ... Allan! ... (*She reaches out to him.*) My dear Allan!

ALLAN (*lovingly, taking her in his arms*): Claireli!

CLAIRELI (*in tears*): Ah! I don't want to live with those two brutes any more. I don't want to see them any more.

ALLAN (*concerned*): Claireli ... please ...

CLAIRELI: How can you be so calm, so composed? Without your composure, earlier today ... yes, you know what I'm talking about ... don't look away from me ... if it hadn't been for you ... (*She passes a finger across her throat.*) You saved him.

ALLAN: That's right!

CLAIRELI: Why did you do that?

ALLAN (*stepping away from her*): Claireli! Claireli! You're frightening me.

CLAIRELI (*taking hold of him again*): Don't pretend that you haven't often dreamt of it yourself. I've sometimes seen it in your eyes, you know, when he's holding me ...

ALLAN: Oh, Claireli!

CLAIRELI: If only eyes could kill.

ALLAN: You're right. But that's the crime of all jealous lovers ... fortunately eyes cannot kill.

CLAIRELI (*with an almost ferocious bitterness*): You're an honest man, Allan. My compliments! But what about me? What am I? What have you done to me? What would become of me if you were to leave? I can't manage without you! Do you know what he said to me earlier? That he would get over it, if he never saw you again. I tell you, the pair of them suspect something! Allan, don't you love me?

ALLAN: Stop it! Stop it! You know that I'm crazy about you!

CLAIRELI (*looking into his eyes*): You're lying. If you had wanted to … if you had wanted to … (*Allan, back to the audience,* Claireli, *looking at him lovingly.*) Coward!

(*They are silent for a second, looking into each other's eyes.*)

(*Mathieu and Mathis enter through the door at the back.*)

MATHIS: There are only two bedrooms.

ALLAN: That's fine. I'll spend the night down here.

CLAIRELI: Why don't we all spend the night down here? We could have a party – Mathis has some playing cards!

THE MAN (*appearing at the top of the staircase*): Good evening, dear guests! (*He comes down the stairs slowly and importantly. He is wearing an old-fashioned coat, silk breeches and stockings, buckle shoes, the elegance of a dandy. He bows grandly before Claireli.*) You must be very tired, Madame, and all I have to offer is the most meagre hospitality.

CLAIRELI: Oh, but, Sir, it is we who must apologize …

THE MAN: But why, Madame? For having brought so much elegance to my modest bachelor's home?

ALLAN (*aside*): He's a right one, the old devil! (*aloud*) Would you allow us to introduce ourselves, good Sir? (*Meanwhile Appenzel finishes setting the table.*) Madame Mathis Brunner and my friend Brunner, originally from Switzerland but living in your beautiful country for some years now; our friend Mathieu – both two old college friends of mine, Allan Danglade at your service, Head of the Medical Faculty at Nancy.

THE MAN (*inviting his guests to sit down*): Madame, Gentlemen. (*Sitting down himself.*) What was it the old woman said? That you'd had an accident?

(*Everybody sits around the table, Mathis and Mathieu rather hesitantly.*)

CLAIRELI: We very nearly had an accident … yes, my husband slipped, but fortunately we were only left a little shaken up …

(*Appenzel carries the soup tureen to the table.*)

THE MAN (*to Claireli*): The mountain is very dangerous in this dreadful weather. If you would allow me, Madame, to serve you myself. It is cabbage soup, the soup of the peasantry.

CLAIRELI: It smells good.

THE MAN (*after having served Claireli*): Appenzel, serve these gentleman and then you can go and find a bottle of my best Neufchâtel. Did the storm catch you by surprise?

CLAIRELI: It was so beautiful this morning.

THE MAN: You don't say! You've been out hunting since this morning? That's very courageous of you!

ALLAN: Courageous? It was because of Madame Bruner that we ended up so far from where we thought we were.

CLAIRELI: And it was because of you, dear friend, that we came back empty-handed. You always lack the necessary composure – unforgivable in a doctor!

ALLAN: That's true. I get very nervous.

CLAIRELI: And very clumsy!

ALLAN (*to The Man*): Isn't she terrible! But I'm used to it. My friends are always teasing me about my clumsiness.

CLAIRELI: He doesn't know one end of a gun from the other.

THE MAN: That sounds very dangerous.

MATHIS (*deciding to join in, churlishly*): And he's always leaving half his equipment at home.

ALLAN (*eating*): Ah! I was waiting for that! Well, what do you expect? They don't teach you how to shoot at medical school, you know! This soup is first-class!

(*Mathis and Mathieu are not eating a single thing.*)

THE MAN (*serving the drinks*): Some of my Neufchâtel?

ALLAN: Excellent! A wonderful bouquet. (*to Mathis and Mathieu*) So, my Swiss friends, are you not eating? I propose a toast to our host ...

THE MAN (*raising his glass*): To your good health, Madame. (*After having drunk, to Mathis and Mathieu who have put their glasses back down without drinking.*) Are you not eating, gentlemen?

MATHIS: I'm not hungry.

MATHIEU: Me neither.

THE MAN (*with disappointment*): No doubt you are overtired. Have you seen your bedrooms? Unfortunately there are only two beds.

ALLAN: If it won't disturb you, Sir, my friends and I have decided to spend the night here in this room.

THE MAN (*astonished*): Not at all ... but Madame Brunner should get some rest.

(*The wind grows stronger.*)

CLAIRELI: How is one supposed to sleep with this storm blowing? (*to The Man*) And besides, these gentlemen have a little something planned …

(*She smiles at Allan.*)

THE MAN: What kind of 'little something', Madame?

CLAIRELI: To spend the night playing cards. It won't be the first time!

THE MAN (*in hollow tones*): Playing cards?! (*Pause.*) Will you be playing too, Madame?

CLAIRELI: But, of course. And you? Don't you enjoy a game of cards?

THE MAN (*darkly*): No … and there are no cards in this house.

ALLAN: We have our own cards!

THE MAN (*slowly getting up*): You brought cards with you? (*To the others who also get up.*) Please, remain seated! Please treat this as your home. Enjoy your game.

CLAIRELI: We've offended you!

THE MAN: No, no, not at all.

CLAIRELI: But we have!

THE MAN: Please, rest assured …

CLAIRELI: Oh, I can tell! As soon as we mentioned playing cards. So there'll be no card games.

THE MAN (*politely protesting*): Oh, Madame!

CLAIRELI: In any case, there's no hurry. Please don't leave us like this. (*With a gracious gesture.*) Please, sit down!

THE MAN (*sitting down again, obediently, in response to Claireli's gesture*): I beg your pardon.

CLAIRELI (*wagging a finger at him*): I can only think that you must be an absolutely terrible card player.

THE MAN (*very seriously*): That's exactly right. Terrible.

ALLAN: So you once lost a game – who hasn't, eh!?

THE MAN (*icily*): I've lost more than anybody else, doctor. I have lost my soul.

ALLAN: Your soul?

THE MAN: Don't you believe in the existence of the soul?

ALLAN: That's a difficult question for a man of science …

THE MAN: Yes, there was a time when I wouldn't have believed in it either. I didn't believe in God, nor …

CLAIRELI: Nor what?

THE MAN: Why are you looking at me like that?

CLAIRELI: I think perhaps you know why.

THE MAN: And you're not frightened?

CLAIRELI: I'm intrigued.

THE MAN: And does it not disturb you to find yourself in my house tonight?

CLAIRELI: No. Why would it?

THE MAN: You'd better ask these gentlemen who've not touched a morsel of my food, nor a drop of my wine. They know full well that this house brings bad luck.

ALLAN (*tapping his chest with his finger, whilst looking at The Man*): What I do know is that there are fools and madmen in the country around here who say that you have met the Devil.

THE MAN (*icily*): Exactly!

CLAIRELI: As you say!

MATHIS (*brutally and with terror*): Shut up, you! Now listen, that's enough! Whatever the gentleman saw or didn't see is his business. It's nothing to do with us!

CLAIRELI: Calm down, Mathis. We're only chatting ...

MATHIS (*brutally*): You shouldn't talk about these things ... (*The wind becomes even stronger.*) Ah, this weather!

THE MAN (*darkly*): Yes, I've never known anything like it ... at least not for many a year.

CLAIRELI: It's true that tonight the wind is making the most horrendous sound.

APPENZEL (*coming in to collect the dishes*): One might say it's like a dog howling in the throes of death.

THE MAN (*to Appenzel*): Be quiet! You know full well that I've forbidden you to use that word! (*He looks at her with venom and she disappears beneath the staircase.*) I beg your pardon. I can't bear to hear that word spoken. You wouldn't know, you're young, but me ... me ... I'm so frightened of death that I would rather be already dead so that I wouldn't have to be afraid any more.

ALLAN: There are people who kill themselves because they are afraid of dying.

CLAIRELI: No?!

THE MAN: It's no laughing matter. I can understand that. It's a terrible thing. When you know that *he* is waiting for you and that *he* is only interested in you and that perhaps *he* is there already, behind the window, outside on the porch ... waiting for you!

(*A sinister howl of wind.*)

CLAIRELI (*deeply affected*): So, it's true then, that you have seen the Devil?

THE MAN (*getting up*): As well as I see you, Madame!

(*They all rise, Mathieu and Mathis take a step back, afraid.*)

ALLAN (*in a mocking tone*): And has it cost you much?

THE MAN (*extending his arms*): Everything in the world!
ALLAN: Really?
THE MAN (*with a malevolent look at Allan*): You don't believe me?
ALLAN: Goodness me, no!
THE MAN (*darkly and hesitantly*): And what if I can prove it?
ALLAN (*smiling*): You were dreaming ...
THE MAN: Yes, of course, the Man of Science is sceptical.
ALLAN (*in a conciliatory tone*): Ah, yes, science ... you know, my dear sir ...
THE MAN: So you don't believe me? Then what do you believe in?
ALLAN: That's tricky ... it's difficult to say ...
THE MAN: And in the meantime you joke!
ALLAN: Not at all. I just don't know what this is all about.
THE MAN: Very well, I will tell you. You were talking of playing cards just now. I was ruined by it, I lost millions ...

(*He stops suddenly in the middle of his story. Pause.*)

CLAIRELI (*expectantly*): And?
THE MAN: At the time I was ruined and in love! Yes, I was madly in love with a very rich young girl, who had no option but to turn me down. (*Pause.*) To cut a long story short, one evening, in my desperation, I found myself in this old house, the only thing from my family that I had left. Everything happened that evening. (*A long pause.*) I was in this room, my loaded gun was in the corner awaiting my final wish. (*He points to the corner where Allan has placed his gun.*) That one over there.
ALLAN: That's mine!
THE MAN: Ah! Suddenly came the calm after the storm. I opened the window. The first thing I saw, up on a rocky outcrop and completely black beneath the moon, a large motionless vulture. This dismal bird unnerved me with its manner of staring straight at me. I aimed and shot just above its head and I'm an excellent shot. But still it didn't move. It just continued to stare at me, cackling menacingly. I moved away from the window and I sat down at this table here to write my final letter to my fiancée, when, lifting my head I saw right in front of me ... Look! (*He gets up and points at the door.*) There, where I've since put the door with the cross, there used to be a large mirror. I saw the mirror start to move and turn all on its own. I got up, captivated. This mirror was used as a door to a cupboard. What could be more simple? Its own weight was causing it to open, that was all! I looked into the cupboard and saw two large

volumes both on the subject of sorcery. The first of the two was called *Sorcery of the Jura* and immediately grabbed my attention because on the cover was embossed a large black vulture, identical to the one that I had shot at just before. (*to Allan*) Oh, I know that proves nothing, but wait! I opened the book. The first two lines leapt out at me. They read: 'If you really want to see the Devil, you need only call him and he will come! But you must call him with all your heart.' I threw the book back into the cupboard and pushed the mirror shut. I must have looked as if I had seen a ghost, or as if I was one myself! But no, alas, the man in front of the mirror was not dead at all! But it was a living being that conjured up the Prince of Death! Yes, I did that, me, who didn't believe in anything. With all my heart I called upon him to help me. To help me! And, suddenly, the figure in the mirror spoke. It said to me, 'Here I am! But I am trapped in here! Open the door! Open it!' And when I didn't dare, there came three knocks from inside the cupboard and the door opened all by itself …

(At that moment, three knocks can be distinctly heard on the front door. Everybody, deeply affected, looks over to the front door and The Man instinctively recoils on seeing the door seemingly open of its own accord, slowly, as if pushed from the outside. Eventually it opens wide and in the doorway stands a figure, completely immobile, covered in a coat and his face hidden by a hat.)

THE MAN (*sharply*): Who's there? Ah! Is that you, Guillaume? Well, come in.

GUILLAUME (*hesitantly sitting down and removing his hat*): I didn't realize you had guests, otherwise I wouldn't have let myself in.

THE MAN: Did you see the solicitor? (*to the others*) I do beg your pardon. This is my manservant, the grandson of the old housekeeper who saw to you earlier.

GUILLAUME (*removing a bag from beneath his coat and pulling out some papers and envelopes*): Here's the paperwork. (*He puts them down on the table.*) And here's the price of the Misère Wood. (*He takes some banknotes out of an envelope and counts out ten.*) Ten thousand … the bill is here.

THE MAN (*counts them for himself, replaces the money in the envelope and leaves the envelope on the table*): Very good. You must be hungry?

GUILLAUME: No, I grabbed something on the way.

THE MAN (*reading one of the documents*): Very well, go and have a lie down, you must be tired.

GUILLAUME: I'll go and sleep over at the farm. I have some business there first thing in the morning.

THE MAN: I need to see you tomorrow morning.

GUILLAUME: Oh, I'll be back nice and early.

THE MAN: Very well. Take the paperwork with you. We'll deal with it all together. (*He takes a wallet from his pocket and puts an envelope into it.*) Ten thousand for the Misère Wood … What did the solicitor have to say about that? (*He puts the wallet back in his pocket.*)

GUILLAUME (*gathering up the papers and putting them in his bag*): That you were getting it for a song!

(*He goes towards the door.*)

THE MAN: We weren't expecting you in such weather.

GUILLAUME: Ah, I would have come whatever the weather. I wouldn't have wanted to carry all that money around with me. Good night!

THE MAN: Good night, Guillaume!

(*Guillaume exits. The Man bolts the door after him.*)

CLAIRELI: And what happened next?

ALLAN: After the cupboard door opened all by itself?

CLAIRELI: What was in the cupboard?

THE MAN: There was something that made my eyes burn … letters all in flames … (*getting worked up*) three words! 'You will win!'

ALLAN: What? 'You will win'?

THE MAN (*harshly*): Don't you understand? With three words in flaming letters at the back of the cupboard, the Devil had pronounced my destiny! 'You will win!' I was a ruined gambler and I wanted to become rich again. It said simply 'You will win!' With those three words I was given all the wealth in the world. 'You will win!' Now do you understand?

ALLAN: Of course! And I know one or two gamblers who would like to meet this devil of yours …

THE MAN: Please, don't make fun of me any more. The next morning, Appenzel found me collapsed on the floor by the cupboard. When I came to, alas, I hadn't forgotten a single detail. I can never forget a single detail.

ALLAN: And *did* you win?

THE MAN (*terribly sombre*): Always!

ALLAN: What? *Always*?

THE MAN: Oh yes, always!

ALLAN: Can you prove it?

THE MAN (*sharply*): Do you think I'm lying to you?

ALLAN: No! But I do think that you have been the victim of an hallucination ...

THE MAN (*edgily*): Yes, I see. But you don't need to be a genius to think of that possibility. I've had the same idea myself. I borrowed some money against the house. A few days later I went gambling, saying to myself, 'Now we'll see if the Devil ...' I never got to finish my sentence. As I entered the room, they were offering the bank to the highest bidder. I got it for 200 louis. I'd hardly sat down before I had won a hundred thousand francs. Nobody had a chance against me. It was frightening how I won every single hand. If I had a flush, nobody else would have one. I started to deal out hands for nothing, for free, just for fun, to see what would happen. I lost every single one of these hands. It was only when money was involved that my luck returned.

CLAIRELI: And then?

THE MAN: I wanted to redeem myself. I went back to playing for money. By the time I left at six o' clock in the morning, I had won every hand.

CLAIRELI: You didn't lose a single hand?

THE MAN: Not a single one.

CLAIRELI: So, what do you say to that, Allan?

ALLAN (*rising from his chair and going over to the fireplace*): I say that I'd like to have a game of cards with this gentleman.

MATHIS *and* MATHIEU (*quickly, in low tones*): Don't, Allan, it won't do any good.

ALLAN: Don't worry!

THE MAN: You still haven't understood, gentlemen, that I cannot lose.

ALLAN (*smiling*): Oh, yes, I understand all right. Give me the cards!

CLAIRELI: And with all your money, did you then wed the woman you loved?

THE MAN: No, Madame. As for me, the one who didn't believe in anything, from that day on I realized that I was damned and when one is damned, you don't worry any more about marrying an angel.

CLAIRELI: What else is there to worry about? There's no need to call up the Devil! (*with fire*) I'm on the side of those who know what they want!

ALLAN: Give me the cards.

MATHIS: Allan, don't do this!

MATHIEU: This is wrong. Don't do it.

THE MAN: You're trying to cure me. I've done everything possible to try to be cured.

ALLAN: You haven't played a game of cards with me. Is it a long time since you played cards?

THE MAN (*sitting down and looking at the cards that Allan has laid out on the table*): Ever since that day, when I returned here to hide away, I have never played cards. Why did you bring a pack of cards with you?

ALLAN (*preparing for the game*): What shall we play?

THE MAN (*placing the wallet with the envelope in it on the table*): Whatever you wish. I will play you for the entire contents of this wallet, as many games as you wish!

ALLAN: Very good. (*Turning to his friends.*) Are we all playing?

MATHIS: No, no, not me!

MATHIEU: Me neither!

CLAIRELI: Count me in!

MATHIS: No, I don't want you to!

CLAIRELI: Very well then.

THE MAN: Ah, gentlemen, silence please!

ALLAN: The first one to turn over a king is the dealer! (*He deals out all the cards.*) There we are! You start!

THE MAN: There you are, already, the first king!

ALLAN: Eh? I didn't expect that. Your deal. (*He passes him the cards.*)

THE MAN (*having shuffled*): Cut!

(*Allan cuts the pack. The Man deals.*)

ALLAN (*looking at his cards*): I'll pass!

THE MAN: No, play!

CLAIRELI (*looking at The Man's hand*): What? You're going to play with that hand?

THE MAN: Of course, Madame. You'll notice that I am doing everything I can to lose.

ALLAN: Very well, I'll see you.

THE MAN: For the entire contents of the wallet. (*He lays down his cards.*) A pair of eights!

ALLAN: Is that all you have? Get ready with your ten thousand!

CLAIRELI (*smiling*): Say goodbye to the Misère Wood!

(*The Man, without answering, wipes his forehead.*)

ALLAN (*lays down his cards*): A pair of queens! I have won, Sir!

(*Mathieu gasps.*)

THE MAN (*incredulous, yet overcome with joy*): That's not possible ... not possible. (*He studies Allan's hand.*) It's true! My God, it's true! I have lost!

ALLAN: Indeed! It seems (*giving The Man a friendly pat on the shoulder*) that you shouldn't believe everything the Devil tells you!

(*At this moment the wind picks up again, growing ever stronger.*)

THE MAN (*trembling with joy, taking the wallet and opening it*): My dear friends! Gentlemen! God bless you! Take it! Take the ten thousand! (*As he speaks, he searches for the ten thousand francs but cannot find them. The others too notice that there is nothing in the wallet, even though they saw him put the money in it earlier.*) Where is it? Where's the money? (*More frantically.*) Where is it?! You saw me put it in there, didn't you?

ALL (*astounded*): Yes, yes, of course. We saw it! It was there! We saw you put it there!

THE MAN (*distraught*): It was there! I put it there! (*He searches his pockets.*) Let me see! It must be here somewhere!

(*Claireli searches through the wallet.*)

CLAIRELI (*putting down the wallet*): Nothing!

THE MAN (*haggard*): I played for the entire contents of the wallet and there was nothing in the wallet! (*There are three loud knocks on the front door. He speaks in a trembling voice.*) Who is there?

GUILLAUME (*outside*): It's me, Guillaume!

(*The Man goes to open the door.*)

THE MAN: What do you want?

GUILLAUME (*approaching*): I beg your pardon, gentlemen. I thought you might have immediately noticed that the ten thousand francs were missing …

MATHIEU (*fearfully*): Well, yes …

GUIILAUME: Strange as it may seem, I still have them! I must have picked them up in their envelope without noticing …

MATHIS (*pointing at The Man*): But this gentleman picked them up …

THE MAN: How did you notice?

GUILLAUME: Just as I was passing the Grande-Marnière, a gust of wind blew my bag open. I put my hand inside to stop the papers blowing away and I found the ten thousand! I couldn't have been more surprised had they walked there by themselves! The wind almost blew them away and then … Well, anyway, here they are. (*He opens his bag.*)

CLAIRELI: That's extraordinary!

ALLAN: Yes ... quite ...

(Mathis and Mathieu look at Guillaume with fear.)

GUILLAUME *(after having given the ten thousand francs to The Man)*: There we are! It's all there and this time I won't take them away again! Good night, everybody ... Actually, I will sleep here tonight, sir, I'll be up early in the morning in a few hours' time.

(He exits through the door to the office.)

THE MAN *(as if hypnotized by the banknotes)*: Come on then, let's play. We won't play for nothing this time. Here's the money. Ten thousand – one hand and the winner takes all! Including Hell itself!

ALLAN: Your deal!

THE MAN: Give me the cards!

ALLAN: Let's play!

THE MAN *(looking at his cards)*: Ah! It's too good a hand this time – four jacks! Let me have four more. *(He throws in his four jacks and takes four new cards.)* What?! Four kings! Let me have four more! *(Frenetically he throws in his four kings and draws four more cards.)* No! Four aces! This always happens! It's always like this! Always! Always! *(He throws his cards into the fire.)* Let the cards burn! *(Raving and tearing his hair out, he staggers to the staircase and exits.)* Why did you have to bring the cards with you? Why did you bring the cards? Why ... the cards?

(Mathis and Mathieu are horrified, the two others are deeply affected.)

MATHIS: Right! I, for one, am not spending a minute longer in this house.

(The storm rages outside. The sound of thunder.)

ALLAN: He's completely mad!

MATHIEU: That's quite possible.

CLAIRELI: But we agreed to spend the night here playing cards.

MATHIS *(brutally)*: Tomorrow morning we have to get up very early and besides there's a perfectly good bed upstairs and we'll be more comfortable than down here.

ALLAN *(sombrely)*: No, I'm staying right here.

MATHIS *(to Claireli)*: Upstairs!

CLAIRELI: I won't be able to sleep now after a story like that. I may as well stay down here.

MATHIS (*furious, exits, pushing open the door*): No, I say, come upstairs!

CLAIRELI: I'll be right up …

(*Mathieu and Mathis exit.*)

ALLAN: Go on upstairs, Claireli!

CLAIRELI (*in hushed tones*): I don't want to leave you, not tonight … I'm afraid to go up with him.

ALLAN: You have to, my darling.

CLAIRELI: That's enough! This is all your fault! We've had the Devil amongst us too. But men can't make their mind up about what they want. Look at our host – one minute he's praying to the Devil to make him win and the next he's praying to God to make him lose! And you're just the same – if you'd been decisive about what you wanted, Mathis wouldn't be upstairs now waiting for me.

ALLAN: Ah! Don't remind me …!

MATHIS (*in the hallway, then coming to the door*): Well, are you coming up or not?

CLAIRELI (*calmly*): Yes, I'm coming. I was just asking Allan if it didn't bother him to be left all alone like this … alone, that is, with the Devil.

(*She exits, smiling.*)

MATHIS: Good night, Allan.

(*Only a single lamp faintly lights the stage, as during the exchanges, Appenzel has extinguished the other lamp on the table.*)

ALLAN (*alone*): The Devil indeed! (*He looks around as if he is just waking up from a bad dream. He goes to the window, opens it, then pushes open the shutters. The blue light of the moon illuminates the room. He leans out of the window.*) What solitude! How desolate! (*Suddenly he hastily closes the shutters and turns around.*) Well, I never! A vulture … perhaps the very bird that old man spoke of … (*He pulls himself together.*) What of it? What's got into me? (*He turns back to the window and looks outside.*) It's always there … as still as ever, as if it were made of bronze. It's certainly very impressive. (*He goes to the door with the cross.*) The old man's story is coming back to me now. Ah, the door! The famous door! (*He looks closely at the door, feels it and rattles it.*) It's shut fast. It won't be opening for me of its own accord! (*At that moment the door with the cross releases its catch and slowly opens, revealing a large mirror.* Allan *cannot prevent himself from recoiling.*) Ah! Ah! The famous mirror! The mirror on the cupboard. Hello there, Allan. You're not a bad looking fellow, are you? Let's have a look at this cupboard. (*He struggles to open the mirror.*) If the Devil's pulling on his side, this may take a while! (*The mirror finally opens with the same movement as the door with the cross.*) Ah! (*He looks inside the cupboard.*) Ah well, there we are, just a straightforward cupboard. (*He takes hold of the lamp and shines it into the back of the cupboard.*) Books! And look! Here ... here are some letters carved into some burnt wood ... (*He lifts the lamp.*) 'You will win.' So the old man wasn't dreaming! Bah! Just an old inscription that started playing on his imagination! (*He says these words a little hesitantly, as he is becoming increasingly unnerved. He now turns his attention to the books in the cupboard. He takes one and closes the cupboard.*) Ah! Look, here's the book about sorcery in the Jura! (*He places the lamp on the table and opens the book.*) Well I never, this is strange ... (*Reading.*) 'If you really want to see the Devil, you need only call him and he will come! But you must call him with all your heart.' (*He reads silently for a few moments, then closes the book and taps the cover with his hand.*) It's a curious thing all the same, this bird here ... and the other one ... the one outside. However, it's nothing that a good bullet won't fix! But what am I saying? I'm sure to miss ... as Mathis says, I'm absolutely hopeless! (*Furious, all of a sudden.*) Ah! Mathis! What a brute! Claireli is right ... when he holds her in front of me ... (*He holds his gun like a hunter lying in wait.*) There are times when I could easily ... (*Feverishly.*) So easily ... (*At that moment the mirror makes a slight noise and* Allan *turns his head.*) The cupboard is opening! (*He slowly places his gun on the table and slowly turns towards the mirror.*) What is it that I want? (*The mirror clouds over so his reflection is no longer visible.*) What is it that I want? (*His voice becomes hollow and choked.*) Who are you? ... What do you want? ... Where are you from? ... Are you the Devil? ... (*The Figure seems to emerge from the mirror and the two of them lean towards each other, face to face, then step back, making identical yet opposite movements as if they are each other's symmetrical reflection.*) You frighten me ... What have you brought me? ... My desire? ... (*Both slowly lower their hand onto the gun.*) Willpower! That is everything! He won't laugh at me any more! Eh? What? What are you saying? That I didn't think the gun was loaded? Not loaded? Are you the Devil in my own thoughts? An accident! Did you say, 'an accident!'? Don't go away! Don't go away, do you hear?! When you're here I feel so strong! You are the real Allan! I'm afraid that the daylight will drive you away! Where are you now? Where have you gone?

(*The Figure has climbed back into the mirror; Allan moves towards him, but at the moment he touches the mirror, it shatters and he faints, whilst The Figure has disappeared.*)

ACT TWO

Same scenery. Darkness.

Allan, stretched out at the foot of the mirror. Enter Mathieu and Mathis already dressed and ready to leave, guns slung over their shoulders.

MATHIEU: Allan!

(*He goes to the window and opens it. The daylight pours in.* Mathis *draws back the bolts on the door and opens it.*)

MATHIEU and MATHIS (*noticing Allan at the foot of the mirror*): Ah! (*They run to him.*) What's happened here?

(*They lift Allan up and carry him to the armchair.*)

MATHIEU: Look! The Devil's door is open!
MATHIS: I said something awful would happen!

(*They place Allan in the armchair and he emits a sigh.*)

MATHIEU: Listen! He's coming round.
MATHIS (*nodding his head*): Yes, but very slowly ...

(*Anxiously, and with curiosity, they watch him come round.*)

ALLAN (*coming round*): What's happening? (*Recognizing Mathis.*) Mathis! It's you! Ah! It's you! (*He takes hold of his hands effusively.*)
MATHIS: We found you in a heap by the mirror. I suppose you were after the Devil, eh?
ALLAN (*quickly*): Ah! I had a nightmare! A terrible dream! Yes, that's right. You said you found me by the mirror?
MATHIEU: That's right! Out cold!
ALLAN (*dazed*): Yes, yes, I remember now ... I was after the Devil ... I opened the door with the cross ... and then ...

MATHIEU and MATHIS: Yes?

ALLAN: And then I came over all dizzy and then crash! That's it ... I had a dream! ... A dream!

(*He gets up and grips Mathis by the hands.*)

MATHIS: What's the matter?

ALLAN (*with increasing tenderness*): My dear old friend! You're my best friend, you know!

MATHIS: I never doubted it ...

ALLAN: This is crazy, these dreams! (*He looks to his right and left.*) This is crazy!

MATHIEU: What are you looking for?

ALLAN: My gun.

MATHIS (*passing the gun to Allan*): Here's your gun.

ALLAN (*feverish*): Give it here! Give it to me! (*He checks the weight of the gun in his hand.*) Ah! It's not loaded! It's not loaded! (*He blows down the two barrels.*) It's not loaded!

MATHIEU: Of course not! Why did you want to know if it was loaded?

ALLAN: The Devil lied!

MATHIS: Did you see him as well?

ALLAN: Yes, I saw him! Certainly I saw him! Ah, my friends! What a dream! I must tell you all about it.

CLAIRELI (*off*): Allan!.. Mathis!

ALLAN: Listen! That's Claireli's voice! Has she gone out already?

(*He puts his gun down next to the staircase.*)

MATHIS: Yes, the door in our bedroom leads directly onto the balcony. She was the first one up.

CLAIRELI (*off*): Come out here! Come and see the sunrise! It's absolutely beautiful!

MATHIS: You can tell us your story afterwards.

(*He leaves and the others follow. The sound of voices outside can be heard: 'Oh, that's magnificent! Wonderful!'*)

(*Appenzel enters through the office door and immediately notices that the door with the cross is open.*)

APPENZEL: Ah! Who did that? Who dared open the door?!

(*She puts the jug of milk and the cups that she has been carrying on the table.*)

GUILLAUME (*at the top of the staircase*): What's going on?

APPENZEL: They opened the door and the mirror is broken!

GUILLAUME (*coming downstairs*): What? The mirror is broken? That's a sign of bad luck! Where have they all gone? The master doesn't want to see them again. I'm supposed to help them carry their things as far as the farm and then, having got them past the Grande-Marnière, say farewell! He doesn't want anything to happen to them but just that they clear off! Ah, here we are! (*He slings the game-bags over his shoulder.*) And now for the guns! (*He puts Allan's gun over his shoulder which is the only gun left in the house, as Mathieu and Mathis have taken theirs with them.*) I think that's everything. (*He goes towards the door.*) All the same ... (*Looking at the door with the cross.*) Why did they have to go and open that door?

APPENZEL: If the master sees it ... it's bound to upset him.

GUILLAUME (*at the door*): Bah! I'll come straight back and patch it up.

APPENZEL (*putting the bowls on the table*): That's good, 'cos you won't get me touching it! Tell them there's some milk if they want it before leaving.

GUILLAUME: Is that a good idea? Let's not hold them up ...

(*He exits.*)

APPENZEL (*looking at the door with the cross*): Heathens!

GUILLAUME (*reappearing at the window*): Ah, that damned vulture is there again!

(*He disappears.*)

APPENZEL (*running to the window*): That damned vulture! Leave it! Leave it be! Do you hear me, Guillaume?!

THE MAN'S VOICE (*from inside his room*): Guillaume! Guillaume!

APPENZEL (*at the window*): Hurry up, Guillaume, the master's calling you!

ALLAN (*enters, followed by Claireli, happily*): Of course! Of course! (*to Appenzel*) Good morning! (*Giving some money to her.*) Please take this for the cost of the mirror.

CLAIRELI (*looking at the mirror*): Ah! Tell me what happened here!

MATHIEU: He's going to tell us all once we're underway.

APPENZEL: Would you like a little warm milk, Madame?

CLAIRELI: I wouldn't say no!

MATHIS: Very well, but quickly now!

(*Meanwhile Guillaume comes back in. Appenzel gives him a nod of the head in the direction of The Man's room.*)

APPENZEL: He's calling you.

(*She pours the milk for Claireli.*)

GUILLAUME (*putting the gun back down in the exact place he took it from*): I'll be right there!

(*He quickly goes up the stairs. The others are too preoccupied to have noticed him.*)

ALLAN (*to Appenzel*): I'd like a drop of milk too, please.
MATHIEU: We'll never be ready at this rate!
ALLAN (*drinking*): We can't possibly leave without thanking our host.
MATHIS: We can leave a note. That will do.
CLAIRELI (*to Allan, whilst drinking*): So, you saw the Devil then? Is he handsome?
ALLAN: He looks like me, Claireli …
CLAIRELI: Not bad then! And what did you talk about?
MATHIEU: We can talk about this outside!
MATHIS: Yes, he can tell us the whole story once we're underway. Time's getting on and we might be able to get to Mont Huon in time for all the game waking up!
ALLAN (*putting down his bowl, taking his gun, jokingly*): Come on then, let's go and bag ourselves some game!
MATHIS (*by the door, to Allan*): And make sure you don't forget anything!
ALLAN: Ah! There you go again! Wait until I tell you my story … In my dream, you were just telling me not to forget anything, when I took aim at you …
MATHIS: So that's why you were checking to see if your gun was loaded!
ALLAN: Exactly! And I said to you, 'Right then, you Swiss fool, what should I aim for? (*He takes aim.*) Your right eye or your left eye?'
MATHIS: The right eye!

(*Allan pulls the trigger and a shot is fired. Mathis is thrown backwards. Cries of horror from everyone. The two men rush to Mathis. Allan is beside himself.*)

ALLAN: I've killed him!
MATHIEU: Mathis!.. Mathis!

(*They both go down on their knees next to the body of Mathis.*)

GUILLAUME (*running down the stairs like a madman*): An accident! There's been an accident! The gun!

(*He throws himself down next to the body of Mathis.*)

ALLAN (*taking the body in his arms*): What have I done? Mathis! My old friend!

MATHIEU: He is dead!

ALLAN (*rests his head on Mathis's chest whilst there is an agonizing silence from everyone, then he gets up, tortured*): Dead!

CLAIRELI (*collapses on the table, then with eyes wide with horror, looking meaningfully at Allan*): Dead!

ALLAN (*finishing getting up, haggard*): Who loaded the gun?

(*He turns to face the door with the cross.*)

GUILLAUME (*still on his knees with his arms stretched upwards*): It was me! It was me!

ALLAN: You?!

GUILLAUME: Yes, me!

ALLAN: But why?

GUILLAUME: There was a vulture out there and I wanted to shoot it. I saw your gun and loaded it. And just then I was called away.

ALLAN (*with a dismissive gesture towards Guillaume and looking continually at the cupboard*): No! No! It was me! I know I was to blame for the loaded gun. (*He suddenly picks up the gun from the floor.*) There should be one more cartridge in there!

(*Guillaume and Claireli rush towards Allan.*)

GUILLAUME: What on earth are you doing?! What are you doing?!

CLAIRELI: There's already been enough bloodshed!

(*Guillaume wrests the gun from Allan.*)

ALLAN (*pushing Claireli away who is helping Guillaume disarm him*): Ah! You! Claireli! I don't recognize you! I don't know you any more! It's you who killed him!

CLAIRELI: Me?

ALLAN (*completely delirious*): Yes, you! You! You killed my friend! It was you who loaded the gun with death! It was you who sent me to meet the Devil last night! It was you! I don't want to see you ever again! Never! Never!

THE MAN (*appearing at the top of the staircase and in a slow, heavy tone*): Why is that door open?!

(*During these final exchanges, Appenzel can be heard continuously saying, "This is terrible! This is terrible!" along with the groaning of Mathieu, who, bent over the body, continuously cries, mournfully, "Mathis! Mathis! Mathis!"*)

CURTAIN

The Man Who Killed Death (*L'Homme qui a tué la mort*, 1928)

René Berton

Characters:
Bricard
Benoit
The Governor
The Judge
Gauvain
Morales
The Priest
Marec
Wardens, Doctor etc.

Act One

Bricard sits at table playing a game of patience and smoking a pipe. There is another table in the room, covered with a black cloth. Benoit sits on a stool, deep in contemplation with his head in his hands. Outside it is night. Occasionally, hammer blows can be heard and we see the glimmers of lantern light.

BRICARD: Lost again, dammit ...! Oh, I've had enough of this ...! (*He gathers up the cards angrily. He looks at his watch.*) Five o'clock ... Time is dragging by ... (*He goes over to the window and looks out into the night.*) They've nearly finished ... What a horrible job! (*He goes over to Benoit, who still sits impassively, and taps his shoulder.*) Come on, old chap, what are you thinking about ...? The death of Louis the 16th ...? Good time to think about that!

BENOIT: God, when will this night ever end ...? I don't think that the sun will ever rise!

BRICARD: It's nearly finished. In an hour it will all be over.

BENOIT: I can't wait for it to be over ... What a nightmare!

BRICARD: You're new to this, aren't you?

BENOIT: It's the first time I've been present at an execution ... (*exasperated*) And my god –

BRICARD: You'll get used to it, believe me.

BENOIT: So you say.

BRICARD: It's true. When you've seen a dozen men executed on the guillotine like I have, you *do* get used to it.

BENOIT: I think it's horrific being involved in a condemned man's last moments ...

BRICARD: Not a bundle of laughs, granted ... But you've got to remember that these men are dangerous criminals – they deserve it. If you think of the suffering their victims went through, you don't feel quite so sorry for the killers.

BENOIT (*without conviction*): Of course.

BRICARD: Besides, this bloke Morales is not worth an ounce of your pity. Just think of those two poor women he butchered for their money ... And the way he tried to dispose of their bodies – such methodical, cold-hearted ruthlessness, the man's a monster.

BENOIT: But don't forget – he never confessed.

BRICARD: What on earth does that matter ...? He was found guilty and there was plenty of evidence to prove that he did it ... (*Pause.*) After all, the law is fair and just: it makes sure that it's not easy to chop someone's head off, you know!

BENOIT: There have been mistakes though, haven't there?

BRICARD (*shrugging his shoulders*): Yes ... I suppose so ... But I wouldn't worry in this case ...!

BENOIT (*stands up and walks over to the window*): I swear the sun does not want to rise today!

BRICARD: Come on, son. Keep it together ... (*Takes a bottle and glass out of the cupboard.*) Have a glass of rum ... It will straighten you out. (*He fills the glass.*)

BENOIT (*reaches out to take the glass then suddenly stops himself*): Is this the same rum that we will give to the prisoner ...?

BRICARD: Yes.

BENOIT: And the same glass ...?

BRICARD: That's right ... Fine drop of rum this ... Really good stuff!

BENOIT (*pushes away the glass with disgust*): No, thank you.

BRICARD (*shrugs his shoulders*): Come on ... What a bloody fuss you're making ...! You really don't want it? (*Benoit refuses again.*) Oh well, your loss, mate! Good health!

(*He drains the glass and wipes his lips with his hand.*) Ah, that's better ...!

BENOIT (*points at the table covered with a black cloth*): What's under there, do you think?

BRICARD: I've no idea ... They brought it up here yesterday ... I think it's just a table.

BENOIT (*lifts the cloth of the table*): Funny kind of table ...! Look, it's some sort of scientific equipment ...! I wonder what they put in this bit here ...? What are all these holes with pipes in them? Looks like they connect to this container ... (*Opens the lid.*) It's empty ...

BRICARD: I can't imagine what it is.

BENOIT (*opens a little box on the side*): Let's see what's in here ...

BRICARD: Ah, I know what that is ... It switches an electrical current on and off ... See the switches and dials there? (*Benoit turns a dial. A low hum can be heard. Bricard is alarmed.*) What the hell are you doing! Stop it! Are you crazy?! (*He hurries over and turns off the dial.*)

BENOIT (*perplexed*): What the devil's all this for?

BRICARD (*hears something at the right hand door*): Someone's coming ...! Put the cloth back! Quickly!

THE GOVERNOR (*enters from the door on the right*): Anything to report, Bricard?

BRICARD: No, sir, all is well.

THE GOVERNOR (*pointing to the left hand door*): How's he doing?

BRICARD: I went to his cell not long ago ... The warden asked me not to make any noise – the prisoner's sleeping.

THE GOVERNOR: Go and check again.

BRICARD: Very good sir. (*Exits.*)

THE GOVERNOR (*looking through the right hand door*): Ah, here come my learned friends! (*Pointing at the playing cards on the table.*) Quick, clear the table please.

(*Benoit puts the cards in the desk drawer. The Judge and Gauvain enter. Benoit exits.*)

THE JUDGE: Good morning, Governor ...

THE GOVERNOR (*shaking his hand*): You're most welcome, your honour ...

THE JUDGE: Allow me to introduce my young colleague to you ... Gauvain.

THE GOVERNOR (*deferentially*): I feel like I already know Mr Gauvain ... I've heard him speak ...

THE JUDGE: Hasn't Morales' barrister arrived yet?

THE GOVERNOR: Mr Lacrouze? I'm not sure he will. He's in bed with a cold I understand. I'm sure he'll send his secretary.

THE JUDGE: I think we may be rather early …

THE GOVERNOR (*looking at his watch*): It's ten past five. At this time of year, the sun rises at about six o'clock. Plenty of time.

THE JUDGE: There's no need to wake the poor chap until the last minute … We'll let him sleep. (*The blows of hammers constructing the guillotine can be heard.*)

GAUVAIN (*nervously*): I think it's appalling, all that noise at this time of night …! Can't they make it quietly?

THE GOVERNOR: The men do their best but I'm afraid they can't do it *silently*.

THE JUDGE: I think you must understand that, Mr Gauvain?

THE GOVERNOR: I followed the Morales trial closely. I must say that the way you argued your case was simply tremendous … Such an eloquent display (*Gauvain gives a modest gesture.*) Yes, yes, it was magnificent. What I admired above all was how sincere you were. I never saw a barrister make such an impression on a jury.

GAUVAIN (*embarrassed*): Please, that's quite enough …

THE GOVERNOR: I mean, that defendant was a difficult bit of work to deal with!

THE JUDGE: Yes, Morales is quite a devilish piece of work.

THE GOVERNOR: His guilt was far from conclusive and after he'd been cross-examined you can see how perplexed the jury was. Myself too, for that matter. But then Mr Gauvain assessed all the evidence in the clear, cold light and all our doubts disappeared. The logic of your argument, sir, came down clean and precise. (*He makes a gesture with his hand.*) Like the blade of a guillotine!

THE JUDGE: I'm pretty sure that in lesser hands Morales would have been acquitted.

THE GOVERNOR: This was a triumph which you deserve to be proud of … And I understand why you wanted to be here to see justice done.

GAUVAIN: It's not that which brings me here to see the condemned man for the last time … Actually, I want to speak to him.

THE JUDGE (*stunned*): You want to speak to him?

GAUVAIN: Yes … I want to speak to him.

THE JUDGE: Why?

GAUVAIN (*lowering his head*): To clear my conscience.

THE JUDGE (*taken aback*): What are you saying …?

GAUVAIN (*lifting up his head*): As you said, it was with absolute conviction that I demanded the head of Morales. I spent days and nights studying the evidence and I remain utterly convinced of his guilt. In demanding his execution I believe we are protecting society. When the jury found him guilty I did not feel proud – I just felt I had done my duty … I have never doubted Morales' guilt –

THE JUDGE: Quite so …! You mustn't forget that I conducted the trial!

THE GOVERNOR: We all agree – the evidence was irrefutable.

GAUVAIN (*developing his argument*): I've never doubted it … (*forcefully*) I believe it was just …! But one thing casts a shadow over this – *he never confessed.*

THE JUDGE: The evidence was all there!

GAUVAIN: But I wouldn't want to see someone condemned by probability …

THE JUDGE (*slapping him on the shoulder*): Reread Pascal, my friend. Doesn't he prove that enough probability equals certainty?

GAUVAIN: Yes … I know … But what is terrifying is that over time this certainty becomes less and less clear …

THE JUDGE: On the contrary! With more time things only become more certain. It's nearly a year since Morales was arrested. All the newspapers talked about the trial. If he wasn't the murderer, some concrete evidence would have emerged by now!

THE GOVERNOR: Absolutely!

GAUVAIN (*collapses into a chair*): Yes … I know … But I can't help it, I find myself extremely anxious …! It's the first time I've been involved in a capital case.

THE JUDGE: Your very first case and you've succeeded in taking an evil man's head in the name of justice …! And you're unhappy …? Do you realize how jealous many of your colleagues are!?

GAUVAIN (*with a weak smile*): You call that a *success* …? (*He dwells on his thoughts.*) But he never confessed! He never confessed …

THE JUDGE (*revealing his impatience*): I do hope you're not starting to think he may be innocent …?

GAUVAIN: I believe him to be guilty, based on all the facts … But now my conscience is beginning to trouble me – what if I didn't interpret everything correctly?

THE JUDGE (*shrugging his shoulders*): Good grief!

GAUVAIN (*speaking with increasing passion*): The idea that we are about to commit a gross miscarriage of justice is haunting me and I simply can't get the idea out of my head … Day and night I'm terrified that I've made a dreadful mistake … (*hesitating for a moment*) I actually went to see the President in secret to discuss my concerns …

THE JUDGE (*shocked*): You did what?

GAUVAIN: Yes … I told him about my concerns … Yes, can you believe it, gentlemen? Me, a public prosecutor, who shouted in the name of justice that Morales must die – I went to see the President behind closed doors to beg that Morales be spared!

THE JUDGE (*with irony*): I'm sure the President was more than a little bit surprised, Gauvain …

GAUVAIN: He was surprised, it's true – but not in the way you might expect. He told me he had followed the case closely and was utterly convinced of Morales' guilt. He said it was impossible to grant clemency, despite my concerns … So that's why I'm here today.

THE JUDGE: You hope that Morales will confess to you before he dies?

GAUVAIN: Yes …! He must …! He *will* tell me!

THE JUDGE (*to the Governor*): What do you think?

THE GOVERNOR: I doubt it, somehow. If Morales wanted to confess he would have done so by now. He has confessed to nothing.

GAUVAIN: If he is continuing to deny it, it's because he's been hoping that his sentence might be commuted to life …

THE GOVERNOR: No. Morales never expected anything like that to happen. He never expected to win an appeal – he only signed it on the insistence of his defence.

GAUVAIN: Maybe when he knew he was going to die, he decided not to confess to anything?

THE JUDGE (*coldly*): Why would he confess?

GAUVAIN: Because … To let the truth be known … Or in an act of defiance … Sometimes when they face execution, I've heard that the condemned not only confess to their own crimes, they also confess to crimes they have nothing to do with, in a spirit of defiance!

THE GOVERNOR: Morales is not one of those, believe me.

GAUVAIN: I'm convinced that he will confess and that my conscience will be at ease. The man is not a brute!

THE GOVERNOR: Yes, I'd agree with you there … The books that he has been reading, and the conversations that he's had with the wardens and myself, prove that. He's a rogue, yes, but not a maniac.

GAUVAIN: I think he'll understand why I must speak to him.

GOVERNOR (*vaguely*): Perhaps.

THE JUDGE: I hope so – for your sake, young man.

(*Bricard enters.*)

THE GOVERNOR: What's he doing?

BRICARD: Morales is an extraordinary man, sir. I have been a warden for twenty-five years and I have seen everything on death row … Every mood and reaction you can imagine. I have seen brave men but Morales surpasses them all.

THE GOVERNOR: How do you mean?

BRICARD: The warden told me that when they started building the guillotine, Morales woke up and sat on the edge of his bed, listening … He said as calm as anything, 'Ha – that's for the morning! That'll put an end to my troubles and not a moment too soon … What time is it?' Four thirty in the morning I told him … 'Oh well, I can get another hour's sleep'. He lay down and fell fast asleep – he still is.

THE JUDGE: It's unheard of!

BRICARD: The man's got guts!

THE GOVERNOR: That, Mr Gauvain, is the man you hope will clear your conscience …

GAUVAIN (*obsessed with his idea*): I must talk to him … I must talk to him!

(*Benoit enters and hands the Governor a calling card.*)

BENOIT: There's a man to see you, sir.

THE GOVERNOR (*reading the card*): Ah yes … But it's much too early … Ask him to wait in my office … I'll call him in when it's time.

BENOIT: Very good, sir.

THE GOVERNOR (*calling Benoit back*): Tell the executioner to start his final checks. We'll bring the condemned man down in a few minutes …

(*Benoit exits.*)

THE GOVERNOR: Professor Fargus has arrived … I'm sure you know him?

THE JUDGE: Who doesn't? The greatest biologist in the country.

THE GOVERNOR: Professor Fargus has obtained permission to attend the execution of Morales … Purely out of scientific interest … He intends to conduct some experiments on the condemned man's corpse.

THE JUDGE: Yes, I know, he's a 'revivalist' – looking for signs of life after death. They've pushed their theories –

THE GOVERNOR: To the point of absurdity! I quite agree.

THE JUDGE: Ha, there's clearly a fine line between genius and madness! These scientific geniuses are more often than not victims of their own deluded imagination!

THE GOVERNOR: I understand that in his laboratory he's built a little guillotine and he's been decapitating all kinds of animals: guinea pigs, dogs, monkeys …

BRICARD (*aside, speaking between his gritted teeth*): The bastard …

THE GOVERNOR: He's made a machine that can, he claims, reanimate severed heads!

THE JUDGE: What an atrocious idea!

GAUVAIN: Cruel and futile!

THE JUDGE (*with irony*): All in the name of science!

GAUVAIN: Yes, science …! What crimes are committed in the name of *that*!

THE GOVERNOR (*looking at his watch*): It's time … (*He looks towards the door or on the left.*) They're waiting for us in the corridor … If you're ready, your honour …

THE JUDGE: Yes, better get this horrid business over with.

THE GOVERNOR (*to Gauvain, who is ready to follow*): I think it's probably best if you wait here. (*Gauvain nods in agreement. To Bricard.*) Get everything ready.

BRICARD: Very good, sir.

THE GOVERNOR: Let's wake him up.

(*The Governor and the Judge exit.*)

(*Bricard opens a cupboard and takes out a pair of scissors, a razor and some rope and places them on the table. He puts a stool in the middle of the stage. Gauvain becomes increasingly nervous, pacing around. He looks at his watch.*)

BRICARD: It won't be long now … For the last fortnight, Morales has gone to sleep with his clothes on, to be ready as soon as he wakes up … I think he regards today as a deliverance.

GAUVAIN: Have you often talked to him?

BRICARD: All the time … I've even played cards with him.

GAUVAIN: Did he say much to you?

BRICARD: He's not much of a talker, but eventually he did start to talk more.

GAUVAIN: Did you notice anything in his gestures or in what he said? Anything that hinted at a confession?

BRICARD: Nothing … The Governor, the wardens, none of us have heard the slightest hint of a confession.

GAUVAIN: It's maddening!

BRICARD: He's no ordinary fellow!

GAUVAIN: Usually, when the condemned man knows his time has come, they confess, don't they?

BRICARD (*giving a vague and evasive gesture*): Usually ... Yes. (*He looks down the corridor on the left.*) Here they come!

(*Enter Benoit, Morales, the Judge and the Governor, along with other figures who are legally obliged to attend an execution: a doctor, senior police officer, the clerk of the court etc.*)

(*Morales is dressed simply in a pair of trousers and a shirt. He is made to sit down on the stool and then Bricard uses the scissors to cut off his shirt collar. When the scissors come into contact with his neck, Morales shudders slightly. There is complete silence apart from the clipping sound of the scissors. Bricard then takes the razor and shaves the neck of Morales.*)

THE JUDGE (*approaching Morales*): Do you have anything to say before justice is carried out?

MORALES (*very calmly*): Nothing.

THE GOVERNOR: Do you have any last requests?

MORALES: No.

THE GOVERNOR: Do you want to send a message to your family?

MORALES: Who would I send a message to ...? I don't have any parents ... I think it's a shame my lawyer's not here – I wanted to thank him for the last time.

THE JUDGE: I will inform him of that.

THE GOVERNOR (*to Morales*): The priest is waiting for you in the chapel ... Would you like to talk to him?

MORALES (*after hesitating briefly*): No ... I do not believe in God.

(*Silence.*)

THE JUDGE (*aside to Gauvain*): I think there is little point in you talking to him. He has nothing to say to you.

GAUVAIN: But I must ...! *I must*!

THE JUDGE (*stopping him*): Gauvain, I beg you ...

GAUVAIN (*breaking free*): Let me pass ... I must talk to him.

(*Gauvain goes up to Morales and then stops, trying to conceal his emotion. Morales stares at him in silence and in his expression we see all the hatred he bears for the man who has condemned him to death. All the same, Morales collects himself and adopts his usual calm demeanour.*)

MORALES: My defence couldn't make it – but the prosecution could!

GAUVAIN: Morales, I know that my presence must seem cruel to you – but I swear that it is for a most important reason.

MORALES (*with a weak smile*): No doubt you're here to make sure that justice is done ... You fought so hard for it, after all. ... A matter of 'professional conscience', no doubt ... Rest assured, your presence does not bother me in the least.

GAUVAIN (*trying to hide his feelings*): Morales, listen to me ... In a few minutes you will pay your debt to society ... Nothing can save you now. The resignation with which you accept your fate proves to me that there is not a trace of human frailty in you. You have no reason to lie or conceal the truth now.

MORALES: I have nothing to hide.

GAUVAIN: Morales, at this moment in time you are no longer a criminal condemned to his fate – you are a man about to die ... You are about to leave this world while we are condemned to live on in it ... In the name of this simple humanity, please tell me the truth and confess your crime, once and for all.

MORALES: I am innocent ... I've always said so and will do so with my last breath.

GAUVAIN: How can you still deny it? Even at the point of death!

MORALES (*remaining completely calm*): If my guilt is so obvious, why are you so determined to hear me confess? (*He stares at Gauvain in the eyes.*) Could it be that you are having doubts ...?

GAUVAIN: You are guilty – I am absolutely convinced of it.

MORALES: You *were* absolutely convinced but something makes me think that now you're not so sure ... (*Gauvain makes a gesture.*) Yes ... Yes ... Your conscience troubles you ... You're having doubts and it's torturing you and you want me to confess to set you free ... And you were the one who denounced me with such conviction, turning a jury against me. You have killed me and before I die you want me to assure you that you haven't made a mistake ...! You have to admit, this is a little unexpected.

GAUVAIN (*his voice strangled*): Of course I have not made a mistake ... I'm giving you a chance to confess your crimes ...

MORALES: It's because of your conscience! You are aware of the terrible burden there will be on your soul and it's destroying you! You're a condemned man too!

GAUVAIN: But your resignation simply proves to me that you accept the judgement – and I'm giving you a final chance to tell me that!

MORALES: I do accept the judgment, because it will put me out of my misery ... Death will set me free ... (*Staring Gauvain in the eyes.*) You refused to listen to me when I swore that I was innocent ... Did you *listen* when I swore that I was not responsible for those crimes? No, never. You never did. I am innocent, but even if I wasn't I would never confess to you ....! Do you hear me? I would never confess to you. I want you to think of me when you fight other cases. I want you to realize how monstrous it is for a man to demand, in the name of 'justice', the life of another based on so-called facts deviously manipulated through rhetoric and artificial logic ...! I want you to be eaten up by doubt ...! I hope that for the rest of your life you will hear a voice deep in your conscience and it's constantly repeating the words: 'Perhaps you killed an innocent man ...!'

(*Silence.*)

MORALES (*regaining his calm*): Give me a cigarette – please.
THE JUDGE (*aside*): Don't say I didn't warn you, my friend.
GAUVAIN (*with his head lowered*): He won't ... he won't give in ...

(*Bricard gives a cigarette to Morales who lights it from a match held out by another of the wardens.*)

MORALES: Thank you.

(*Silence.*)

(*The Governor looks at his watch and gives a sign to the wardens. They approach Morales to tie him up.*)

MORALES: A moment please.

(*The wardens look at the Governor who indicates that they will listen to Morales. Morales takes a long drag of his cigarette, blows out the smoke slowly, watching it disperse into the air. Slowly his hand lowers and he puts his hands behind his back.*)

MORALES: I'm ready.

(*A warden ties Morales' hands behind his back while another holds his legs.*)

MORALES (*remaining very calm*): There's no need for force ... (*The wardens take the ropes and prepare to tie him up more thoroughly.*) Let me go ... I'll walk by myself. (*He walks with a solid step heading towards the exit. The priest arrives with a crucifix. Morales shudders, stares at the cross then lowers his head.*)

(*Silence.*)

MORALES: I wonder, sir, could I have a few minutes more ...? I'd like to speak to the chaplain.

THE GOVERNOR: If you so wish.

MORALES: Thank you. (*He walks towards the priest, his eyes fixed on the crucifix.*)

THE PRIEST (*placing an arm on Morales' shoulder and leading him out*): Come with me, my child.

Act Two

The same set. Professor Fargus's table has been moved centre stage. The sun is rising. The noise of the crowd can be heard. Gauvain is near the window looking outside. Marec, the Professor's assistant, is checking the laboratory equipment in a white lab coat.

THE GOVERNOR (*coming in from the right and standing aside*): Please come in, Professor. You can do your experiment in here.

THE PROFESSOR (*coming in followed by the Judge*): It's perfect!

THE GOVERNOR (*presenting Gauvain to the Professor*): Allow me to present Mr Gauvain to you.

THE PROFESSOR (*shakes his hand*): Delighted to make your acquaintance ... And many congratulations on your tremendous victory ... (*Gauvain fidgets.*) The Governor knows how interested I am in the challenges of psychology, and he's told me about all the efforts you've made trying to talk to the condemned man this morning.

GAUVAIN: All in vain, unfortunately.

THE PROFESSOR: The conflict going on in your conscience between the barrister and a human being proves the strength of your character and it has all my admiration. But now, if I may say so, there is no reason to torment yourself any more. Morales is incontrovertibly guilty.

THE JUDGE: Well said!

THE GOVERNOR: If you need anything Professor, I'll make sure the wardens are at your disposal.

THE PROFESSOR: Thank you ... My assistant is all that I need. Are we ready?

MAREC: Yes sir. I have poured the blood into the receptacle on the table.

THE PROFESSOR: Good. Check all the connections.

MAREC: I've already done that, sir.

THE PROFESSOR: Do it again ... Quickly, quickly!

THE GOVERNOR: You've got plenty of time, Professor. The execution's already terribly delayed.

GAUVAIN (*anxiously*): Oh ... Why?

THE GOVERNOR: Because, after Morales saw the priest, he decided he wanted to go to mass. We're obliged to let him do so ... Yes, this man who boasted that he was an atheist evidently wants to find some solace in the divine after all. I must say I wasn't expecting that!

THE PROFESSOR (*while he's examining the apparatus on the table*): All men are the same ... During their life they do not believe in God or the Devil ... But when death is near and they behold the cross, religious sentiments suddenly awake in them and they fall to their knees in prayer ...!

GAUVAIN (*beginning to breathe heavily*): If Morales confessed to the priest, maybe he admitted his guilt, yes? Maybe he's confessed to everything?

THE JUDGE: Well, only the priest would know that ...

THE GOVERNOR: And no-one can break the sanctity of confession.

GAUVAIN (*rubbing his hands in despair*): Oh god ... How can I find out ...? I must know ... I must find out!

THE JUDGE (*to the Professor*): No doubt you intend to conduct an experiment to explore your theory of revivalism on the body of the executed man?

THE PROFESSOR: On his body ...? Not exactly. I have no interest in his body. All that interests me is his head or, to be more precise, his brain.

THE JUDGE (*with irony*): Am I right in assuming that you have the notion that you'll be able to bring the dead brain inside a severed head back to life? ...

THE PROFESSOR (*looking him in the eyes*): Yes, sir, I do have the notion to believe that ... If we have enough time I will explain to you precisely how.

THE JUDGE: But, Professor, the truth about life is –

THE PROFESSOR: What exactly *is* life ...? Life is simply the coming together of a number of organic functions which work against the forces of mortality ... These functions are sustained by the organs within our body. Each one of these organs possesses individual functions which resist the agents of destruction which constantly bombard us. Together all of these organs create what we might call 'the life force' ... But in order for life to function in this way, the human body must have some key principles in equilibrium. There are three key areas: the brain stem through which the nervous system is mediated, operating our senses and movements; the lungs, which bring oxygen into the body which is essential in all the chemical processes within the body; and the heart which pumps the blood needed to nourish the body.

THE JUDGE (*listening carefully*): If you take any one of those components away – life immediately stops.

THE PROFESSOR: Now wait a moment …! In a man like Morales, at the peak of health, physically perfect, the life force is at full strength. We remove his head from his body …

THE JUDGE: And he's dead, obviously.

THE GOVERNOR: Instantaneously!

THE PROFESSOR (*looking at them closely one at a time*): No, gentlemen, he is not …

THE JUDGE (*astonished*): What on earth do you mean?

THE PROFESSOR: At least, he's not dead *immediately* … He's *beginning* to die … When a person is executed, life is not immediately extinguished; we've demonstrated this many times in our laboratory. Moreover, if we open up the corpse immediately after execution, we find that the heart *continues* to beat, the stomach *continues* to digest and the glands *continue* to secrete … So although the body may seem to be completely dead, it is full of life!

THE JUDGE: But for how long ….? Seconds … A few minutes at the very most.

THE PROFESSOR: In actual fact it can last for hours. The organs of the body continue to fight against their destruction … They strive to stay alive … We have detected this in the *body* of an executed man, so why not inside his *head*?

THE JUDGE: Because it's simply impossible …! Surely the organs of the body continue their functions for a limited amount of time because they are merely, for want of a better word, mechanical … But the brain is another matter altogether. The brain is part of an organic system but it functions *inorganically*!

THE PROFESSOR: One of our greatest physiologists, Cabanis, declared 'the brain secretes thoughts like the liver secretes bile'.

THE JUDGE: That's just some materialist's quip …! When we start to talk about the mind and its thoughts, we are entering the realm of metaphysics. We go beyond the world of the body; we enter the realm of the soul, and science has nothing to offer us there, it's powerless … Science cannot explain the 'mechanism' of the mind and the soul. In the face of that, science just disappears … It's the story of Pascal, isn't it? A scientific genius who converted to Christianity and believed that geometry could prove the existence of God! No, Professor, the brain inside a decapitated head cannot think, for longer than a split second … It's impossible!

THE PROFESSOR (*smiling*): Impossible …? There's no such word in science …

THE JUDGE: When a man is decapitated the brain is effectively obliterated …

THE PROFESSOR: No, it will continue to function until vitality is finally extinguished from the body … We have to admit that noise would continue to be perceived by the ears of a dead man, and images would still be reflected on the retina of the dead man's eyes. And these will be conveyed into the brain … The brain, therefore, is like a motor that continues to function while it cools down. It is simply like putting a piece of equipment 'on hold'.

THE JUDGE: Can you prove it?

THE PROFESSOR (*shows his table*): By using my invention, I can … Before long I will place Morales' head in here … And an electric current will be passed through his brain while blood begins to pump …

THE JUDGE (*unnerved*): Human blood …?

THE PROFESSOR: Obviously, human blood would be preferable but it's difficult to obtain it in sufficient quantity. I've used ox blood – the chemical composition is very similar. It's fresh and still alive. I prepared it so that it retains all its fluidity. Oxygen is being passed into it and it is being kept at a temperature of 37° centigrade, the temperature of the human body.

THE JUDGE: And you'll inject that blood into the dead man's brain?

THE PROFESSOR: Yes … We will pump it into the brain with the same force and rhythm of the cardiac muscle. With the electric current I will re-establish nerve activity within the brain. The injected blood will give the brain both the nutrition and temperature it requires … In other words, I will be re-establishing, artificially, the physiological conditions to permit life to return and reveal itself … It's rather like how a drop of water can revive a dried flower, even after many years … It's pretty much the same thing.

(*Silence.*)

THE JUDGE: Very well, Professor, but tell me: if your horrific experiment is a success, what exactly are the benefits?

THE PROFESSOR: The benefits ...? I believe there are two of them ... Moral and scientific ... I believe that for our humanitarian friends, it'll prove that death does not follow decapitation instantaneously and an individual continues to think and, therefore, suffer ... It will also demonstrate that it is possible to bring things back to a full state of apparent life. In other words, it'll prove that we can kill death ... I'm sure you remember gentlemen, the story of the woman who was asphyxiated but brought back to life after nine hours – *nine hours*, gentlemen! With my work, there is no illness or trauma which can terminate life permanently.

THE GOVERNOR: So you're saying it's impossible to kill someone instantaneously?

THE PROFESSOR: Perhaps. Of course, immediate death *is* possible. The hangman's noose in England and the electric chair in America kill instantaneously by destroying the essential organs. The guillotine merely cuts through a section of the vertebrae leaving the brain intact. What might be immediate would be a great weight falling from the height of a guillotine onto the head of the condemned, crushing the brain to pulp ... That would be instant death.

THE GOVERNOR: Clearly yes, I'm sure it would ... But that would be butchery rather than capital punishment.

BENOIT (*entering*): Sir, the condemned man has left the chapel.

THE GOVERNOR: Gentlemen, it's time.

(*The Judge and Governor exit.*)

THE PROFESSOR (*to Marec*): We're all set ... Let us begin! Marec, what is the current?

MAREC (*turning a lever and looking at the dial*): Four amps.

THE PROFESSOR: Good ... What temperature is the blood?

MAREC (*looking at the monitor*): 37.6° C.

THE PROFESSOR: Perfect ... When you inject the blood be sure to expel all the air out of the connecting tube. As you are well aware, the smallest pocket of air in the capillaries can immediately prevent circulation ... You just need to give the pump a single push to expel all the air.

MAREC: Of course, sir.

(*We hear a crowd start to murmur.*)

GAUVAIN (*running to the window*): There he is!

THE PROFESSOR (*approaching the window and looking out*): How calm he looks ...! Look how calm and collected he is as he walks towards the guillotine ...! He's standing still ... He's looking up at the blade ... Not a single emotion on his face – not even a bead of sweat! It's incredible! He's stepped on to the platform ... He's turning around ... My goodness, he's looking towards us ...

GAUVAIN (*suddenly turning and grabbing the bars of the window*): He's looking for me ...! He's seen me! Oh, how he's staring at me! ...

THE PROFESSOR (*gesturing for quiet*): I think he's going to speak ...

GAUVAIN (*overwhelmed*): Oh my god ...! The confession – he's going to confess ... (*He listens anxiously.*)

THE VOICE OF MORALES: Can you hear me? Yes, you, Gauvain. Listen to me, I am –

(*At that moment we hear the noise of the blade as it comes down and chops off Morales' head. Gauvain screams.*)

THE PROFESSOR (*very calm*): The blade didn't give enough time for him to finish his sentence ... Oh well ... Now my work begins!

GAUVAIN (*wringing his hands in despair*): What did he want to say ...? Oh, we'll never know ...! *We'll never know*! (*He rushes over to the Professor and talks to him in a breathless voice.*) Professor ... I must ask you something ... It sounds absurd, it sounds mad ... All the things you've talked about make me feel that I may be losing my sense of reason ...

THE PROFESSOR: What is it?

GAUVAIN: You're planning to bring that severed head back to life on this table ... Do you think you could ... You could ...

THE PROFESSOR (*staring him in the eyes*): make it speak ...?

GAUVAIN (*in a breath*): Yes ...

THE PROFESSOR: I think it is possible ... It's certainly not impossible, theoretically or practically ... You see, we have a special valve there which can pump air into the trap here and permit it to speak ... However, it all depends if the blade came down below the larynx ...

GAUVAIN: He must finish his words – he must speak!

(*The warden enters carrying Morales' head wrapped in a black cloth. The Governor and the Judge follow.*)

THE PROFESSOR: Put the head on the table.

(*The warden and the assistant do so and everyone crowds around to look at it, concealing from the audience the substitution of the false head with a concealed actor.*)

THE PROFESSOR: Yes, it looks like the larynx is intact … Perfect … Where the blade cut through means that the vertebrae are preventing the spinal fluid from draining out which is excellent for our experiment … So, Marec, pass me the needles and I'll push them into the marrow … I'll attach a tube into each of the major vessels and the air valve into the trap here … We have now re-established communication between the brain and its blood supply with this receptacle of blood taking the place of the heart … Put the head into the clamp … It's too far forward … There … That's it, perfect.

(*The Professor stretches his arms. Everyone moves away and the head of Morales can be seen on the table wrapped in a black cloth. The professor sweeps the cloth off. Everyone recoils in horror. The human head, its eyes closed, its face splattered with blood, is there in plain view.*)

THE PROFESSOR (*placing his hand on the head*): Yes, good, the revitalization is beginning to take effect … Switch on the current and stop the pump.

(*Silence. Everyone stares forward anxiously.*)

THE JUDGE: Nothing's happening.

THE PROFESSOR: We have to wait for the network of capillaries to fill with blood and circulate through the cranium … (*triumphantly*) Look! The blood is pulsing through the jugular vein! This proves, without doubt, that circulation has been re-established throughout the entire head … (*Touches the head.*) The temperature is rising … Colour is slowly coming back into the skin … Gentlemen, it is returning to life …!

THE GOVERNOR: You're right … The skin does not have the pallor of death …

(*Silence. Suddenly the dead man's eyes open wide. Everyone recoils with a scream of fright.*)

THE PROFESSOR (*exultant*): Wonderful! The nervous system is instigating movement! It's alive …! Didn't I tell you?

THE JUDGE: Couldn't it just be the electric current that made the eyelids move?

THE GOVERNOR: It can only be a reflex movement!

THE PROFESSOR (*still exultant*): No, no! That movement is *voluntary*!

THE JUDGE: But look at its expression! The eyes are *dead*!

THE PROFESSOR: And I maintain that those eyes are alive! They can see us!

The head can see us … It can hear us, I am absolutely sure of it. I will prove it!

(The eyelids tremble and then the eyes look around. It slowly looks at each person, one by one.)

THE GOVERNOR (*breathless*): It's as if he's looking for someone …

(The eyes fix their gaze on Gauvain.)

GAUVAIN (*mad with terror*): It's staring at me …! No, no, cover it up …! I can't bear it! Close its eyes! I'm losing my mind! In the name of God, close the eyes!

(The eyes close themselves.)

GAUVAIN: Ah …!

THE PROFESSOR: It heard you …! (*triumphantly*) Well, gentlemen, are you convinced now? Wasn't my experiment an unmitigated success?

GAUVAIN (*uttering a scream of fright*): Look! … There … There … There …! The lips are moving!

THE JUDGE: It's trying to speak …

THE PROFESSOR (*to Marec*): Quick, pump some air into the trachea!

(Marec operates the equipment. The lips continue to move. Silence. Everyone watches and waits anxiously.)

GAUVAIN (*breathlessly*): Oh my God, what is he trying to say …?

THE JUDGE: Gauvain, talk to it – go on.

GAUVAIN (*recoiling in fear*): No, no! I don't want to speak to him …! I don't need to … I know what he wants to say …! He wants to confess his guilt …! He wants to tell me I was completely right …! I told you he was guilty …!

(The mouth opens slightly and one can hear, quietly but very distinctly, these lengthily and lugubriously uttered words.)

MORALES: *I … I … I am innocent …*

GAUVAIN (*screams*): Ah …! He spoke …! He told me …! *He was innocent* …! I've killed an innocent man …! In the name, in the name of justice!

(Gauvain screams with laughter. He suddenly starts behaving as if he were summing up in court.)

GAUVAIN: Members of the jury … In the name of the society I am sworn to protect, in the name of justice I am sworn to uphold, with complete conviction and a clear conscience, I declare that this man is guilty and I demand his head …! (*He becomes demented again, laughing wildly.*) Ah, ah …! And here it is … The head I have asked for. I want it …! Give it to me! He belongs to me …! It's mine! I want it! I want it!

(*Gauvain dashes towards the table, the Professor struggles with him trying to protect the head.*)

THE JUDGE (*appalled*): The poor man!

THE GOVERNOR (*to the wardens*): Take him away!

GAUVAIN (*bundled away by the wardens, shouting*): In the name of society … In the name of justice, with all my conviction and my conscience, *I demand this man's head*!

THE END

Bibliography

Antona-Traversi, Camillo, *L'Histoire du Grand Guignol* (Paris: Librairie Théâtrale, 1933)

Artaud, Antonin, *Collected Works Volume Four* (London: Calder and Boyars, 1974)

Barker, Clive, *Theatre Games* (London: Eyre Methuen, 1977)

Barker, Clive and Maggie B. Gale (eds), *British Theatre between the Wars, 1918–1939* (Cambridge: Cambridge University Press, 2001)

Boal, Augusto, *Games for Actors and Non-actors* (London: Routledge, 1992)

Brophy, Philip, 'Horrality: The Textuality of the Contemporary Horror Films', *Screen* (27, 1986), pp. 2–13

Berkoff, Steven, *East, Agamemnon, The Fall of the House of Usher* (London: Calder, 1977)

Blair, David (ed.), *Gothic Short Stories* (London: Wordsworth, 2002)

Bonis-Charancle, Marc, *La Maison hantée* (Paris: Georges Ondet, 1903)

Brenton, Howard, *Plays for the Poor Theatre* (London: Methuen, 1980)

Burke, Edmund, *Philosophical Enquiry into the Origin of our Ideas of the Sublime and Beautiful* (Oxford: Oxford World's Classics, 2008)

Dash, Mike, 'Some experiments with severed heads', *About A Blast From The Past* http://allkindsofhistory.wordpress.com/2011/01/25/some-experiments-with-severed-heads/ (accessed 5 February 2015)

Deák, Frantisek, 'The Grand Guignol', *The Drama Review* (March 1974), pp. 34–52

de Beauplan, Robert, 'Introduction' to *En Chemin de Fer*; *Une Robe de Soie*; *Séparation*: *Pièces en une acte par Henriette Charasson*, in *La Petite Illustration* (9 December 1933)

Gilbert, Sandra and Susan Gubar, *The Madwoman in the Attic: The Woman Writer and the Nineteenth-Century Literary Imagination* (New Haven: Yale University Press, 1979)

Goodland, Patrick, *Games Galore!* (London: Scripture Union, 1969)

Gordon, Mel, *The Grand Guignol: Theatre of Fear and Terror* (New York: Amok Press, 1988; rev. ed.; Da Capo Press: New York, 1997)

Gordon, Mel, *Voluptuous Panic: The Erotic World of Weimar Germany* (Port Townsend: Feral House, 2008)

Goulding, Sylvia, *Hilarious Adult Party Games* (Boston: Lagoon, 2003)
Gritzner, Karoline, 'Introduction', in Karoline Gritzner (ed.), *Eroticism and Death in Theatre and Performance* (Hatfield: University of Hertfordshire Press, 2010), pp. 1–11
Grose, Carl, *Grand Guignol* (London: Oberon Books, 2009)
Hand, Richard J., 'Half-Masks and Stage Blood: Translating, Adapting and Performing French Historical Theatre Forms', in Katja Krebs (ed.), *Translation and Adaptation in Theatre and Film* (London: Routledge, 2013), pp. 143–61
Hand, Richard J., 'Labyrinths of the Taboo: Theatrical Journeys of Eroticism and Death in Parisian Culture', in Karoline Gritzner (ed.), *Eroticism and Death in Theatre and Performance* (Hatfield: University of Hertfordshire Press, 2010), pp. 64–79
Hand, Richard J., *Octave Mirbeau: Two Plays* (Bristol: Intellect 2011)
Hand, Richard J., 'Staging an "Unbearable Spectacle": The World Premiere of Joseph Conrad's *Laughing Anne*', *Studies in Theatre and Performance* (21:2, 2001), pp. 109–17.
Hand, Richard J., 'Theatres of Interactivity: Video Games in the Drama Studio', in Nathan Garrelts (ed.), *Digital Gameplay: Essays on the Nexus of Game and Gamer* (Jefferson: McFarland, 2005), pp. 208–20
Hand, Richard J. and Mary Traynor, *The Radio Drama Handbook: Audio Drama in Practice and Context* (New York: Continuum, 2011)
Hand, Richard J. and Michael Wilson, *Grand-Guignol: French Theatre of Horror* (Exeter: University of Exeter Press, 2002)
Hand, Richard J. and Michael Wilson, *London's Grand Guignol and the Theatre of Horror* (Exeter: University of Exeter Press, 2007)
Hand, Richard J. and Michael Wilson, 'Transatlantic Terror: French Horror Theatre and American Pre-Code Comics', *Journal of Popular Culture* (45:2, 2012), pp. 301–19
Hossein, Robert, *La sentinelle aveugle* (Paris: Bernard Grasset, 1978)
Kristeva, Julia, *The Severed Head: Capital Visions* (New York: Columbia University Press, 2011)
Lemarié, Yannick and Pierre Michel, *Dictionnaire Octave Mirbeau* (Paris: Editions l'Age d'Homme, 2011)
Lothian, Alice, 'Plays and Novels of St. John Ervine', *The North American Review* (215:798, May 1922), pp. 644–56
McGrath, John, *A Good Night Out: Popular Theatre, Audience, Class and Form* (London: Methuen, 1981)
Mack, Robert L., *The Wonderful and Surprising History of Sweeney Todd: The Life and Times of an Urban Legend* (London: Continuum, 2007)
Nohain, Jean and François Caradec, *Le Petomane*, revised edition (London: Souvenir Press, 1992)
Phillippon, Jacques and Jacques Poirier, *Joseph Babinski: A Biography* (Oxford: Oxford University Press, 2009)

Pierron, Agnès, *Le Grand Guignol: Le théâtre des peurs de la belle époque* (Paris: Robert Laffont, 1995)

Pierron, Agnès, 'House of Horrors', *Grand Street* (Summer 1996)

Pierron, Agnès, *Les Nuits blanches du Grand-Guignol* (Paris: Éditions du Seuil, 2002)

Pierron, Agnès, *Maxa, la femme la plus assassinée du monde* (Montpellier: L'Entretemps éditions, 2011)

Rebello, Stephen, *Alfred Hitchcock and the Making of Psycho* (London: Marion Boyars, 2013)

Rivière, François and Gabrielle Wittkop, *Grand Guignol* (Paris: Henri Veyrier, 1979)

Rubin, Martin, *Thrillers* (Cambridge: Cambridge University Press, 1999)

Scher, Anna and Charles Verrall, *100+ Ideas for Drama* (London: Heinemann, 1975)

Sedlack, Henrietta, 'Henriette Charasson, Ecrivain Catholique' (Unpublished MA thesis, Loyola University, Chicago, 1938)

Swale, Jessica, *Drama Games for Classrooms and Workshops* (London: Nick Hern Books, 2009)

Swale, Jessica, *Drama Games for Devising* (London: Nick Hern Books, 2012)

Thomson, Helen, 'Welcome to the body shop', *New Scientist* (225:3010, 28 February 2015), pp. 10–11

van Itallie, Jean-Claude, *The Serpent: A Ceremony* (New York: Atheneum, 1969)

Villiers de l'Isle-Adam, Auguste, *Contes cruels* (Paris: Calmann-Lévy, 1883)

Wells, Paul, *The Horror Genre: from Beelzebub to Blair Witch* (London: Wallflower Press, 2000)

In addition, the authors have also made reference to a number of short newspaper articles and reviews from the contemporary French, British and American press, principally from the following publications:

Le Soir
Excelsior
Le Matin
L'Eve nouvelle
Time
Observer

Websites

There are a number of Grand-Guignol related websites available, containing a wealth of information (and occasionally misinformation) about the genre. By far the most comprehensive and reliable is www.grandguignol.com, maintained by Thrillpeddlers in San Francisco.

Select Filmography

The Alfred Hitchcock Hour (television series, 1963–65)
American Horror Story: Coven (television series, 2013–14)
Between Us Girls (Henry Koster, 1942)
Carry on Screaming (Gerald Thomas, 1966)
A Cottage on Dartmoor (Anthony Asquith, 1929)
Les Diaboliques (Henri-Georges Clouzot, 1954)
Final Destination (James Wong, 2000)
Frankenstein (James Whale, 1931)
Psycho (Alfred Hitchcock, 1960)
Re-Animator (Stuart Gordon, 1985)
Resident Evil (Paul W.S. Anderson, 2002)
See No Evil (Richard Fleischer, 1971)
See No Evil, Hear No Evil (Arthur Hiller, 1989)
Sweeney Todd: The Demon Barber of Fleet Street (George King, 1936)
Sweeney Todd: The Demon Barber of Fleet Street (Tim Burton, 2007)
Taxi Driver (Martin Scorsese, 1976)
Texas Chain Saw Massacre (Tobe Hooper, 1974)
Theatre of Blood (Douglas Hickox, 1973)
Thriller (television series, 1973–76)
Wachsfigurenkabinett (*Waxworks*) (Paul Leni, 1924)
Wait Until Dark (Terence Young, 1967),
Les Yeux sans visage (Georges Franju, 1959)

Index

Note: French plays that are included as translations in either this volume or our previous two Grand-Guignol books are listed by their English title, followed by their French title. French plays that are not in those books, but exist elsewhere in translation and/or have an English production history are listed by their French title first, followed by their English title. French plays that have no translation or English-language production history are listed by their French title alone. Plays and novels are listed by their title with the name of the author in brackets. Films are listed by their title with the name of the director and year of production in brackets. Emboldened page numbers indicate the location of the script itself within this volume. Images from the Gallery of Production Photographs between pages 48 and 49 are referenced as Ill. in bold italic.

Abertoir Horror Festival 39, ***Ill. 8***
Aguirre, Wrath of God (Werner Herzog, 1972) 199
Alfred Hitchcock Hour, The (television series, 1963–65) 42
Alvarez, Arcedio 54
American Horror Story: Coven (television series, 2013) 200
Antoine, André 2, 3
Antoine, André-Paul 125
Arden, John 20–21
Artaud, Antonin 23–24, 26, 38
Asquith, Anthony 42
At the Telephone/Au téléphone (André de Lorde and Charles Foleÿ) 124, 196
Atelier des Aveugles/Seven Blind Men (Lucien Descaves) 55–56
Au petit jour (André de Lorde and Jean Bernac) 196, 197
Au rat mort, cabinet 6/Private Room Number 6 (André de Lorde and Pierre Chaine) 35, 128
Autier, Paul and Paul Cloquemin 27
Aveugles, Les (Maurice Maeterlinck) 56

Baker, Josephine 5n
Barker, Clive (horror writer) 13n
Barker, Clive (theatre academic) 5, 13, 13n, 14, 23, 24, 33–34
Barker, Howard 198
Berkoff, Steven 26
Berkson, Eva 6, 7
Berton, René xii, 4, 14n, 24, 57, 196–97, 198

Better Half, The (Noël Coward) ***Ill. 4***
Binet, Alfred 25 (see also André de Lorde)
Birds, The (Alfred Hitchcock, 1963) 27
Bizou, Clara 6
Blind Man's Buff/Aveugle! (Charles Hellem and Pol D'Estoc) 52, 55–57, **83–97**
Blind Man's Buff (game) 34
Bloomfield et Cie/Shepherd's Pie (Léon Frapié and Georges Fabri) 41
Boal, Augusto 14, 15, 35
Bonis-Charancle, Marc, 52, 52–54
Brain That Wouldn't Die, The (Joseph Green, 1962) 200–1
Brenton, Howard 26
Brontë, Charlotte 53
Brophy, Philip 10
Bruant, Aristide 2
Bulldog Drummond 5
Burke, Edmund 195
Burton, Tim 42

Carry on Screaming (Gerald Thomas, 1966) 28
Casson, Lewis xi
Castle of Otranto, The (Hugh Walpole) 194
Castle, William 18
Cat and the Canary, The (1939) 191
Cat and the Canary, The (John Willard) 191
censorship xii, 197n
Cercueil flottant, Le (Eddy Ghilain) 36
Chaikin, Joseph 37
Chaine, Pierre 35, 128
Charasson, Henriette xii, 6, 124, 127–28
Chimier, René 195n
Choisy, Camille 4–5, 5n, 6, 197
Chop-Chop!/La Veuve (Eugène Héros and Léon Abric) 196–97, ***Ill. 5***
Christie in Love (Howard Brenton) 26
Circle Violence (game) 34
Clouzot, Henri-Georges 7, 11
compagnie acte6 (Paris) 7
Conrad, Joseph 39
contes cruels 10
Cottage on Dartmoor, A (Anthony Asquith, 1929) 42
Coward, Noël xi
Crime dans une maison de fous ou Les Infernales/The Old Women (André de Lorde and Alfred Binet) 56
Cyclops (game) 34

Dard, Frédéric 125
de Beauplan, Robert 126–27
de Lorde, André xii, 3, 6, 56, 127, 128, 129; (with Alfred Binet) 24, 25–27, 56, 128, 200; (with Pierre Chaine) 35, 128; (with Eugène Morel) 38; (with Henri Bauche) 124, 128–29, 196; (with Charles Foleÿ) 196; (with Jean Bernac) 196, 197
Descaves, Lucien 55–56
de Maupassant, Guy 2
Diaboliques, Les (Henri-Georges Clouzot, 1954) 7, 11
Doctor Damage (game) 24
Donoghue, Emma 54
douche écossaise 2–3, 10, 11, 38
du Maurier, George 129

Ecco (1965) 38
eroticism 35–36
Ervine, St John, 57, 124–26
Euthanasia/Euthanasie (René Berton) 196

faits divers 10, 13, 194, 199
Fall of the House of Usher, The (Edgar Allan Poe) 26, 54
Fantôme de l'Opéra, Le (*The Phantom of the Opera*) (Gaston Leroux) 129, 194
Fight in the Dark (game) 34
Final Destination (James Wong, 2000) 27
Final Kiss, The/Le baiser dans la nuit (Maurice Level) xiii, 18–19, 35, 56
Fleischer, Richard 56
Franju, Georges 7, 56n
Frankenstein (James Whale, 1931) 6, 26
Frankenstein (game) 24
Frapié, Léon and Georges Fabri, 41

Game of Thrones (television series, 2011) 199
Gerbidon, Marcel 5
Ghilain, Eddy 7, 36, 40
Ghost Stories (Jeremy Dyson and Andy Nyman) 18, 19
Gignoux, Régis 35, 52, 54–55, 125
Gilbert, Sandra and Susan Gubar 53
Gladiators (game) 34
Gordon, Mel 13n
Gordon, Stuart 200
Gothic 7, 11, 14, 17, 21, 26, 27, 39, 53, 190, 194, 195
Gothic Drama 27, 194
Grain de poivre, Le (Marcel Gerbidon) 5
Grand-Guignol Laboratory (University of Glamorgan/South Wales) xi–xii, xiii, 19, 22, 27, 35, ***Ills 1–8***
Great Terror, The/ La Grande épouvante (André de Lorde and Henri Bauche) 124, 128–29, **156–88**, 196
Green, Joseph, 200–1
Gritzner, Karoline, 36
Grose, Carl, 17
Guillotine, the 196–97, 198, 199

Hammer Studios (Hammer House of Horror) 7, 194
Hand of Death, The/Horrific Experiment, The/L'Horrible Expérience (André de Lorde and Alfred Binet) 24, **25–33**, 40, 43, 128, 200
Haunted House, The/La Maison hantée (Marc Bonis-Charancle) 18, 22, 35–36, 52–54, **60–69**
Heart of Darkness (Joseph Conrad) 193
Hellem, Charles and Pol d'Estoc, 52, 55–57, 196
Héros, Eugène and Léon Abric 196–97
Herzog, Werner 199
Hickox, Douglas 42
Hiller, Arthur 57
Hitchcock, Alfred 7, 11, 11n, 18, 19
Hooper, Tobe 54
Hope, Bob 191
horrality 10
Horror and Laughter: A Night at the Grand-Guignol (Abertoir Horror Festival, 2009) 39, ***Ill. 8***
house doctor (*médecin de service*) 3, 18
Hum Circle (game) 20
Hunter and the Hunted, The (game) 34
Hypnodrome, The 17

Jane Eyre (Charlotte Brontë) 53
Journey's End (R.C. Sherriff) 52, 58
Jouvin, Jack 5–6, 126

Judith: A Parting from the Body (Howard Barker) 198

Kama Sutra or Never Play with Fire..., The/Kama Soutra, ou Il ne faut pas jouer avec le feu (Régis Gignoux) 35, 52, 54–55, **70–82**
Karloff, Boris 57
King Lear (Shakespeare) 56
King, George 41
King, Stephen 54
Kiss of Blood, The /Le Baiser de Sang (Jean Aragny and Francis Neilson) 18, 38, 39–40, 190, 196, 198, **Ills 1, 3**
Knott, Frederick 56
Kristeva, Julia 198

Lantern Theatre, The (Liverpool) 17
Laughing Anne (Joseph Conrad) 39
Lavery, Bryony 58
Leni, Paul 190–91
Leroux, Gaston xii, 129, 194–95
Level, Maurice xiii, 35
Levy, José xi, xii, 55
Librarie Théâtrale, La xiii
Licence to Thrill (Liverpool) 17, 19
Light in the Tomb, The/Gott mit Uns! (René Berton) xiii, 18, 22, 52, 57–59, **98–122**
Lighthouse Keepers, The/Gardiens de phare (Paul Autier and Paul Cloquemin) 27
Little Theatre xi, 55, 125
Lord Chamberlain xii, 5, 52, 55
Lottery of Death, The/La Loterie de la Mort ou Sept crimes dans un Fauteuil (Eddy Ghilain and Pierre Larroque) **40–48**
Lovecraft, H. P. 200
Lovers,The/ Les Amants (Octave Mirbeau) 35, 190, 193–94, **221–31**
Lyric Theatre (Hammersmith) 18

Mademoiselle Fifi (Oscar Méténier) 2
Maeterlinck, Maurice 56
Maltby, H. F. 57, 125
Man Who Killed Death, The/L'Homme qui a tué la mort (René Berton) 18, 57, 190, 196–201, **256–75**
Man Who Met the Devil, The/L'Homme qui a vu le diable (Gaston Leroux) 190, 194–96, **232–55**
Marchard, Raymonde 7
master of ceremonies 19
Maurey, Denis and Marcel 7
Maurey, Maurice (Max) 2–4, 5, 18, 52
Maxa, Paula (Marie-Thérèse Beau) 5, 5n, 6
McGrath, John 16
melodrama 2, 4, 7, 11, 25, 26, 37, 38, 40, 41, 126, 191, 194, 195
Méré, Charles 57
Méténier, Oscar 2, 3, 4, 16–17, 19
Mirbeau, Octave xii, 35, 190, 192–94
Misery (Stephen King) 54
Molotov Theatre (Washington DC) 7
Montmartre xi, 2, 3, 7, 17
Moulin Rouge, Le 2

Nancey, Marcel and Jean Manoussy 52
Night at the Grand-Guignol, A (Edinburgh Fringe, 1999) 17
Nin, Anaïs 7
Nonon, Charles 7

Oedipus (Sophocles) 56
Orientalism 55, 128, 129, 196

Paulais, Georges 5
Person Unknown, The (H.F. Maltby) 57, 125
Petite Illustration, La xiii
Petit Journal, Le 2
Petit Parisien, Le 2
Petomane, Le (Joseph Pujol) 2
Pierron, Agnès xii–xiii, 5n, 197n
Pigalle (see Montmartre)
Plague (game) 23
Poe, Edgar Allen 26
Pornography (Simon Stephens) 58
Progress (St John Ervine) 57, 124–26, **130–45**
Psycho (Alfred Hitchcock, 1960) 7, 11, 18, 19, 39–40

Rat Mort, Le 2, 128n
Ratineau, Paul 3, 6, 27 190n
Re-Animator (Stuart Gordon, 1985) 200
Resident Evil (digital game) 22
Rohmer, Sax 129
Rome (television series, 2005–07) 199
Room (Emma Donoghue) 54
Rubin, Martin 10

Scarf Seduction (game) 36
See No Evil (Richard Fleischer, 1971) 56
See No Evil, Hear No Evil (Arthur Hiller, 1989) 57
Serpent, The (Jean-Claude Van Italie) 37
Sherriff, R.C. 52, 58
Silk Dress, A/Une Robe de soie (Henriette Charasson) 6, 124, 127–28, **146–55**
Slaughter, Tod 41
Sondheim, Stephen 41
Sophocles 56
Southwark Playhouse 17
Stephens, Simon 58
storytelling 20–22
Survival Horror Game, The 22
Swale, Jessica, 14, 15, 16, 20, 21, 23, 24
Sweeney Todd 40–41
Sweeney Todd: The Demon Barber of Fleet Street (George King, 1936) 41
Sweeney Todd (Stephen Sondheim) 41
Sweeney Todd: The Demon Barber of Fleet Street (Tim Burton, 2007) 42

Tales from the Crypt (comic) 201
Taxi Driver (Martin Scorsese, 1976)
Texas Chainsaw Massacre (Tobe Hooper, 1974) 54
Théâtre de la Vice et de la Vertu 6
Théâtre des Variétés 4
Théâtre du Rire et de l'Epouvante (Théâtre Saint-Georges) 5
Théâtre Libre 2
Theatre of Blood (Douglas Hickox, 1973) 42
Theatre Royal (Plymouth) 17
Thomas, Gerald 28
Thorndike, Sybil xi, 25
Thriller (television series, 1973–76) 56
Thrillpeddlers (San Francisco) 7, 17
Thursday (Bryony Lavery) 58
Tics, or Doing the Deed/Après Coup!... ou Tics (René Berton) 24, 52, 196
Tin Shed (Newport) 7
Torture Garden, The/ Le Jardin des supplices (Octave Mirbeau) 192–93

Toulouse-Lautrec, Henri 2
translation xiii
Trilby (George du Maurier) 129
trust 34

Ultimate Torture, The/La Dernière Torture (André de Lorde and Eugène Morel) 38, ***Ills* 2, 6, 7**

Vampires of Strasbourg (game) 35
van Itallie, Jean-Claude 37
Ventouse, La (Marcel Nancey and Jean Manoussy) 52
Vers l'au delà (Charles Hellem and Paul D'Estoc) 196
Vigor Mortis (Brazil) 7
Villiers de l'Isle-Adam, Auguste 10
violent theatre games 13–16, 33–35

Wachsfigurenkabinett (*The Waxworks Show*) (Paul Leni, 1924) 190–91
Wait Until Dark (Frederick Knott) 56
Wait Until Dark (Terence Young, 1967) 56
Walpole, Hugh 194
Wax Museum, The/Figures de cire (André de Lorde and Georges Montignac) 190–92, **202–20**
Wells, Paul 10
Whale, James 6, 26
Wiegant, Christiane 7
Willard, John 191

Yeux sans visage, Les (Georges Franju, 1959) 7, 56n
Young, Terence 56

Zibell, Charles 4, 5
Zola, Emile 2, 10, 191, 192